Safe Among the Germans

Safe Among the Germans

Liberated Jews After World War II

Ruth Gay

Yale University Press   New Haven and London

Printed in the United States of America

Library of Congress Cataloging-in-Publication Data
Gay, Ruth.
Safe among the Germans : liberated Jews after World War II / Ruth Gay.
p.   cm.
Includes bibliographic references (p.   ) and index.
ISBN 0-300-09271-7 (cloth : alk. paper)
1. Jews—Germany—History—1945–. 2. Holocaust survivors—Germany.
3. Refugees, Jewish—Germany—History—20th century. 4. Jews, East European—
Germany—History—20th century. 5. Holocaust, Jewish (1939–1945)—Influence.
6. Germany—Ethnic relations. I. Title.
DS135.G332 G35 2002
943′.004924—DC21   2001006897

A catalogue record for this book is available from the
British Library.

The paper in this book meets the guidelines for permanence
and durability of the Committee on Production Guidelines for
Book Longevity of the Council on Library Resources.

10 9 8 7 6 5 4 3 2 1

To my wonderful daughters,
Sarah, Sophie, and Lizzie,
with all my love

Contents

Introduction

This book is about what happened to the Jews afterward—after the killings in the death camps had stopped, after the slave laborers had been freed, after the deportees to the Soviet Union had come home. These moments of release and deliverance are so powerful that most of the survivors who have told their stories stop and draw breath at that endlessly longed-for moment. When danger ends and life begins again, there no longer seems any reason to go on with the story.

Most of the Jews who survived had experienced not only physical suffering but the dehumanization so thoroughly practiced by the Nazis. The pendant to that moment of liberation was then the critical incident during which they felt their dignity restored. One woman whose camp was liberated by Americans described her first encounter with an American soldier, who held open a door for her as they left a building. That simple, conventional action overwhelmed her. "It gave me back my humanity," she said. Gita Glazer, who returned to her native Lodz after years in a forced-labor camp, was overjoyed to discover that several members of her family had also come back and were living together in an apartment. When she appeared at the door, emaciated and still in her prisoner's uniform, they did not recognize her. She was so hungry that she put off all questions until they had given her something to eat. At the end of the evening, they brought her to a room with something that amazed her: as she put it, "a real bed, with sheets and pillows." When her family left, she stood for a long time in front of that unfamiliar luxury, contemplating whether she shouldn't sleep on the floor. Getting into that bed was her first step toward reclaiming her life.

What happened in those first years after the war is the chronicle of a kind of heroism that has been unrecognized for the most part even by its actors. The heroes in this case are largely the Jews who grew up in interwar Poland. Roman Vishniac knew even in 1938 and 1939 that the moving photographs he was making in Poland were capturing what he called even then "the vanished world": the poor but picturesque shtetl Jews; the angelic little boys, their faces framed by sidelocks, clustered around their study table; marketwomen on a snowy day; shabby synagogue interiors; store owners in front of empty shelves. Parallel to this world, a new secular Jewish culture was emerging in which Jews lived both in an inhospitable modern Polish world and also apart. In a time when the fantasy of the nation-state still dominated Europe, the Jews could only be at a disadvantage. But they were no longer content with the enclosed life they had accepted for nearly a thousand years. Our story begins, therefore, with the metamorphosis of Polish Jewish life in those interwar years, with the growth of a vital, secular Jewish culture, with the Jewish leap into modernity. But this was only a very brief two decades in Jewish life in Poland, and it was halted by the onset of the Second World War.

All but destroyed in those years by the murderous Nazi regime, the surviving Polish Jews returned from concentration camps and deportation after 1945 only to discover that Poland had also become a killing ground. In the first two years after the war ended, between 1,500 and 2,000 Jews were killed in pogroms in Poland. Instead of a welcome and a homecoming, the exhausted survivors found themselves in a dangerously hostile atmosphere and urgently in need of elemental safety. With Palestine and most of the Western world closed to them, their situation was desperate. But in one of the great ironies of the postwar world there was one place in Europe that was safe and accepted refugees. That was, improbably, Germany. The Jews of Poland fled for protection to the Allied forces who had divided Germany into four occupation zones and who seemed to the displaced Jews like sheltering angels.

In the three years before Israel's independence in 1948, before other countries were willing to open their doors to immigrants, Polish and other Eastern European Jews piled up in what the United Nations relief organization called assembly centers and others called displaced persons camps. In time 270,000 Jews made their way to Germany to wait for their future.

This became an unexpected moment in Jewish history, a final irony, as the last flowering, the last living moment of Polish Jewish culture, played itself out in the D.P. camps in Germany. Surviving Jews were convinced, in the first years after their liberation, that their stories would never be adequately understood. What they found again and again was disbelief and incomprehension, and sometimes even outright rejection. The survivors drew closer to one another, therefore, with certain passwords that conveyed instantly their link. "Amhu"— they called one another—a Hebrew word meaning "His People," a seemingly harmless but bitterly ironic reflection on the sufferings of His People in the preceding six years.

With substantial populations sometimes reaching 7,000 or 8,000, the displaced persons camps became Jewish villages where for the last time Yiddish was still a working language. What emerged spontaneously and powerfully were original music, poetry, theater, and literature. A brilliant flicker of life before the culture of Polish Jews disappeared. But by 1949 the mass migration from the D.P. camps following the opening of Israel, the United States, and other parts of the world ended this incandescent final moment of Eastern European Jewish life.

The Eastern European Jews were not the only Jews in Germany. Nearly two-thirds of the half-million Jews in prewar Germany had been able to emigrate before the war. Of those who remained, 170,000 had been deported by the Nazi regime and killed. The handful who survived to see the war end numbered a mere 15,000 German Jews still alive on their native ground. In their postwar newspapers and in their private conversations they agonized over whether to stay or to go. Although the Eastern European Jews, even those with secular allegiances, always felt themselves a people apart and saw Germany as only a "waiting room" until they could settle somewhere permanently, the German Jews had lived for a century with the belief that they were Germans. But after twelve bitter years under the Nazis, they no longer knew who they were or how they were to live in a Germany that had embraced Hitler.

These were the partner communities that made an uneasy alliance in postwar Germany. Their situation was complicated even further as they attempted to work out a new Jewish destiny in the divided Germany that became a Cold War reality after 1949. Although all these developments elicited powerful feelings among the Jews in Germany, the Jewish communities abroad hardly understood what was happening and adopted a remarkably intransigent position, condemning out of hand the Jews who chose to live in that hated country. Universally criticized by Jews abroad, the Jewish communities in Germany found themselves being treated as outcasts and pariahs.

Their story as it unfolded in the half-century after the end of the war provides one of the most gripping chapters in modern Jewish history. Largely ignored by the outside world, the Jews in Germany developed a complex new identity. No longer "German Jews," they insist they are "Jews *in* Germany," a country that is still absorbing the shocks not only of its Nazi past but also of the post-Communist world. Tripled in numbers now by an influx of Jews from the former Soviet Union, the Jewish communities in Germany are undergoing yet another metamorphosis. Far from being a community of "remnants," as they were at first, they are energetically building a complex new Jewish life, now eagerly watched by Jewish organizations abroad which have discovered this interesting, sophisticated community and are vying for influence in it.

As this book is completed, the city of Berlin, in partnership with the federal government, is planning to build a huge Holocaust memorial and has already contributed to the construction of a daring new Jewish museum—both of which are extremely controversial architecturally. What is not controversial, however, is the vitality of the burgeoning Jewish community.

This book is quite frankly an attempt to win the attention of a public that had long been either indifferent or hostile to the idea of Jews settling in postwar Germany. The mourning for the dead of the Holocaust seems to have preempted the place of the living and left a strange lack of interest in history both before and after the Nazi period. I hope here to pay homage to those who survived and courageously built a new Jewish world in the most unlikely of all places. Numbering no more than thirty thousand at their peak, they bequeathed a complex identity to their children who grew up in a country they were hesitant to call their own. But Germany, with its eight million foreigners, is beginning to learn the meaning of a plural society and so is the once tight Jewish community. The Jews from the former Soviet Union are not only Russians but come also from Bukhara, Uzbekistan, Ukraine, and other republics—each with its own distinctive Jewish past. However faintly remembered, these differences add yet another dimension to the newly expanding community. The Holocaust survivors knew how to greet such complexity. "Am Yisroel khai—the people of Israel lives!" they said triumphantly of the surviving remnant. They would repeat that slogan in today's Germany.

Safe Among the Germans

CHAPTER ONE

Where They Came From

The phenomenon of thousands of Jews from Eastern Europe freely choosing to migrate to Germany in the first years after World War II was a source of wonder to the Germans as well as to the Jewish communities elsewhere in the world. What these onlookers did not know was that the Jews in Eastern Europe came from a long past that had prepared them for nothing else but the disembodied life of the perpetual stranger in their quotidian lives. Among the most enduring images of twentieth-century art are the paintings of Marc Chagall depicting the eternal shtetl—with its tumbledown wooden houses and synagogues, its fiddlers and denizens colored in lurid green and purples flitting through the air, their feet never touching the ground. These seemingly dream-like representations of the lost shtetl correspond closely to the daily reality of Jewish life in the East. The Jews, as the pictures convey, were not bound to the soil on which they lived. They established no

. They were prepared at every moment to leave. The substance ~~or their~~ lives lay elsewhere: in their laws, in their community, and in their history. The actual world around them—the churches, military barracks, government buildings, peasant houses—were all part of an evanescent scene that might be exchanged the next day, if the Jews were expelled by government decree from their village, for a different set of churches, barracks, government buildings, and peasant houses. The detached quality of this life is what Chagall has so vividly represented in his floating figures.

This detachment, which the Jews share, perhaps, with the Gypsies in Eastern Europe, was an attitude toward the world that was neither arbitrary nor sudden. It was grounded in centuries of experience and offered the only viable way of living in an inhospitable and intermittently dangerous environment. These Jews could not harbor any sentimentality about their Polish homeland, or revel in the beauties of its rivers and forests. Those rivers and forests were never meant for Jews.

How all of this came about, the sort of life that the Jews evolved in the millennium of their existence in Eastern Europe, is fundamental to our understanding of what happened in 1945. The decision of Eastern European Jews to settle in Germany at that time seemed unthinkable to the rest of the world in view of the nearly realized intent of the Nazi regime to kill every one of them. How could they emigrate to the land of their killers? And yet, as we shall see, they had their reasons—which not only brought them to Germany in the first place but sustained them in their lives when they got there.

When World War II came to an end in May 1945, hundreds of thousands of Jewish prisoners in concentration camps and forced-labor installations across Europe greeted the peace as the cessation of their torment on this earth. One man always said thoughtfully as he described the day of his release: "On May 1, 1945, it snowed," as if one miracle had succeeded another. On the eve of the war, seven million Jews had been living in Eastern Europe, mostly under precarious conditions. In each of the main centers of Jewish life—the Soviet Union, Poland, Romania, Hungary, Lithuania, and Latvia—the cause for their uneasiness was different, but nowhere were they freely accepted citizens with all the rights and privileges of the native born, as Jews were in the West, or even in Czechoslovakia—a border country. Instead, Jews were regarded as a hereditary class of outcasts, different in ancestry and religion from the majority. Although they had lived for nine hundred years in Poland, for nineteen hundred years in the Crimea and Hungary, for eighteen hundred years in Romania, the passage of time had done little to change their status.[1]

They lived under constraints that restricted their choices and twisted their lives at every turn. They were limited in their ability to enter trades and occupations, to acquire land, to enter schools of higher learning. And each individual branch of government seemed to have its own methods of marking the difference between Jews and other citizens. In the army, in the courts, even in routine encounters with bureaucrats, Jews had learned to expect discrimination rather than justice. And those who were poor could expect even greater maltreatment than those who offered an imposing presence, or who perhaps could "pass." Pervading all these experiences was the sense of an unbridgeable social gap.

In contrast to his coreligionists in the West, a Jew in Eastern Europe began life in a world that was overtly and even dangerously hostile. In the film *Image Before My Eyes*, which depicts Jewish life in Poland between the wars, one well-dressed, cultivated Jew, wearing a homburg and pin-striped suit, indicates that his fashionable appearance and flawless Polish would immediately accord him respect from strangers. But if anyone—even a taxi driver or a waiter—were to discover that he was a Jew, he could expect their attitude to turn immediately to scorn. The historian Celia Heller sees in these events the rigidities of a caste system in which the Jew always remains inferior to the Pole, no matter what his social status or wealth.[2]

Even those who flirted with Polish patriotism found their position anomalous or indeed unwelcome. Between the wars, the Yiddish poet Moshe Shimmel commented ruefully on his earlier years, when he wrote in Polish, empathetically exploring patriotic Polish feelings: "Even if you were to sing of the homesickness of generations of Polish immigrants or hymn Poland's fallen heroes, the sigh of their last breath and their trembling dreams, . . . even then they will gird themselves against you with their spears."[3] Similarly, if less poetically, a resolution of the Polonist Society at the Jagiellonian University in Cracow passed in February 1937 simply and brutally barred Jews from membership.[4]

Isaiah Berlin, the brilliant historian and polymath, made another kind of distinction, in a conversation with the grandson of the Russian-born economist Alexander (Shura) Gerschenkron. Reflecting on "Shura," who had been born in Odessa around the turn of the century, Berlin, who lived in England, said, "Odessa was a very unRussian Russian town. Doesn't mean you couldn't be Russian there. Your grandfather was. Fundamentally he was Russian. Culturally he was a Russian. But his home was not Russia, it was Russian literature."[5] In the same way Isaiah Berlin himself, despite his many honors, his distinguished career, the knighthood he was awarded in middle age, always insisted that in England he was "a Jew from Riga."

While our image of Jews from Eastern Europe has been formed by pictures of poor immigrants arriving at Ellis Island in New York or the famous series by Roman Vishniac of impoverished street vendors and Talmud students in Poland in the the 1930s, not all of the Jews were poor or picturesque. In each country, despite the impediments that applied to most Jews, a thin layer had risen to affluence, and in

Hungary in the days of the old Hapsburg monarchy some wealthy Jewish families had even been ennobled.

But whatever their rank, the Jews did not fit into the world in which they had been born. Those who came to Germany after the Second World War and remained there had been shaped by their earlier lives, by the attitudes those lives formed, by the political positions they dictated. These Jews expected to be lifelong strangers. Group portraits are always suspect, but I believe that there is a common profile among the Eastern European Jews who moved to the West: certain convictions, principles of behavior, ways of thinking. The memoirs of the survivors of the concentration camps and interviews with these and other Eastern European Jews reveal a varied and highly nuanced response to the world, but one that at its core shows a fundamental alienation from their homelands. It is this core conviction, with its presumption about the nature of the world, that lay behind their decisions about where to settle after the war. It gives us some clue to how they made choices about their postwar lives and the emotional momentum that carried them forward.

The fundamental alienation of the Eastern European Jews from their homelands, as it turned out, also had its uses during the frightful war years, because their lifelong wariness led them to be careful with their trust. In this connection, I have long meditated on a story told to me by Gita Glazer, a young woman who was living in Lodz when it was annexed to the Third Reich in September 1939 following Germany's invasion of Poland. After renaming the city Litzmannstadt, the Germans turned its 160,000 Jews into a slave-labor force dedicated to producing goods for the German army. In May 1940 Gita, together with the other Jews of the city, was forced into the sealed ghetto set up by the Germans, who supervised not only production, but every detail of life.[6] Food was kept to a bare subsistence level, and the Jewish inmates were crowded together under such dangerously unsanitary conditions that outbreaks of typhus were not unusual. At the end of 1941 the half-starved, debilitated Jews in the ghetto suddenly had to make room for new transports from the West. In the months of October and November 1941, the Germans began to "cleanse" Jews from cities in the "Old Reich," as well as from Austria and Czechoslovakia, by deporting them to the East. In these first transports, 20,000 German Jews were sent to the Lodz ghetto.

When they arrived, according to Gita, the Polish Jews were astonished at how well nourished the new arrivals seemed, at the good, warm clothes they were wearing, at their seeming health. And yet, as she put it, once in the ghetto, "they died like flies" of no apparent cause. Her impression is substantiated by statistics showing that 3,000 of the new arrivals died in the first weeks after their arrival.[7] The reason the appalling death rate may have been less than metaphysical, for the aged and the sick were heavily represented among those "selected" for this transport. Yet even so, the numbers are provocative. What Gita was saying was that the Lodz Jews were somehow better prepared morally and psychologically to withstand the hardships imposed on them by the German occupiers. For the German Jews, whatever their physical condition, this final shock destroyed them. What has haunted me about this story are the assumptions behind it: that the Polish Jews' widespread expectation of the enmity of the outside world, and their psychological armoring against this hostility, played a role in their ultimate survival. Although the captive Jews knew that they were in a deadly situation dependent on chance and the whim of their captors, they also discovered that where there was a sliver of hope, ingenuity and the will to struggle played a role in their preservation. Unlike the Jews from the West, the Jews of Eastern Europe had gone to a hard school.

As the German-imposed ghettos gradually enclosed more and more Eastern European Jews, the inmates had two responses: the first and most immediate was to maintain their humanity despite the calculated German strategy to destroy not only their bodies but every shred of self-respect. The second was the universal desire to leave evidence behind of the events as they were happening. In the ghettos, then, the Jews doggedly did what they could to ameliorate their day-to-day situation by carrying on some semblance of a cultural life. They ran clandestine schools for the children, wrote subversive songs, produced plays and cabaret evenings. The banning of schools for children was part of a long-range German strategy, as spelled out in a memorandum, labeled "secret," written in Lodz by a Nazi officer on November 18, 1940. "Some Thoughts on the Management of Foreign Peoples in the East" lays out the permissible curriculum for the ghetto schools: "Simple reckoning until, at the highest, 500; writing of one's name; the teaching that it is God's law to be obedient to the Germans; and also to be honest, industrious and conscientious. I think that reading is not necessary."[8] However much Nazi ideology may have attempted to reduce the Jews to a state of pure brutishness, the Jews themselves insisted on their civilization and demonstrated it in their illegal cultural activities.

Hardened though Eastern European Jews may have been to the endemic anti-Semitism to which they had grown accustomed, even they knew that something extraordinary and extraordinarily frightful was happening. In the long Jewish tradition of recording and remembering for future generations, those trapped in the ghettos early determined that their story should be set down. The impulse was of long standing, as old as Jewish history; it derived its strength from the injunction in Deuteronomy that concludes the biblical story of Amalek, the king who led his people in a triumphant slaughter of the Jews as they emerged from their wandering in the desert. "Remember Amalek," the biblical verse reads, "and what he did to you on your journey after you left Egypt—how, undeterred by fear of God, he surprised you on the march, when you were famished and weary, and cut down all the stragglers in your rear. Therefore . . . you shall blot out the memory of Amalek from under heaven. Do not forget!" (25: 17–19).

They did not forget. Over two millennia, the Jews have accumulated many enemies. Persecutors may come and go, but their murderous interchangeability remains. Haman and his evil deeds are revisited at Purim every year in the reading of the story of Esther; the torments of the Inquisition, of the tsars of Russia, and of Hitler's time were all variants on the theme of Amalek. It was a history in which time was blurred and Amalek was as immediate as Hitler. In fact, in the ghettos and the concentration camps, no Jew would utter the name of Hitler. But "Amalek" as his pseudonym was clearly understood by the initiates.

The scholars in the ghetto early realized that they might not survive to tell their story in person, but they were determined to leave behind a systematic account of the life around them, a record of all that Amalek had done. Their sense of their place in history and their passion to record the horrors of the Nazi crimes were fueled in part by the conviction that no one would believe what they had endured unless it was carefully and clearly documented. The inmates of the Lodz ghetto, as well as those of many others, deliberately kept a collective journal, supplying statistics, names, details of daily life—all in an attempt to leave behind a sober, irrefutable report that would plead their cause, should the keepers of the journal not survive. One of the first such documents to be published after the war was the diary kept by Emanuel Ringelblum and his associates in the Warsaw ghetto and buried for safekeeping in three different places in rubberized metal milk cans. His purpose, Ringelblum wrote in December 1943, was to "make sure that not a single fact about Jewish life at this time and place will be kept from the world."[9]

Marcel Reich-Ranicki, a Polish Jew who after the war became a prominent literary critic in Germany, spent several years working in the Jewish administrative office in the Warsaw ghetto where he had access to documents of historical importance. One day Ringelblum appeared in his office and asked the young Reich-Ranicki to help in collecting material. In Ringelblum's archive, reports Reich-Ranicki, "everything was gathered up: directives, posters, diaries, circulars, street-car tickets, statistics, illegal newspapers, scientific and literary works. These were intended to be of use to future historians." They also had a more immediate use. "On the basis of these materials," Reich-Ranicki continues, "reports were drawn up for the Polish underground movement and also for the Polish government-in-exile in London."

Ringelblum himself, whom Reich-Ranicki describes as a "tireless organizer, always in a hurry . . . was hunted down by the SS together with his family in Warsaw in 1944 and shot in the ruins of the no longer existing Ghetto."[10]

There were also other kinds of documentation that Jews caught up in the horrors of Nazi persecution felt impelled to preserve. In the last weeks of the war, as the Germans in occupied Poland realized that they would soon be overtaken by the advancing Red Army, they determined to erase some of the grossest evidence of their crimes. A group of Jewish prisoners from Bialystok were marched into the nearby forest, having been first outfitted with especially visible uniforms and laden with twenty-five-pound chains to prevent their escape. Their task was to unearth a series of mass graves of Jews who had been shot, to stack the corpses in alternating layers with wood sawed from the surrounding trees, and then to burn the resulting pyre. Aware that the Nazis hoped in this way to destroy the evidence of their murderous operations, a number of the so-called Burners, at enormous risk to themselves, decided to deposit some of this grisly evidence where it could be found after the war.

"Even in the very first days," Simon Amiele and Salman Edelman, two of the Burners from Bialystok wrote, "we decided to take steps that later could be brought to the attention of the whole world. Once one of the Germans said to us, 'None of you will survive this. But even if you do and report it, no one will believe you.'" This only spurred the Burners on to devise a means of gathering proof. They watched their guards carefully, and when their attention was diverted for a moment, the workers would "drag the arm of a corpse, a rib, a skull . . . throw it into the ditch and cover it with sand. . . . We firmly believed that one of us would survive and that one day we would be able to testify before a court as to all the horrors that we had endured."[11] In the depths of the forest, no less than in Lodz, these Jews believed in the final justice of history.

Nine hundred thousand Jews perished at Treblinka, a camp dedicated solely to killing. Richard Glazar, one of the fifty-four survivors, was able to escape with a friend, Karl Unger during the astonishingly well organized uprising of the prisoners on August 2, 1943. Believing that they were the sole survivors from the burning camp, the two invented new identities for themselves as Czech laborers and moved west across the Polish countryside. Eventually they were picked up by the Polish police and sent to Germany as conscripted workers for a factory in Mannheim. But as the Allied bombers and artillery closed in on the house they shared with a fellow worker named Heinrich, Glazar and Unger began to worry lest the story of the crimes of Treblinka and the names of the murderers perish with them.

"We were now a group of three," he wrote in his memoir, "no longer just a pair. And one of three has a better chance of surviving than one of two. Nor could we imagine a more appropriate stage-set for our story than the drama that was taking place outside. 'Heinrich,' we said, 'take a good strong pull on the bottle, and listen to us. We are going to give you a testimony—and you will take over the responsibility for it—in the event that we two . . .'"[12] As it turned out, Glazar survived to write a detailed memoir of life and death at Treblinka.

Whether they were recording the history of a community or their own experiences, Jews shared a passion for remembering and keeping a permanent account of what had happened to those caught up in the Nazi juggernaut. The Germans had done their best to camouflage their intentions, deceiving their victims to the very last moment, persuading them that they were being sent to the "showers," which, as we know, released only the gas that would kill them. Trains arriving at the death camp Treblinka stopped at the elaborately painted facade of a nonexistent railway station, with windows labeled "Tickets" and arrows showing the way to a "Waiting Room." To prevent panic, special guards were assigned to escort the aged gently to a building labeled "Field Hospital," where they were simply shot.

But even in tightly guarded Treblinka, in September 1942, in the midst of war, the working Jews managed to send two emissaries to Warsaw to warn the Jews there to take action to defend themselves against deportation. Their aim was nothing less than global. "The task is," one of the organizers instructed the messengers, "to report about Treblinka. To give testimony to the underground organization in Warsaw. They will then try to convey the information abroad by way of the Polish underground—to England." How can we measure their success? Ten months later the last survivors of the Warsaw ghetto were brought to Treblinka, received by their fellow Jews almost with reverence. They learned that the two who escaped had at least succeeded in letting the world know, even if they were not able to save the Jews of Warsaw. Their bitter accomplishment was that "the Germans had to resort to tanks and heavy artillery to defeat the rebels [in the Warsaws ghetto], with its women, and aged men and children.

Their legacy was the injunction to 'throw away all the last bric-a-brac of life, give up hope that you may be the last to survive, but show the world and yourself' what you can do."[13]

After the war these accounts took on a different urgency. All those lives had been taken, and now it was time for the executioners to pay for their crimes. It was for this purpose that those who had felt the barbarism in their own flesh or had seen it with their own eyes earnestly hoarded evidence. This hunger for justice was bound up not only with a need for revenge but also with a sense of history. Some remnants of the Jewish people would survive even this catastrophe, and those who had passed through it wanted it reported correctly and the evildoers punished. What lay at the root of these stratagems to leave a record was the victims' awareness that they were not just randomly selected individuals who were being destroyed. They had been marked for murder as Jews—a fact of life that may have been more salient in the East, where it had been burned into their consciousness, than in the West. They had turned that very separateness into a strength.

Among German Jews who had fled in time, the concept of Amalek also retained all its Old Testament force. After the war the German Jews wrestled with the problem of whether it was permissible to visit Germany much less to return to live there. In New York in 1959 the Representative Committee of Former German Jews passed a resolution to the effect that "no former Jewish citizen of Germany should ever again claim German nationality, unless he does it by his express personal wish," an escape clause presumably provided for those seeking to reclaim property. This formula was adopted by other organizations, among them the Council for the Protection of the Rights and Interests of the Jews from Germany. Commenting on the discussion that swirled around these issues, the historian Harry Maor noted, "This was the reawakening of the old Biblical concept of the arch-enemy Amalek whose place was now taken by Germany."[14]

In the same way the old concept of the Diaspora—galuth, in its Hebrew form—was invoked somewhat defensively by those Jews who had either returned or decided to stay on in Germany. At a meeting of the Jewish community of Württemberg in 1959, the membership reflected that "there was a difference between the new return of Jews to Germany who had earlier emigrated to Israel—the Promised Land—on the one hand and those who came from all other countries. What all these other countries have in common, in contrast to Israel, is that they are all part of the galuth. Whoever goes from Germany to America or from America to Germany has simply exchanged one stay in the galuth with another. From the Jewish point of view, there is no essential difference whether one finds oneself in Germany or America, although, of course, after all that has happened one would prefer every other galuth land over Germany."[15]

These were feelings that had deep roots in Jewish tradition but had dimmed in the two centuries before Hitler amid the Westernization of German Jewish life. In the postwar world, German Jews, shaken by their experiences of the previous twelve years, were re-examining the principles that had served them in the past. The basic belief in Jewish separateness, which was antithetical to the principles of the Enlightenment, had been suspended for them during the heady years of emancipation. And their sense of being part of Germany had only increased during the Weimar years, when the very constitution of the new Republic had been drafted by a Jew.

For a hundred years, German Jews had thought of themselves as Germans. But in the aftermath of the Nazi terror, the old biblical and Zionist distinction between homeland and galuth took on new force. All this came to the fore in the first years after the war, when the few

German Jews who had survived in their homeland confronted the delicate and difficult question of whether to stay or to go. For those who accepted the idea of galuth, it meant abandoning the aspirations cherished by Jews since the age of Moses Mendelssohn and accepting the Zionist view that only the land of Israel was home; all other countries were places of temporary domicile. But the homeland-galuth distinction also served to neutralize the decision of those who decided to remain in Germany. All of galuth was equal and equally alien. There was nothing more reprehensible, therefore, about living in Germany than in America.

For the Jews in Eastern Europe, however, their centuries-old sense of alienation from their surrounding world had hardly changed during the interwar years, even though young Jews in Poland were speaking more Polish than Yiddish and more Jewish children were attending state than Jewish schools. But even as Jews participated more fully in the culture around them, official, politically driven anti-Semitism kept them from ever feeling truly a part of their native land. In the classroom they learned early that they could not recite with the other children in the room the "Polish child's credo":

Who are you? A little Pole.
What is your sign? The white eagle.[16]

In Eastern Europe the Jews lived under particularly anxious circumstances, but they were not the only minority in their part of the world. In spite of the myth of homogeneity that went with the official national histories, in Eastern Europe every boundary had been bitterly fought over for centuries. With maps being steadily redrawn as a consequence of war or diplomacy, whole populations could wake up one morning to find that their nationality, ruler, and even their official language had been changed overnight. Sometimes large populations seeking to align their inherited culture with the new boundaries, migrated en masse as people sought to join their kinfolk. Border areas in particular reflected these changes in their many layers of peoples.

Czernowitz, a flourishing multinational city of 94,000 in the old Austro-Hungarian Empire, then predominantly German-speaking, is a good example of this mixture. After the First World War, when the Empire was broken up, Czernowitz was ceded to Romania and re-named Cernauti. But it still had its old polyglot population of Ger-mans, Poles, Austrians, Romanians, German-speaking Jews, Yiddish-speaking Jews, and Ladino-speaking Sephardic Jews, as well as Ukrainians and Russians, not to mention the regularly visiting Gyp-sies. After the Second World War, Czernowitz/Cernauti was awarded to the Ukrainian Republic in the Soviet Union and renamed yet again, this time Chernovtsy. Under such circumstances, it would have been hard for anyone to remember where his patriotic loyalty lay. Adminis-trations were transitory, governments were far away. What survived was nationality.

Under all rulers, however, the Jews were a people apart. In the culture of Eastern Europe, where language and religion were funda-mental identifiers, the Jews had never been allowed to forget that their forefathers had killed the God of the Christians. It is no wonder that they felt themselves born into a different society from their neighbors. And this led to a development of Jewish life in Eastern Europe that in the previous two centuries had diverged widely from that in Western Europe. For a long time Eastern Europe had been the cradle of Jew-ish learning, so that Jewish communities in Western Europe imported their rabbis, cantors, teachers, kosher slaughterers, and other func-tionaries from the East in order to carry on their religious life. By the end of the eighteenth century a more critical view of these experts began to prevail in the Jewish communities of the West. Influenced by the range and methods of Western learning, a new generation sud-denly began to find the teachers from the East ignorant, barbaric and superstitious—adjectives that appeared again and again in the writings of the "Enlightened" Jews.

It was only gradually that this intellectual freedom and these fresh ideas began to move East; with few exceptions the rabbis and teachers in the religious academies—the yeshivot—regarded them as little better than sacrilegious. Although the battleground at first was in the advanced schools of learning, these disputes were not just scholarly but were rightly perceived by the heads of the yeshivot as ideas profoundly dangerous to the received tradition, threatening to bring fundamental changes in the structure of Jewish communities both East and West.

In the West modernity implied a change not only in the status of the Jews in society but also in the attitude of their Christian neighbors. In Eastern Europe, however, the rigid separation of peoples retained its medieval character into the twentieth century. For the Jews in the East, this meant the construction of an entire parallel world. A community of any size had its governing body—the *kehillah*—as well as its institutions: synagogue and cemetery, schools, slaughterhouse, and ritual bath. Larger centers maintained schools of higher learning, orphanages, hospitals, hostels for travelers, a poorhouse for the indigent and elderly, and a network of voluntary associations to meet every human emergency. There were societies to provide dowries for poor brides, credit and loan banks, institutions for the support of students, holy brotherhoods for the burial of the dead. All these institutions as well as the necessary employees and officials were maintained out of the taxes and fees the community levied on its members.

Because the Jews often lived in densely populated segregated villages, these often took on a quality that travelers from abroad and even those who lived in them could not overlook. They were marked by a sense of decay and neglect. Buildings rotted and crumbled, streets were unpaved, the mud in spring and autumn was legendary, and

Jews in interwar Poland lived in many different knds of environments, from the capital, Warsaw, to the famous muddy villages, the *shtetlach* of legend. This is Wysock, a tiny village in Volhynia in 1937. Photographer Moshe Raviv. YIVO—Institute for Jewish Research, New York.

amenities were few. The surviving photographs of the old synagogues and houses of study show cluttered rooms, shabby furniture, tattered books leaning on shelves in disarray. Was this poverty? Was this, as anti-Semites intimated, a sign of depraved Jewish character? Or was it quite simply how people lived who had no right to the land they occupied, no guaranteed future in the place where they lived? At any moment, their meager possessions could be expropriated; they could be expelled without recourse or set upon by neighbors or government forces suddenly turned savage. This mood was perfectly captured by Sholem Aleichem in one of the last of his Tevya stories. After the revolution of 1905, which badly misfired, the Jews were being expelled from the villages where they had lived for generations and pushed into the cities. Tevya, pondering the hardships around him, reflects that now, at last, was the time for the Messiah to arrive on his white horse. As he sits on a bench in front of his house, musing in this way, he actually sees in the distance a white horse and rider approaching. In a perfect ironical touch, the horseman turns out to be not the Messiah, of course, but the agent of the *starosta,* the head man of the village, who tells Tevya that he has come with orders to destroy Tevya's property. Because he and Tevya have known one another for a long time, he finally relents, though for appearances' sake he must at least break Tevya's windows, even if he doesn't empty the feather beds and otherwise loot the house. But he has much more important news: Tevya must vacate his property immediately and move to "his own people" in Berdichev, the nearest big city. Tevya protests—reminding the rider that his ancestors for generations have been buried in the Jewish graveyard, that his family has lived in the village longer than many of the peasants who are now its residents. But his protests are of no use. The new ordinance clearly specifies "Jews," and they are to be herded into the cities. Their past is of no interest to the lawmakers.

The historian Ben-Cion Pinchuk remarks on yet another aspect of the Jewish villages. "Very little attention," he points out, "was paid to external decoration, painting or gardening—these were more characteristic of their non-Jewish neighbors."[17] Nor did Jews keep pets. They kept horses, poultry, and cattle for use, but not even a dog for protection. Jewish travelers on the road were so often set upon by peasants' dogs that the animals had become in themselves a symbol of vicious anti-Semitism. This conviction was so deeply rooted in Eastern European Jewish feelings that a playwright could set a whole theatre laughing by arranging a tableau with the right elements. In Sholem Aleichem's play *The Big Win,* a little elderly couple discover that they have won the lottery. The next scene is devoted to demonstrating their new splendor. The curtain goes up to show them sitting practically lost in baronial chairs in front of an immense stone fireplace. What makes this paradise ludicrous, for a Jewish audience, is that at their sides are two huge Great Danes. This was existence at its most absurd.

Added to the sense of life as a temporary sojourn was the traditional Hasidic caution against building synagogues that were too beautiful lest they presume to compete with the destroyed sacred Temple in Jerusalem. This injunction was perhaps not always observed, and certainly did not apply to traditional Jews who were not Hasidim. Nonetheless, aesthetics was not high on the Jewish cultural agenda, a fact viewed with some irony by the more worldly members of the community. Writing lovingly about the Yiddish writers' center at number 13 Tlomackie Street in Warsaw during the interwar period, Y. Y. Trunk noted, "If a Jew from the provinces who only knows the little Hasidic prayer houses would suddenly come upon Tlomackie 13, he would have been very surprised. . . . [He would see that] the great distance from secular literature to, as it were, 'the way of the prayer-house' is not at all so great as the unclean witnesses [the secular Jews] would have him believe. Already on the steps of the Literary Union such a Jew would feel the spirit of the Hasidic prayer-house. The steps were dirty and twisted, and one always smelled the smells of all kinds of Jewish cooking."[18]

In their long sojourn in Eastern Europe, then, the Jews had developed not only a physical world but also a style of life that grew out of their special circumstances. Despite centuries of settlement in the East, the Jews had remained rigorously separate, at least spiritually, from the life around them. On a folk level, of course, there was a natural sharing of homemade remedies, foods, and superstitions without either the peasants or the Jews recognizing the common elements in their lives. They all ate kasha and rye bread and borsht, and they shared the same fear of the Evil Eye. But all the while each group remained firmly convinced of its superiority to the other.

Apart from a few well-publicized—and aberrant—episodes of conversion, the Jews continued soberly and steadily in their religious belief and practices. In Eastern Europe unforced conversion was rare, and adherence to Judaism was more than simply a belief in a body of religious dogma. In everyday rituals, as well as in the celebration of many holidays, the Jews were steadily reminded of their long history as a people. In the yearly cycle of reading the Scriptures in the synagogue, they remembered their exodus from Egypt, their acceptance of the Law from the hands of Moses, their rescue from extinction in Persia, the miraculous triumph of the Maccabees over encroaching Hellenism, the day of mourning for the destruction of the Temple by the Romans. (In fact, the Yiddish word for this destruction, *khurbn,* has retained its resonance over the centuries and returned in full force in the Yiddish press and literature to describe the Holocaust of the twentieth century.)

Jewish communities turned inward, seeing themselves always and forever as a people in exile, in goles (as Yiddish-speaking Jews would say, using the Yiddish pronunciation of the Hebrew word *galuth*). This powerful word represents not only a physical fact but also a state of mind: the Jew who lived everywhere and was at home nowhere. Fifty years after the Holocaust, Felix Zandman, a Jew from the neighborhood of Grodno who had become a successful entrepreneur in the United States, showed in a brief interview how profoundly this feeling shaped his thinking. He did not speak only for himself, of course, but expressed the deeply rooted attitude of his world. Zandman grew up in a small town with five thousand Jews. As a child he once asked his grandmother whether the house in which they lived belonged to them. "Nothing belongs to us," she answered, "only that which we have in our heads and can pass on to others."[19]

Eleven years old when the war began, Zandman soon began to see the truth of this maxim. He was saved from the German search parties by a Polish woman who hid him and a few other Jews, including his cousin, in her house. To pass their long days in the darkness of their hiding place, his cousin, who was a scientist, taught him mathematics and physics. By the end of the war, Zandman was seventeen and the sole Jewish survivor of his town. He decided to leave Poland and made his way to France to study science—this time more formally at the university. Eventually, he came to the United States, where he started a successful electronics business with branches in several countries, including Israel.

Although he is now an American citizen, he has lived in many parts of the world, which provoked an inevitable question during an interview with a reporter for the Israeli newspaper *Ha'aretz*. He was asked how he defined himself. "I have an American passport," he answered, "and an Israeli passport. Formerly I had a French passport, as well as a Polish one. But from my point of view my passport always was and remains a Jewish one. I am a goles Jew."[20] All his many stops, in many countries, were to him mere accidentals. What was immutable was goles. This concept which shaped the way Eastern European Jews thought of themselves, was also inseparable from their condition.

One of the premises of Eastern European Jewish life was its dense uniformity, its adherence to a highly organized, traditional Judaism which governed every action, profane as well as sacred. In addition to the conventional religious services in the synagogue, Jewish laws governed the business world, with regulations on property and trade. In the domestic sphere it included food, dress, manners and mores, and even sexual practices. Where there was serious dispute on matters of business, property, or even domestic affairs, Jews had recourse to their own court—the Beth Din—which protected the litigants from the vagaries or humiliations of official justice. Unlike the Jewish communities in the West, however, the Kehilla—the governing body of the Eastern European Jewry—was unbending in its opposition to innovation. This practice of living a complete life among themselves became the cornerstone, as we shall see, of the Jews' immediate postwar existence.

Some who fell under the spell of Western philosophy, science, or literature fled to the West to study in the universities and take up a profession closed to them in the East. Some of them fled simply to escape what had become an intolerable way of life, as they saw it, deformed by its superstition and insularity.

Jews in the East who were enticed by the Enlightenment but who stayed, responded to it in characteristic Eastern European fashion. The typically young Maskilim—the followers of the Enlightenment—did not seek to join the majority culture or attempt to integrate Jewish thought with Russian or Polish language and literature. Rather, they created a parallel secular world within the Jewish community. Like their earlier counterparts in Germany, they nourished Hebrew as a living language for the writing of poetry and other profane literature, for the development of political ideas, for the creation of a new kind of Jewish culture.

The Jewish world of Eastern Europe, then, was far from static. Especially in the last century of its existence, it was full of ferment as it dealt in its own way with the currents of secularism: such liberating philosophies as socialism, nationalist ideas of separatism, Yiddishism, Zionism. All these gave Jewish youth at the end of the nineteenth century many alternatives to the theocratic society into which they had been born. In time, even the religious sphere became less than monolithic.

Although scholars made up a visible and perhaps picturesque part of Eastern European life, they were hardly representative of the working world. On the whole those young men who entered on a life of study also entered on a life of poverty and dependence, supported by their wives or their in-laws. But even in Eastern Europe, by the end of the nineteenth century alternatives to the traditional theocratically centered life began to create a stir.

The issue was goles. How was a Jew to live in the modern world? For most Jews of Eastern Europe, goles was their way of living both within and apart from the physical world into which they happened to have been born. By the end of the nineteenth century, however, the young and the poor of Eastern Europe were listening attentively to passionate—and conflicting—views on what their future ought to be. The great secular movement that stubbornly insisted on the Jews' right to stay where they were born and to conduct their lives as Jews in a just, socialist society was the Bund, or the General Jewish Workers' League in Russia and Poland. Founded in 1897, the same year as the Zionist movement, the Bund cherished the variety of Jewish life in the Diaspora—its languages, its culture, the Jewish sense of self as a people, with its own destiny. They affirmed and embraced Jewish rootedness in the Diaspora, referring to it in Yiddish as *doikeyt*—hereness. The socialist Bund had principles that went far beyond a conventional trade union program for better wages and working conditions. They even campaigned for more humane conditions for Jewish soldiers in the army. But above all, the Bund was a secular, nationalist counterweight to the Zionist movement. After World War I the Versailles accord, which gave official minority status to the Jews in Poland, was a step in exactly the right direction for their policy. It accepted the wide dispersion of the Jewish people but insisted that wherever a Jewish community might find itself it should have the right to cultivate its own culture and its Jewish consciousness.

For the Zionists, goles was a condition not to be endured but to be fought. Their purpose was to negate goles and claim the ancient

Two views of girls' education in Poland during the interwar years: above, girls at
a *cheder* (traditional elementary school) in a small town, Lakarev in Lublin
province. They have a woman teacher and are probably learning prayers.
Note the ragged pages from which they are reading. Below, girls in a laboratory of
a trade school for girls. YIVO—Institute for Jewish Research, New York.

Land of Israel (Eretz Israel, then called Palestine) as the homeland in which Jews would build a new Jewish state. Although the Zionists won hundreds of thousands of adherents, the conditions of life in Palestine required a courage and a hardiness that only the most dedicated could summon up. But its appeal, in principle at least, can be measured by the fact that 400,000 Jews in Poland signed up to to vote in the 1921 Zionist election for its international officers.[21] The Zionists—although divided in their beliefs as to what the future Jewish state should look like—were united in their conviction that there was no future for Jewish life in the Diaspora in general and in Poland in particular. What was needed was a Jewish state in the land of Israel.

Even before the Balfour Declaration of 1917 in which the British seemed to promise "a Jewish national home," and well before the formal creation of the Zionist Organization in 1897, the idea had circulated with increasing force, especially among the idealistic young, that the Jews, like other peoples, were entitled to their homeland.

Since the 1880s pioneering groups had been buying land in Palestine, training themselves in agriculture, animal husbandry, the cultivation of vineyards—whatever they envisioned as useful to the establishment of a new Jewish state. Some 120,000 dedicated settlers emigrated there between 1881 and 1930. But the lure of Palestine could not begin to compete with the siren charms of the New World, the Golden Land.[22] In a movement that was almost messianic in its force, a fever to emigrate to America swept across Eastern Europe at the end of the nineteenth century, reaching into the smallest towns and villages. German and English shipping companies vied with one another for this trade, building larger and larger ships—some big enough to hold a thousand passengers. In the three decades before World War I some two and a half million Jews, mostly young families or single young people, left their homes in Eastern Europe to settle in America. By the time free entrance to the United States was closed in 1924, nearly one third of the Jewish population in Eastern Europe had left.

For many of those who remained, the new political movements, with their proposals for a different and better life, challenging the age-old rabbinical system, all had their appeal, but so did the traditionalists. The religious Jews, who spurned Zionism on the ground that it anticipated the coming of the Messiah, who rejected America as an unholy land, and who, of course, rejected the secular attitudes of the Socialists and Bundists, found a home in the Agudas Israel—the Union of Israel. The very conservatism of this party's program was a great virtue in the eyes of Jews who feared the encroachment of secular ways on the old theocratically organized society. Fighting the powerful forces of modernization that were invading the Jewish community from all sides, the Agudas understood that its schools were its main weapon in the battle to capture and indoctrinate the next generation. Although each of the competing movements also set up schools to further its particular ideology, the Agudas schools, which had the weight of tradition behind them, made up the largest and most influential network in the Russian Empire.[23]

Immutable as this old system had seemed to those who were in flight from it, ultimately even this society was fractured by the First World War. As boundaries changed, monarchies tumbled, and even the vast Russian Empire was overthrown by a revolution, the old tightly closed Jewish community was also caught up in the cataclysm. The official minority status awarded to Jews after World War I only underlined the difference between Jewish aspirations in Eastern Europe and Jewish expectations in the West. During the French Revolution, when the Jews had won the right to be citizens of the Republic, they had wanted nothing less than to be Frenchmen, just as German Jews wanted to be counted as Germans. In the classic formulation in 1893 of the most important Jewish defense organization in Germany, the German Jews defined themselves as "German citizens of the Jewish faith." It was a formula that would have applied as well to Jews anywhere in the Western world where birth and culture determined nationality while religion remained a private matter.

In Poland, however, a country where Polish nationalism had been honed to a fever pitch by a century of Russian repression, nationality was defined more narrowly. It was not easy for Polish patriots to recognize that by the time the Versailles Treaty established the boundaries of their new republic, it actually contained only a slim majority (55.5 percent) of people who called themselves Poles. In the passion for "self-determination" that gripped the makers of the Versailles Treaty, they also accorded minority rights to other definable groups on Polish soil. Suddenly the three million Jews, who made up 11 percent of the population, were only one of a number of officially designated nationalities: a position that they had, of course, occupied de facto all along. The largest minority was the Ukrainian, accounting for 18 percent of the population, followed by smaller numbers of Germans, White Russians, and Lithuanians.[24] Each nationality had the right to send representatives to the new Polish Seym or parliament. In the Jewish community this only served to reinforce the boundaries between the existing parties, each of which hoped to play a major role. Ultimately eleven Jewish parties were represented in the Seym, although their voices counted for less than they had hoped, as the politics of the country took a sharply undemocratic turn.

With their formal standing as an official minority within the new Polish boundaries, the Jews no longer existed solely on sufferance. Yet apart from a small number of adventurous intellectuals, there was little rapprochement between the majority Polish Catholic population and the minority Jews. In spite of the formal political changes at Versailles, it quickly became apparent that Poland between the wars was less than an ideal place for Jews. The Poles, at last masters in their own house, had no intention of turning their country into a pluralistic society. And the drive toward Polonization became a dominating political force.

The postwar liberal constitution was quickly abrogated in 1921, when the Pilsudski regime took over in a coup d'etat. During the next fourteen years Pilsudski was able to keep the clamorous anti-Semitic parties in check. Yet it was the Pilsudski government that signed a nonaggression pact with Nazi Germany in 1934 and invited Propaganda Minister Goebbels to lecture at Warsaw University.

After Pilsudski's death in May 1935, the right-wing parties came into their own, particularly the violently reactionary and anti-Semitic National Democratic Party known as the Endeks, whose aim was to force the Jews out of Poland by instituting an economic boycott. In the midst of a worldwide depression, what was more convenient than to blame all of Poland's problems—especially its economic ones—on the Jews? Poland was still an agricultural country, and overpopulation in the villages as well as the unemployment in the cities led to an inevitable lowering of wages. The mass emigration that had been the solution to domestic difficulties for Jew and Pole alike was now much reduced as a result of new American legislation that severely limited immigrants from Eastern Europe. At home the Jews were doubly disadvantaged.

Many parties concurred with the Endek proposition that the Jews should emigrate. This position had a long history in Poland, and sometimes the persuasion took the form of pogroms. On the very day that World War I ended, for example, there was a murderous pogrom in Kielce, and a few days later a pogrom in Lwow claimed sixty-four

Jewish lives. In April 1919 a pogrom in Vilna resulted in the death of sixty-five Jews and the looting and destruction of two thousand Jewish homes and businesses.[25] These eruptions continued sporadically throughout the interwar period. As late as 1935–36, more than twelve hundred Jews were wounded in such outbursts.[26]

But most effective in cutting off Jewish means of self-support was the economic boycott. Jews had long been disadvantaged by laws restricting where and how they could work. They were all but excluded from the civil service, so that by 1931, out of 87,640 government employees, only 599 were Jews.[27] In the same year only some 2 percent of elementary and high school teachers were Jewish. Jewish doctors and lawyers could conduct private practices but were not admitted to posts in state institutions. These and other limitations forced Jews to work for whatever wages they could get, wherever they could, and this often meant in Jewish-owned enterprises. Even these businesses were endangered, however, by a rising level of anti-Semitism led by the National Democratic Party. If no one would hire them, if no one bought in their stores, if no Pole went to a Jewish doctor or lawyer, according to Endek reasoning, the Jews would soon be forced to move to Palestine, or perhaps to Madagascar, an island that was to figure later in Nazi schemes for ridding themselves of the Jews.

Isolating the Jews was not a new idea. Even before the First World War, the masthead of the National Democratic Party's daily newspaper had carried the slogan "Patronize your own."[28] But now this demand was meant in earnest, and it did not stop at slogans. The nationalists carried on a program of terrorism, photographing and publishing the names of Poles who patronized Jewish stores. And the campaign had its desired effect. Although until the mid-1930s the Jews had had a virtual monopoly of retail stores in the little towns and villages where they lived, by 1938 the number of Jewish businesses had been cut in half, and in Galicia, the Jewish population had become so impoverished that at Passover more than a third of the Jewish households applied for help to tide them over the holiday.[29]

A numerus clausus was proposed for admission to the universities, and although it did not become law, it was tacitly in effect for the medical schools. Nor did the hostile atmosphere in the universities stop short of real violence: there was at least one murder at Warsaw University and several others elsewhere. One newspaper graphically described the methods of discouragement: "The youth movement blocked the way of the Jews so that it was difficult for them to complete all the formalities [for registration]. . . . Those who persisted in making their way to the university campus faced being beaten up with knuckle-dusters and sticks decorated with razors."[30] The effect was measurable. In 1928 Jews had accounted for 20 percent of Polish university students; a decade later they numbered only 7.5 percent.

By 1937 the anti-Semitic forces in the government had gained enough momentum to insist on the "bench ghetto" in the universities to separate and mark out the Jewish students. Indignant, the Jewish students agreed among themselves that rather than sit in the bench ghetto, they would stand either at the left side of the hall or in the aisle. Moshe Prywes, a medical student at Warsaw University, was able to report that several "left-wing liberals" who were not Jews joined them, in a gesture of defiance and solidarity. When in 1939, just before the war, the last twelve Jewish medical students graduated from Warsaw University, they were not invited to the graduation ceremonies but instead were summoned to the dean's office, where they were simply handed their diplomas.[31]

Even the secondary education necessary to qualify for the university was hard for Jews to acquire, for the preparatory schools all required school fees. In view of the impoverished state of the Jewish population, only the well-to-do could afford even to attend the high schools. As a consequence, the Jewish students were members of a small elite class whose very emergence into the public arena exposed them to humiliation and hardship. But whether they were privileged or working class, the unemployment and poverty that awaited them sapped the hopes of the young. In an essay contest conducted in 1936 in Poland by YIVO (the Yiddish Scientific Institute), some six hundred young Jews submitted their autobiographies. Their life histories, written in Yiddish and Polish, express their desperate frustration as they describe their inability to find work, to embark on a career—even to obtain training, because they were excluded from apprenticeship programs.[32] And all this because they were Jews. One young man summarized his feelings in a single sentence: "If one were to ask me to give a single definition of the period in which I live, I would answer: a hopeless generation."[33]

It was not a hopelessness that led to inactivity, however. Many young Jews saw politics—either Zionism or Socialism—as a way out of their unjustly thwarted and impoverished lives. Although America was closed, Palestine was the hope of the Zionists. But after 1936 even emigration to Palestine grew difficult, as British policy became more pro-Arab, imposing quotas on Jewish immigrants. As a consequence, by 1939 only 4,500 Polish Jews were allowed to enter the country, compared with 30,500 in 1935.

In this difficult world, what was surprising was the rich cultural and intellectual life that the Jews of Poland built. At the end of the nineteenth century a new secular Jewish culture had flowered in the medium of Yiddish and in the emergence of new Jewish literary forms. The Yiddish theatre, newspapers, periodicals, Yiddish music, and a network of schools in Yiddish and Hebrew combined to offer an active Jewish cultural life. Jewish schools, though they had to levy school fees, accounted for 20 percent of Jewish school children, and the secular political parties commanded the majority of the political public. In the 1930 national election for the Jewish parties, the Bund

The Maccabee of Warsaw, a Jewish sports club, supported all kinds of
athletic activities, from soccer to skiing to gymnastics. This was its
first motorcycle team, photographed in November 1929.
YIVO—Institute for Jewish Research, New York.

won 10 percent of the votes, the Zionists 65 percent and the Agudas
Israel 21 percent, a convincing secular majority.

United by their common language—Yiddish—millions of Jews
across Eastern Europe read the same books and periodicals, attended
the same plays, and sang the same songs no matter where they lived.
The development of a fresh secular culture rooted in Jewish folk life
continued with unabated energy until it was extinguished along with
the Polish Jews in World War II. As Yiddish writers like the future
Nobel laureate Isaac Bashevis Singer fled to the United States, an outpost of Yiddish culture and publishing sprang up in the New World.

But uprooted from its natural audience and overwhelmed by the force of American life, Yiddish literature, theatre, and even politics gradually became an exercise in nostalgia. The great names of the Warsaw Yiddish Pen Club were somehow only quaint in New York. The audience of Yiddish-speakers was aging and dying, and the new, native-born generation had plunged headlong into American life. After a thousand years in Europe, Yiddish failed to take root on American soil. Like most of their contemporaries, the children of the Jewish immigrants embraced America and, with it, its language.

While Jewish hardship in Poland during the interwar years followed the long-familiar course of discrimination and exclusion, salted with outbursts of violence, in the Soviet Union history took a truly revolutionary course. There the government was able to accomplish in the first half-century after the Revolution what had never occurred before in two thousand years of Jewish exile. It succeeded in destroying memory.

The Russian Empire had been the birthplace of the greatest Yiddish writers, and in cities like Odessa, Warsaw, and Vilna a unique and confident Yiddish-speaking culture had flourished, with schools, periodicals, and clubs that were the basis for an complete cultural world. In 1897 the last census before the Revolution showed that 96.9 percent of the five million Jews in tsarist Russia were Yiddish-speaking.[34] Marc Chagall spent his entire painterly career reincarnating in dreamlike landscapes the homely features of his birthplace, Vitebsk. Newspapers, magazines, and an active publishing industry in both Hebrew and Yiddish were reflections of a flourishing cultural life. The Jewish theatres not only produced plays in Yiddish but, in Moscow, also started the Hebrew-speaking drama company Habima, which in 1931 moved to Tel Aviv. The greatest modern Hebrew poet, Chaim Nahum Bialik, who also emigrated to Tel Aviv in 1924, began his career in Russia. Yet all this came to an abrupt end. In their eighty-year reign of terror and hardship, the Soviets were able to wipe out not only the Jewish religion but also the rich and famously contentious cultural life of Russian Jews as it had been before the revolution.

The overthrow of the tsarist regime in March 1917 was an event that every oppressed element in the population could only greet with joy. The Jews were among the first to rejoice in and embrace the Social Democratic government of Kerensky. But there were two stages to the revolution with very different faces. Under the social democratic Kerensky regime, which took power after the overthrow of the tsar, the Jews received, for the first time in their history in Russia, the right to free and equal citizenship. As one observer wrote: "Suddenly their chains fell off. . . . The Jews could straighten their backs, and look to the future without fear."[35]

Eight months later, however, in October 1917, when the Bolsheviks seized power, the Jews found themselves caught between sides in the ensuing civil war. Freed from the tsars, the long-suppressed nationalist forces in the old Russian Empire broke out of the new Soviet Union to declare their independence. The Ukraine, Poland, the Baltic States, Armenia, and Azerbaijan formed their own governments. At the same time, forces loyal to the old monarchy organized the White Army, giving the newly established Red Army, with its few Cossack allies, a major task as it attempted to contain the rebellion and sustain the new regime.

In the civil war the Jewish loss of life was immense, especially in the Ukraine. In the three years after the revolution there were 1,520 pogroms, and between 180,000 and 200,000 Jews were killed.[36] If we include all those killed wounded, raped and orphaned by the violence, the victims number no fewer than 1,000,000.[37]

The Bolshevik regime which overthrew the Kerensky moderates, while paying a certain lip service to human rights, did not scruple to use terror and force in order to bring a helpless population into line with its program. We now know the price in human lives and suffering that was exacted for the collectivization of agriculture and the subsequent famine of the 1920s. The destruction of domestic animals, the interruption of farm production, and the paralyzing effect of arbitrary arrests dedicated to rooting out dissidents and the independent farmers, the *kulaks,* led ultimately to the deaths of seven million people. The peasants, barely a century out of serfdom now, became the servants of the state.[38] It is no wonder that they greeted the change grimly and again found an enemy in the Jews, who appeared prominently in the first years of the Bolshevik regime as the agents of the oppressive new government.

For once, the peasants' perception accorded in part with the facts. In the small towns and cities of Tsarist Russia, the Jews had played a special role as the merchant class: proprietors of stores, market stands, and taverns. They were independent artisans, horse and cattle traders in the country, estate managers for the often absentee landlords, and money lenders in a premodern society where banks were scarce and not geared to the needs of small borrowers. After the Revolution of October 1917, these occupations, which had been the mainstay of Jewish economic life, became anathema to a Bolshevik government that was determined to wipe out the "petty bourgeois" trades. At the same time, the Bolsheviks saw in the Jews a pool of relatively educated people in a sea of suspicious and illiterate peasants. Although the number of Jews who were prominent in the Bolshevik party was small, their visibility was great. Figures such as Trotsky, Zinoviev, Kamenev, and Sverdlov were close collaborators of Lenin and were used to confirm a popular impression that Bolshevism was a Jewish movement.[39] Young Jews especially were susceptible to the appeals of the Revolution. It spoke not only to their idealism, to their desire to change the wretched world in which they lived, but also to their own immediate situation. Without work and without prospects for a future in the old order, they seized on this opportunity to make a place for themselves in the new. By joining the party, they could become clerks, administrators, government functionaries, as the new revolutionary government organized its bureaucracy.

There was, however, a difference between the cold-blooded calculation on the government's side and the idealism that motivated many of the first Jewish advocates of the Revolution. Isaac Babel, in one of his stories about the Red Cavalry, describes the death of just such an idealist—Elijah, the son of Rabbi Motale Bratslavsky of Zhitomir. Badly wounded in fighting for the Bolsheviks during the civil war and abandoned by his comrades, Elijah is recognized by Babel, who pulls him onto the "political section" train. As Elijah lies on the floor of the car, Babel catalogues his possessions, evoking the duality of his life. "His things were strewn about," writes Babel, "mandates of the propagandist and notebooks of the Jewish poet, portraits of Lenin and Maimonides lay side by side. . . . A lock of a woman's hair lay in a book, the resolutions of the Party's Sixth Congress and the margins of Communist leaflets were crowded with crooked lines of ancient Hebrew verse." Babel reminds Elijah that when they had met at his father's synagogue in Zhitomir only four months earlier, the boy had not even belonged to the party. "I did," Elijah answered, "only I couldn't leave my mother." "And now, Elijah?" Babel asks. "'When there's a revolution on, a mother's an episode,' [the boy] whispered less and less audibly. 'My letter came, the letter B and the Organization sent me to the front . . . ' He died before we reached Rovno." Babel concludes: "He, the last of the Princes, died among his poetry, phylacteries, and the coarse foot-wrappings."[40]

As the society was remade, the Jews were forced out of their usual way of life, their usual trades, into various collectives or jobs in state enterprises. By 1926 the profile of Jewish occupations had changed radically. The small traders, storekeepers, and peddlers who had made up a third of the Jewish employed dropped to a mere 11 percent, while the number of "nonmanual salaried workers"—that is clerks, party functionaries, and the like—more than doubled from 10 percent to 23 percent. But this was hardly the good news it seemed to be. The Bolsheviks (after 1919, the Communist Party) were interested only in using the Jews until they could develop loyal cadres among the rest of the indigenous population. Then the Jews were faced with a campaign far more virulent, one that struck far more deeply into their sense of identity, than any of the pogroms of the tsars.

What was to be done about the Jews? The nationality question had been carefully discussed at each of the Communist Party congresses since 1917, with the Bolshevik leadership showing itself less and less inclined as time went on to allow free cultural expression to the many minorities that inhabited the vast new state. By 1921 at the Tenth Party Convention, Stalin laid down the latest official position. National self-determination, he said, "has become an empty slogan."[41] Although he could not avoid recognizing the many languages spoken in the Soviet Union, he expected all nationalities to "assimilate" to a "universal proletarian culture," rejecting in one sweeping statement all those folkways, customs, and other aspects of daily life that make up "national culture."

Of all the cultures in the Soviet Union, especially outside Russia, that of the Jews was the most vulnerable. It had no territorial base and no central authority. For as long as anyone could remember, each community of Jews had governed itself through the locally elected kehillah. In this world, where wealth ensured prestige, the kehillah generally drew its members from the more prosperous members of the community, whose political power was sealed in this theocratic society by one of the coveted seats on the east wall of the synagogue. As part of their duties, the officers determined the taxes by which the kehillah supported the vast array of communal institutions and paid their own functionaries. The kehillah as an institution and its leaders as individuals now became targets of the new regime.

A Commissariat for Jewish National Affairs, which was intended as the government's executioner, was appointed by the Bolshevik government in January 1918. By June 1919 the commissariat characterized the Central Boards of the Jewish Communities (the kehillot) as "rallying points for undisguised enemies of the . . . October Revolution" and decreed that they should "be dissolved forever."

This meant not only that all Jewish communal property was turned over to the government but that all religious activity came under close and suspicious government surveillance. Jews who persisted in the old observances laid themselves open to persecution for "counterrevolutionary leanings." The Jewish religious schools were absolutely prohibited. As we know, these were the backbone of Jewish continuity, and the government understood that without them, the Jews in the Soviet Union would in short order lose all knowledge of their history, their sacred texts, their tradition. In their place the government established official schools—conducted in Yiddish, because this was the language of their students, but without any Jewish content. Instead of Jewish history, for example, students were taught a course in "The Class Struggle Among Jews." By 1933 even these schools were regarded by the Stalin regime as a dangerous "deviation," and Jewish parents began sending their children to the Russian schools. By the outbreak of World War II only 20 percent of Jewish children were still in Jewish schools.[42]

Many Jewish children, however, faced a grim future in the new Soviet Union because of their parents' history. Nearly half of the Jews in the old regime had been engaged in trade, which made them "bourgeois," a crime for which they were classified as *lishentsy*—persons deprived of rights. Their children soon discovered that because of this blot on their records, they were barred from schools of higher learning and were ineligible for state housing and for many kinds of employment. Jewish origin, it turned out, was no less a liability under the new regime than under the old, and there was no escape. Under Stalin every Soviet citizen carried an internal passport, whose fifth line gave the bearer's nationality. For Jews, no matter where in the Soviet Union they were born, the line always carried the word *Evreii*— Jew. It was another way in which Jews were clearly marked as different from their fellow citizens.

In a move that had many hidden motives, the government decided in 1928 to improve the condition of the expropriated and unemployed Jews by granting them the territory of Birobidzhan in which they could devote themselves to "productive" agricultural labor. Acquired by Russia in 1858 and located on China's northern border, Birobidzhan was as large as Belgium, though its entire population amounted to some 30,000 people, largely transplanted Cossacks. Some observers believe that the opening of the territory in 1928 may have had less to do with the welfare of the Jews than a need to establish a Soviet presence in the East on the vulnerable Chinese border.[43] The figures for the recruitment and duration of settlement in this "Palestine" of the Soviet Union speak for themselves. In the first ten years that the territory was opened 35,000–40,000 Jews came to Birobidzhan, and large numbers promptly left. By 1939 only 14,000 Jews remained, of whom less than a third, some 4,000, were still on the land.[44] Although Birobidzhan was always displayed as a showpiece of the regime's benevolence toward the Jewish population, it was never more than a strange and backward outpost of an isolated Jewish community.

By the end of the civil war, the government had embarked on a wholesale dismantling of Jewish life in Russia. Such independent political movements as Zionism and the Bund were, of course, totally unacceptable, and Jewish newspapers, like all the newspapers under the new regime, were now required to conform to the official government position. By 1922 all Jewish periodicals were simply taken over by the regime. Not content with regulating the structure of Jewish life, Soviet regulations reached even into the spelling of Yiddish, requiring Jewish publications to be spelled phonetically. This meant that the thousands of Hebrew words embedded in Yiddish would lose their identity and their historical resonance. The language, with its new simplified phonetic spelling, would be wiped clean, as it were, of its memory. Both biblical and modern Hebrew were entirely forbidden in Communist Russia, presumably as carriers of unwelcome nationalism.

With the Stalin-inspired political purges in the 1930s, it became not only inconvenient but dangerous to be a Jew, especially a prominent one. Between 1935 and 1939 the most prominent Yiddish writers and intellectuals disappeared: deported to remote labor camps or executed. Among them was Isaac Babel, who died in a prison camp in 1939. Although the number of victims is not known, what is clear is that Yiddish literature was cut off, and its readers learned to hide their interest and their books.

The crimes of the Stalin era are too well known to be recounted here. But they were dissembled under smiling lies for those who would believe. In the end the Soviet regime destroyed the morale and culture of a people who had lived a rich life inside the borders of Russia despite a thousand years of hardship. Cut off from the Jewish communities of the West by a government which forbade travel, which censored mail, which eavesdropped on telephone conversations, the Soviet Jews were gradually lost to the world Jewish community, locked away behind guarded frontiers. It was only as World War II opened borders by force that they emerged again—but much changed.

CHAPTER TWO

Return to the World

After six years of war, Europe in 1945 was a mass of destroyed cities, displaced populations, and ruined industry, as its inhabitants awaited the future with confusion and anxiety. Immediately following the joy of peace came the realization of how much work lay ahead to rebuild a habitable world. As the war ground to a halt, nearly twelve million people in Western and Central Europe were not where they wanted to be. Coming originally from some twenty countries, they had been displaced through captivity, flight, or the search for safety. Now they were seeking reunion with their families and their homelands.1 While all of this was true for the civilians far from home and the returning soldiers, as in so much else, the Jewish situation was catastrophically worse.

At the end of the war the Jews who had survived the destruction of their communities and the slaughter of their people were scattered across thousands of miles of Europe, from hideaways on Dutch farms to the fastnesses of the Urals deep inside Russia. Those who had gotten out before the war were scattered across the globe, on every continent. During the war, when the Germans desperately needed labor to keep their factories going, they conscripted laborers wherever they could find them. Some were prisoners of war, others were taken from the subjugated peoples in newly occupied countries; some were collaborators from these territories who saw an advantage in serving the Germans. Some of the Jews herded together in ghettos or concentration camps were also drafted for the Nazi chain of slave-labor camps established to aid German industry in the war effort. I. G. Farben, in fact, went a step further by establishing its notorious Buna factory for the manufacture of artificial rubber right on the outskirts of Auschwitz.

Usually, however, the Jews, the collaborators, and the prisoners of war were brought to the sites of the factories and housed in makeshift barracks, with the men and women separated. Guarded day and night by the Wehrmacht and the SS, the slave laborers were routinely marched back and forth from their camps to the factories where they worked. Sometimes they passed through pleasant little villages and sometimes through peaceful city streets as the neighborhoods grew accustomed to their spectral forms. One woman from Munich remembered seeing as a child a troop of emaciated prisoners marching by. She was haunted forever after by the words of her father, who said, "We will pay for this." Stephan Stolze, who lived near Magdeburg, describes in his memoirs how, as a teenager, in the spring of 1944, he and a friend set out early one morning on a fishing expedition. As they approached a bridge to cross the Elbe, he writes, they heard "coming up from their right the sounds of a shadowy column of about a hundred people, closely pressed together: convicts in striped jackets, with caps and wooden clogs, surrounded by uniformed guards and shepherd dogs. These were prisoners from the small concentration camps that were situated on the east bank of the Elbe near the

Dessauer-Junkers Works. The wooden clogs clattered, the dogs pulled at their leashes panting." Stephan and his friend were challenged by an SS man but allowed to pass. "In the meantime," he continues, "the column of prisoners had moved entirely onto the bridge, enclosed by their uniformed guards with dogs. We went the next hundred meters very quickly, then more slowly. Whether we talked about the prisoners, I no longer recall. But if we had talked about them, I would surely not have forgotten it. When something was dangerous, the habit of lying applied even between us thirteen-year-olds."[2]

At the same time Gita Glazer, a Jewish girl of nineteen who had been "selected" at Auschwitz for work in an airplane factory in Wittenberg-on-the-Elbe, marveled on her daily march through the town that there were still charming houses, with pretty curtains at the windows and well-tended gardens. These symbols of a normal existence, at a time when for her every day was a struggle for survival, were almost incomprehensible. But she also knew what her column of marching women must have looked like to the inhabitants of those houses. She and her comrades had only their cotton prison uniforms, winter and summer, with not a stitch of underwear to shield them from the cold. In their highly visible stripes, they marched five abreast through the village streets and down the road—a thousand young girls moving back and forth between their barracks and the factory twice a day. "They cannot say," she concluded, "that they did not know about us."[3]

They were soon joined by others. Although the major death camps, such as Auschwitz, Treblinka, and Sobibor, were located in Poland, Germany itself was seeded with slave-labor camps. When the war ended it was estimated that there were sixty thousand Jews scattered across Germany in such camps.[4] There, too, prisoners died, but more slowly: of malnutrition, disease, exhaustion, and the brutality of their guards. Martin Gilbert in his *Atlas of the Holocaust* gives one example for the area around Stutthof, a town on the Baltic Sea in East Prussia. In spring 1944 the Germans set up sixty work camps in this area, to which they brought fifty-two thousand Jews, among them thirty thousand women. By the end of the war, only a year after their arrival, no more than three thousand had survived the appalling conditions of their daily lives.[5]

Although the official armistice was signed on May 8, 1945, the war actually ended in stages, as the American army moved east and the Russian army moved west, liberating cities, villages, and camps as they came upon them. It is worth noting that although today the Jews who came out of the camps alive are usually called "survivors" in the Holocaust literature, they themselves consider their coming through alive as the culmination of a victorious struggle, the result of a thousand tiny strategies that had preserved them to the end. For them the significant event in their lives was the liberation, the day of their rescue. In telling their stories, they often begin with the ringing sentence, "I was liberated on such and such a day." In their writings after the war, they refer to themselves, still with a taste of jubilation, as "liberated Jews." They also used the term *She'erith Hapletah*—the "surviving remnant" or the "saving remnant"—to describe themselves and their extraordinary fate.[6]

Many of the SS men and the other guards at the prison camps are remembered for their murderous dedication until and beyond the very last moment. Often exceeding their orders, they pushed their prisoners on death marches away from the oncoming liberators and toward the interior of Germany. Eventually, though, even these paradigms of loyalty fled before the advancing Allies. Once the war was lost the more ordinary German soldier wanted only to fade into anonymity. One Berliner observed to a journalist about the last days of fighting: "No one was part of it any more. It happened very quickly. They suddenly were dressed differently, all uniforms were gone, no insignia at all, and they'd all been 'forced' [to participate in the war]. The turnabout happened so fast, it was a joke. I never saw anything like it."[7]

For the Austrian and German refugees who returned to Europe as American soldiers and then interviewed Germans in the denazification process, the denial of the Nazi past was less than a joke. These interviewers uncovered one lie after another among former Nazi Party stalwarts seeking a certificate attesting to their political reliability. For petitioners from the humble corner grocer to such celebrities as Herbert von Karajan, the once-coveted Nazi Party emblem in their lapels now became an embarrassment or worse. Yet in the popular perception, too many of the high bureaucrats, especially in the judiciary, were cleared and continued to hold important posts. Von Karajan himself was unimpeded in his postwar career despite his having joined the Nazi Party in Austria as early as 1935 and then again in Germany.

For many Germans, the Nazi past was to take longer to resolve than the time it took to remove the party emblem. But for all of those uprooted by the war, the search for family and homeland was the paramount concern. By the first winter after the end of the war, most of the twelve million displaced persons in Central Europe had found their way home. This is particularly remarkable, as the historian Michael Marrus has noted, because it was not accompanied by the expected epidemics of typhus or dysentery that typically afflict such large movements of people with only the most makeshift sanitary arrangements.[8] Although Europe's railway system was shattered by wartime bombing and the trains ran only irregularly, everyone seemed to need to be somewhere else and crammed onto whatever was moving. Soldiers trying to get home; refugees who had fled from the path of battle; prisoners of war, political dissidents, common criminals, and forced laborers brought to factories in German-occupied territories all wanted to go back to their homelands. *Volksdeutsche*, ethnic

Germans who had been living in Russia since the seventeenth century, were being expelled from the East and trying to find some refuge in Germany. Some groups had good reason to remain in Germany: the foreign collaborators with the Nazis who feared punishment if they returned, and those from the Soviet Union who were opposed to the regime and dreaded a return to the oppression they had escaped. There were, of course, many other reasons for people to stay or go in the upheaval wrought by the war. Yet even more remarkable than the numbers who remained was the speed with which so many had found their way back.

Among the Eastern European Jews, who again had a unique position in this welter of needs and desires, three motives put them in motion: finding family, finding safety, finding a home. By the end of the war, having seen the crematoria, the shootings, and other atrocities, many of these Jews suspected that the rest of their families had perished. Nevertheless, they wanted to return home in the slim hope that anyone else who had survived would also come back to that center from which they had started six years earlier. Some Jews who found family members alive could not suppress a feeling of shame before those who had lost everyone. They wondered how it was possible to go on without any intimate connection in the world. It was, in fact, just this need for family bonds that inspired much of the postwar journeyings and searches, that led people to claim alliances, however distant, in the hope of reestablishing some context for their lives.

Most Jews went directly back to their villages. Or a seeker might return to the last address where the family had still been whole. If he found no one there, his second stop was Lodz, which became a gathering point for Jewish refugees trying to reorient themselves in the postwar world. Yankel Pomerantz, originally from Radzyn, did both. A Jew who had fled east to the Soviet Union, he returned to Poland in April 1945 after hard service as a member of a Polish unit in the Soviet Army.

Pomerantz was one of the many thousands of Jews who served in the Polish wing commanded by Gen. Zygmunt Berling and dedicated to freeing Poland from the Germans. Eventually 100,000 strong, this First Army (as it was called) included as many as 20,000 Jews by one estimate. One reason for the uncertainty about the number of Jews is that many who served in these Polish units hid their Jewish identity while in uniform.[9]

When Pomerantz returned to his parents' home in Radzyn, he was told by his neighbor's son that he himself had been part of a detail of men who had marched Pomerantz's parents into the nearby forest and witnessed their execution and burial in the woods. "He told it to me," Pomerantz writes, "in a very abstract way, as if my family had not lived for years behind his family, as if he had not seen my mother and my father nearly every day for his entire life."[10]

Chilled by the news and by the hostility of his former neighbors, Pomerantz asked to be taken to any Jews who were still left. The young man told him that only six were left, including a child, but it was now too late in the evening, too dark, to be moving about the streets. Pomerantz agreed to stay but remained awake through the night with his gun at the ready by his side. The next morning he again asked to be taken to his friends and was told by the son, "I cannot take you. Last night they were killed. Some Polish Fascists found them and they were killed." "From that moment on," writes Pomerantz, expressing the feelings of thousands of other Polish Jews, "all I wanted to do was leave, to run. Suddenly Radzyn had become a very sinister place. I wondered who was lurking behind every corner. I felt nothing but fear around me. I did not want to walk around . . . to see the streets, the faces of those who had stood silently by while so many died."[11] This was a feeling echoed by other Polish Jews for whom the hostility of their fellow townsmen was a signal that they no longer had a place they could call home.

In May 1945, with the war over, Pomerantz went to Lodz with a friend. In a makeshift arrangement, a building in central Lodz had become the unofficial Jewish headquarters for information. In a large hall, under the letters of the alphabet, were long white sheets with the names and addresses of survivors. Newcomers scribbled their own names and addresses on the margins. "Inside that brick building," writes Pomerantz, "everyone looked like little children after a fire or some catastrophe, calling out and searching for their parents. . . . Even being able to find someone from your home town was like finding a relative; you wanted so much to believe that someone was still left, that you were not so completely alone."[12]

Jewish survival in Poland had been the product of many accidentals, especially on which side of the border the Jews found themselves after the Germans declared war on Poland on September 1, 1939. Poland was then divided, according to the German-Soviet treaty of August 1939, between the two nations, Germany annexing the part adjoining its borders, and the Soviet Union taking the eastern half. Many of the Jews in the German zone fled to the Soviet area, which seemed safer than Nazi-occupied Poland. Some few in the East returned to the German-held areas, seeking to be reunited with their families.

But the refugees in the east soon became a burden to the authorities since they were without shelter or means of support. The Soviet solution was simply to ship the unemployed newcomers to work in mines and other enterprises in the interior that needed labor. Large numbers were sent to the coal mines in Donbas in the Ukraine, where they lived under extremely primitive conditions and worked in mines notorious for their lack of safety. With so many of the newcomers inexperienced, the accident rate soon became deadly, leading some of the refugees to escape illegally to find some alternative.[13] In their newly acquired territory, the Soviets also began a program of arrests, seeking to forestall all those who might harbor a shred of opposition to their regime. In the first twenty-one months of their control, they imprisoned half a million people in Ukraine and Byelorussia who were suspected of "nationalism" and therefore of disloyalty to the Soviet Union. In the same period they deported 1.5 million Polish citizens, among them some 400,000–500,000 Jews, to the interior of the Soviet Union.[14]

The last transports were sent off in June 1941, just before the Germans launched their attack on their erstwhile Soviet allies, beginning with an advance into Soviet-held eastern Poland. This attack also marked the first steps toward the realization of the ultimate goal of the Nazi leadership: the elimination of the Jews. With their invading troops, the Nazi command sent in four *Einsatzgruppen*—mobile killing units that rounded up the Jews in the villages that the army overran and murdered them in marathon shootings. Between July and December 1941, these special units reported that they had killed 300,000 Jews.[15]

Although they did not know it at the time, the Jews who had been deported by the Soviets before the invasion were saved from the certain destruction that awaited those who fell into German hands. Given only a few hours to pack and then herded into cattle cars, they were sent east to work in the vast Soviet Gulag. They served in penal colonies beyond the Urals and in Siberia; they logged in the forests of Archangel, and some were sent to the collective farms in Kazakhstan and other agricultural areas in the south.

Some adventurous young Jews even trekked south on their own, hoping to reach the borders of Iran and Afghanistan. Their plan was to cross into these neutral countries and make their way to Palestine. Their grand scheme was thwarted, however, by the all too effective Soviet border patrols so that they, too, had to turn to the collective farms for work as a way to subsist. For all these newcomers life was hard because the farms did not raise their own food, but under Soviet central planning were required to raise such single cash crops as cotton. In exchange they would be supplied with their basic necessities from elsewhere. With the war, this system of exchange broke down so that the supply of food became erratic and scarce. Under such circumstances, the commercial crops became a human disaster for their growers, who were without the means of subsistence. Unlike the landless newcomers, however, the members of the collective could eke out their diet from their own kitchen gardens, which provided some minimum of food. But this system left the new arrivals in a desperate condition.[16]

Moshe Prywes, a young doctor, has described how his flight from Warsaw with his wife and her parents to Bialystok, which was then in the Soviet sector, ended in their deportation. In June 1940 he and his family were rounded up with thousands of others and loaded into baggage cars, forty people to a car, to start their journey. For a toilet, they cut a hole in the floor. With the car sealed, there was no light except during brief stops once or twice a day, when the doors were opened and the deportees were given their rations of tea, bread, and a thin soup. They traveled in this way for six weeks until they came to the end of the railroad line in the town of Kotlas on the Vychegda River. There they were loaded onto barges—four hundred people to a barge. These, under equally primitive conditions for food and sanitary facilities, floated north on the river into what seemed like a trackless and uninhabited forest.

After traveling for forty-five days, the Prywes family and their fellow passengers arrived at an uninhabited part of a forest. This, they were told, was their destination, and they were allowed to disembark. There were no houses, or other preparations for them, and they slept on the ground until they themselves built their barracks. "It took a few weeks," wrote Prywes, "before ten of us, chopping trees, sawing logs and cutting notches into their end had constructed a small log dwelling. The final step was to pack the spaces between the logs with pitch. It did not take long," he continues, "to discern the dual nature of Soviet prison life. On the one hand our labor was productive and highly valued." At his camp, for example, the prisoners operated a sawmill and made wooden ammunition boxes. "On the other hand the very conditions of prison life were inherently dehumanizing."[17]

When the war was over, it took the Soviet Union nearly a year before it promulgated the decree that allowed deported Poles to return home. Unknown to the deportees, the Polish government and the Soviet Union had signed a repatriation agreement in Moscow on July 16, 1945. The first to be released were the soldiers like Yankel Pomerantz, who had served in a Polish unit of the Soviet army. Then, between February and July 1946, the mass of Polish civilians were allowed to return home. This was an astounding development in a country that in many respects was a giant prison camp. The Polish Jews did not need to be urged; longing and hoping for reunion with their families, they returned to Poland, again transported in primitive boxcars—though on the return journey some were luxuriously fitted with wooden bunks. These Jews made up a large proportion of the survivors. And unlike those who came out of the camps, they returned in family groups. Their exile in the Soviet colonies had indeed saved them from the killing camps of the Nazis, but it left them with little more than the bundles they had brought with them five years earlier. They swelled the numbers of Jews returning to Poland whose first move was to seek news of who was alive and who was dead. During the official repatriation period between February and July 1946, the first wave of some 173,420 Jews returned. In the course of the next decade, Polish Jews continued to find their way home. Another 11,300 returned between 1947 and 1949, and by 1956, a total of about 230,700 Jews had been repatriated.[18]

In those first years after the war, most, like Yankel Pomerantz, were quickly disabused of the idea that they were welcome or that Poland was even a probable place for Jews to rebuild their lives. Many of the Jews who returned reported that they were greeted by their former neighbors with such remarks as: "What, are you still alive?" and "What are you doing here?" This hostility was sometimes a camouflage for the fear that former Jewish property now in Polish hands would have to be returned to its owners.

Moshe Prywes, like others who had shared his experiences, made up his mind about his future very quickly. "For almost all the Jews who had spent the war years in the Soviet Union, Poland was now no more than a way station," he writes, "a country of transfer. After Auschwitz, there were not even proper tombstones of our lost ones to keep us anchored there. For all of us Poland had become little more than a graveyard."[19]

The old anti-Semitism was given a fresh political twist in postwar Poland, as the Jews were blamed for the imposition of the new Communist regime. Neither the Polish government-in-exile nor the Polish people, it turned out, had much to say in determining their postwar future. Poland was only one element in Stalin's plan to control Eastern Europe and as much of Germany as he could get. Well before the war ended, in fact, Poland's fate had been sealed in the four-power agreement at Yalta, culminating in what the historian Michael Steinlauf has called the "rigged national referendum of 1946." In the election of 1947 Boleslaw Bierut, who all through the war had been groomed in Moscow for this role, was elected president of Poland. Once again the Poles saw themselves as the victims, not only of the

Russians, but also of their agents—the Jews—because many Jews had joined the new Communist regime. This new grievance on top of the existing folk prejudice, augmented by years of exposure to German anti-Jewish war propaganda, escalated into the old accusations of blood libel.

By July 4, 1946, a little more than a year after the end of the war, a pogrom erupted in Kielce, a town in central Poland, south of Warsaw. Of the twenty-seven thousand Jews who had lived in Kielce before the war, some two hundred had returned and, though visibly unwelcome, had begun to rebuild their community house.[20] Without any other living quarters, they all camped in this house as they straggled back to their town.

On July 1 an eight-year-old Christian boy named Henryk Basczyk set off from home for a neighboring village without telling his parents. Two days later, when the boy came back, the father appeared at the local police station with his son, claiming that his child had been held prisoner in the Jewish community house, taken into a cellar and tortured. And there in the cellar, the boy stated, he had seen "murdered Christian children, and it was only by a miracle that he had been able to escape." As it happens, there was no cellar under the Jewish community house, as the police later ascertained.[21] But the old blood libel rumor quickly spread—that Jews killed Christian children in order to use their blood to make matzot. Several thousand people gathered in front of the Jewish community house carrying homemade weapons and seeking revenge. The bloodthirsty mood was heightened by the sinister propaganda of the Armia Krajowa—"the home army," an anti-Semitic force of ex-soldiers who had been whipping up a frenzy against the Jews for having brought Communism into a Catholic land. The pogrom in Kielce, with no interference by the police, ended in the murder of forty-two Jews; fifty more were wounded.

The violence did not stop at Kielce. In the two years after the war, between 1,500 and 2,000 Jews were killed in Poland in a variety of anti-Semitic incidents. In this agitated situation, Christians who had hidden Jews or taken in Jewish children even asked their grateful friends not to identify them publicly. But for Jews throughout Poland who had been pondering whether to stay, the Kielce pogrom became the turning point in the decision to go.[22]

In 1946 Jews who were arriving in Berlin from Poland were telling frightening stories of the danger to Jewish life. Leo Schwarz, the head of "the Joint" (the American Jewish Joint Distribution Committee), wrote in his report for 1946:

> A man who recently came in from Stettin tells of viewing an incident in which, before his very eyes, an 18-year-old Jewish boy was thrown by Polish ruffians from a streetcar, falling to the ground dead, with a knife sticking in the back of his neck. Another Polish traveler tells of four Jews in Cracow killed within recent weeks by Poles who had entered their home and shot them dead. Others tell of the constant insults and threats which they meet at every turn. A Jew tells of entering a bus with his wife and immediately being met by a chorus of jeers from the other occupants who tell him to go to Palestine and to get out of Poland if he values his life. All Jews speak of the impossibility of venturing out into the streets after dark or of travelling alone in rural areas.[23]

To a people shaken by the horrors of its war experiences, yet in peril at home, the only question was: Where was safety? The answer was strange: the safest place for Jews at that perilous moment was in the Allied Occupation Zones in Germany, the last country it would have occurred to a Jew to choose. There they could contemplate their future without worrying whether they would be alive the next day. And their first question was where to settle—in Palestine, in the

United States, in Canada, in South America? Germany, for these twice-displaced Jews, was only the "waiting room," as the journalist Ernst Landau called it, until they were admitted to a place of permanent settlement.

While the Jews were preoccupied with finding their families and finding safety, a new Europe was being redivided around them by the four Allied powers. Germany itself was split into four zones, and although Berlin lay deep within the Soviet zone, it, too, was carefully separated into four occupying sectors. The world soon became familiar with the inspection point at the American and Soviet boundary in Berlin—the famous Checkpoint Charlie, with its prominent and somewhat ominous notice: "You are now leaving the American Sector."

Each of these sectors soon developed a character in the popular mythology of the displaced persons. The American zone quickly became the principal goal of those who sought what seemed the invincible protection of the American army. Others, who wanted to emigrate to Palestine, believed that getting to the British zone in Germany would be the first step on the way, for Britain was the governing mandate power in Palestine. This was, as it turned out, a mistake, because the British were adamant about preventing more than a trickle of Jewish immigration to Palestine.

In the three years after liberation a quarter of a million Eastern European Jews, mostly from Poland, accumulated in the waiting room that was Germany.[24] And so it happened that the last episode in the saga of Eastern European Jewry, the last chapter in the history of Yiddish as a working, living, and literary language, unfolded, strangely enough, in the land of Amalek. Hitler had succeeded after all, not only in killing six million Jews but also in obliterating two Jewish cultures: that of the German Jews, with its 1,600-year history, and that of the Eastern European Jews. It did not take long for the surviving Jews to recognize this fact. As early as November 1946, at a conference of the Federation of Polish Jews in Augsburg, Dr. Samuel Gringauz, originally from Kovno, reflected on their fate. "Polish Jewry today," he said "is a closed historical category, just like, for example, that of the Sephardic Jews. In the tenth century the Jews first stepped on Polish land. In the twentieth century they are leaving it. . . . But between these points, between the beginning and the end, lie a thousand years of historical greatness . . . of spiritual achievement and political-social activity."[25]

The elegiac mode was a little premature, because for a single phosphorescent moment the old self-contained Jewish life flared into existence in the displaced persons camps of Germany. Even as they waited for a place of permanent refuge, the Jews formed dense communities in these camps, once again with their own government, synagogues, newspapers, theatres, schools, workshops, medical facilities. They also reestablished a thriving cultural life. They organized orchestras made up of members of the Saving Remnant, who toured the D.P. camps playing both Jewish and classical music.[26] They improvised cabarets and set up dance bands to play American jazz, while a number of theater groups performed not only the familiar Yiddish stage classics but also new works based on their experiences in the war years.

One notable group of musicians crossed musical boundaries playing not only in the displaced persons camps but also for the American army. This was a group of young men originally from Lodz who managed to find one another after their searing experiences in the camps. On April 23, 1945, three of them were liberated by American troops on the road near Cham as they were being pushed forward in the last stages of a death march. An American captain who heard their story took them under his wing. He sent to Czechoslovakia to find instruments for them; ordered the Bürgermeister of Cham to get them proper clothing, which included matching tailor-made suits for their performances, and nursed them back to health. Their leader, Chaim Baigelman, was the only survivor of a dynasty of musicians. He had had three sisters and four brothers, among them David Baigelman, a renowned composer and conductor whose songs were so popular and so widely known that they were often taken for folk songs. In the Lodz ghetto David had continued to write, and two of his lullabies, composed on the death of a friend's daughter, have been steadily performed in the postwar years as part of the canon of resistance music.

In homage to a band called "The Jolly Boys" that had played in Cracow before the war and had not survived, Chaim Baigelman and his orchestra called themselves "The Happy Boys." During the interwar years, Baigelman's band had been at the height of its popularity, specializing in American jazz. To keep up with the current scene, they had even arranged to receive a weekly package from the Chappell Music Company in New York, with the words and music to the latest American hits. Although they did not know a word of English, Baigelman and his fellow musicians had studied these songs and made them part of their repertoire. When he and his new band began to play for the American troops, they did not need English. A hummed phrase from a tune was enough for them to start playing.

But when "The Happy Boys" performed in the D.P. camps, as they did all over Germany, then they played Yiddish songs, mostly contemporary compositions. The music was sometimes based on old tunes, but the words reflected the shared experiences of the musicians and their listeners. One song with a new text by Baigelman "Es bengt zich nuch a hajm"—One Longs for Home—seems to promise a sentimental piece of nostalgia. Instead, one hears a fierce account of how every Jew in the D.P. camps thought about his situation. In this song, which looks both backward and forward, the text moves gradually away from the past. By the end the future wins.

It must have been a bad dream.
But now I know what has happened.
The best are gone; it is a horror, a terror, a terror.
How does one continue to walk and talk when it shouldn't
    have happened?
All around us, one hears the same lament.
Each one is filled with the same deep hurt as me,
    because . . .

One longs for home.
How does one find it on this earth?
One longs for home.
Every way is blocked to us.
But we continue to hope. It cannot be otherwise!
Once again life will become beautiful.
One longs for home.
A warm home, the way it once was.
One longs for home.
Our mourners must have retribution.
It was once terrible,
But it has changed for the better.
Now one must live
Because the time has come!

I have always been puzzled by the famous dictum by Theodor
Adorno that there could be no more poetry after Auschwitz. In actuality, those who came out of Auschwitz and the other camps alive
wrote volumes of poetry and much more, in a fever to record what
had happened. In their years in the D.P. camps in Germany, it was as
if they needed the poetry, plays, stories, songs, and music to give expression to their experiences. And all in Yiddish. In the intimate atmosphere of the camps, every nuance of expression was understood.

The Happy Boys, a Jewish jazz band led by Chaim Baigelman, originally from Lodz, fourth from left. The other musicians, from left, are Sam Spaismacher, Henry Eisenman, Abraham Mutzman, Edward Silberszac, Ickhak Lewin, Abraham Lewin, and Josef Lewin. Henry Baigelman, personal collection.

Chaim Baigelman reconstituted his band when he emigrated to America in 1949, but he rarely had such passionately attentive audiences again.

In the D.P. camps the newly freed Jews found that they needed official spokesmen to deal with the authorities on their behalf. In the British zone, three days after the liberation of the concentration camp at Bergen-Belsen, Josef Rosensaft, the former proprietor of a foundry in Bendzin, Poland, and a born leader, organized a provisional representative committee, later confirmed by a camp election. In the American zone, a few months later, in July 1945, the displaced Jews organized the Central Committee of the Liberated Jews in Bavaria and elected Zalman Grinberg, a thirty-three-year-old doctor from Kovno, as its head. In January 1946 the committee widened its jurisdiction to the entire American zone and also began publication of *Undzer Weg*— Our Way—a zone-wide Yiddish newspaper, the first postwar Jewish newspaper in the camps. Bearing the subtitle "The General Jewish Newspaper in Golus Germany," it was at first issued weekly, later twice a week. Through the efforts of the American relief organizations, who procured the type, it was printed in Hebrew letters, a fact that was greeted with extravagant exclamations of joy in an article in the first issue. "A Jewish newspaper!" wrote Israel Kaplan, who became editor of the newspaper of the Historical Commission, "actually printed in the radiant, four-square Yiddish letters—the golden little letters, the dear letters which have been welcomed by Jews, for generation after generation with a burning kiss."[27] The first issue, which appeared on October 12, 1945, carried on its masthead in Hebrew and Yiddish a slogan from Deuteronomy familiar to every camp inmate: "Remember what Amalek did to you!"

Starting just six months after the end of the war, *Undzer Weg* spoke directly to the hearts of people bereft of family and homeland and facing only a most uncertain future. Its manifesto on the front page bore the name of the memorial service for the dead: "Yizkor— He shall remember . . ." Indeed, the statement begins with the remembrance of "our parents, sisters, and brothers, our wives and children who were cruelly killed by brutal thugs," but it goes on to celebrate "the heroism of the ghetto fighters, who sacrificed their lives in the underground movement, and the heroic partisans." This was not the voice of people who saw themselves as defeated but rather that of people triumphant in their survival. The manifesto concludes in a rush of feeling:

> Holy remain the rays illuminating our eternal history through
> the glorious heroism of those who fell: Jewish fighters in the

regular armies, especially the armies of the Jewish Brigade and all those who fought and sacrificed their youth for the honor of the Jewish people. In holy reverence and deepest awe, we stride ahead to a great future. . . . The People of Israel Lives [Am Yisroel Khai].

The newspaper was only the first stroke in the reawakening of Jewish cultural life. Throughout the liberated areas, groups and individuals began to come forward to record or reflect on what had happened. Sometimes it was a letter or poem or short story submitted to a newspaper. Sometimes it took more ambitious form, as artists, historians, and teachers attempted to resume their prewar life. But much of the cultural activity in the D.P. camps was marked by the bursting need for expression—for an examination of the cataclysmic experience from which they had all just emerged.

At the end of 1945 Polish Jewish actors who had survived the war in Tashkent and elsewhere in the Soviet Union formed a theatre troupe on their arrival in the Soviet zone of Germany. In homage to their teachers, they took for their name the initials of the famous Moscow Jewish Art Theater (MIKT), but they quickly came into conflict with the Soviet authorities, who wanted the group to abandon its repertoire for the approved "Socialist Realism" that would serve a propaganda purpose. Rather than submit, the troupe arranged to have itself smuggled across the border to the American zone in the spring of 1946. With a new base in Munich, it retained the old initials, becoming the Munich Jewish Art Theatre. For the next three years it toured the camps and communities where Jews lived, playing the classics of the Yiddish theatre. In 1947 alone it gave performances in fifty-eight camps to a combined audience of forty thousand persons. Another Munich-based group, which split off from the original company, specialized in musicals and variety shows.

By 1948, in fact, there were three professional Jewish dramatic troupes and three amateur groups performing in Germany, quite apart from such visiting actors and singers as Herman Yablokoff, himself a native of Grodno, who came from the United States to tour the camps.[28] Yablokoff, who was well known to Yiddish-speaking audiences on both sides of the Atlantic, describes in his autobiography his first appearance at a D.P. camp in Germany, in April 1947. Although his name had drawn a packed house, he could feel the hostility in the hall to the appearance of yet another condescending visitor from America. Rather than begin with his prepared program, he stepped forward to make an impromptu speech, and ended by saying: "I have not come to you as an American philanthropist or politician. I have come as a Jew to his fellow Jews in despair. Of one thing you may be certain—the Jewish communities in the free world have not forsaken you, and never will. . . . I too am a wandering Jew, a displaced person."[29] This assurance, as well as the sound of his Grodno Yiddish, broke down the barriers and permitted him to go on.

But professional entertainers were not enough for a people burning with a story to tell. In time some sixty amateur groups sprang up spontaneously in the camps. Some had such success that they, too, toured to their compatriots in other camps. It was all part of the ferment of the period, in which a freed people sought every possible means to capture and present its history.[30]

In time, each camp of displaced persons published its own newspaper. In fact, every organization functioning in the camps or communities—all the Zionist political parties, the Writers' Union, and the sports and cultural clubs—had some kind of bulletin or newsletter. Some were no more than a few mimeographed sheets. But what they all shared was a sense of intimacy as demonstrated by the frequent use of the word *our* in the titles: Our World, Our Goal, Our Word, Our Hope, Our Front, Our Courage, Our Voice, Our Struggle, and, of course, Our Way. As the names indicate, these newspapers were not addressing a general public. They were written by Jews for one another, Jews who were bound together by their wartime sufferings, for whom these papers were a forum.

Jewish publications in Germany in the three years between the end of the war and the disbanding of the camps had an unparalleled character in their personal style and in the vigor of their self-expression. More than two hundred newspapers, periodicals, and books were published in those years, almost all in Yiddish, giving vivid voice to the inmost feelings and hopes of these young Jews. There was a newspaper in Hungarian, another in Rumanian, one in Polish, and one in Hebrew, *The Spark,* which began life in 1940 as an underground publication by Zionist students in the Kovno ghetto. When they were deported to Dachau in 1944, they persisted, even in the camp, in the dangerously illegal production of their handwritten newspaper. They published its first legal issue in July 1945, only two months after liberation, in the hospital for displaced persons at St. Ottilien, near Munich, and it continued to appear until April 1948.[31]

One of the enduring accomplishments of the period was the publication, under the supervision of Rabbi Samuel S. Snieg of a She-'erith Hapletah (Saving Remnant) edition of the Talmud. With some financial help from "the Joint" and with the balance provided by the American army from the resources of the German economy, the nineteen-volume set was printed in an edition of 750 copies and dedicated to the United States Army of Occupation.[32]

However fleeting their stay in these camps, the Saving Remnant had an indefatigable sense of history. They were also systematic. One of the first acts of the Central Committee of Liberated Jews was to set up a Historical Commission "to gather documents and material on the history of the just past *khurbn* [destruction]." (The commission was using the traditional Yiddish word, heavy with history, which is

כָּל דּוֹר וָדוֹר
חַיָּב אָדָם
לִרְאוֹת אֶת
עַצְמוֹ כְּאִלּוּ
הוּא יָצָא מִמִּצְרָיִם.

"In every generation one should regard oneself as though he had come out of Egypt." A sentence from the Passover Haggadah. The letter *beth* of the Hebrew alphabet from a page of the *Survivors' Haggadah,* written and illustrated by the Lithuanian writer Yosef Dov Sheinson, with additional woodcuts by the Hungarian Miklos Adler. At the top of the letter are shown the pyramids of Egypt. In the long stroke the words "Bad-Bath," with its evocation of the gas chambers. At the bottom the barbed wire, guard towers, and chimneys of a death camp. This Haggadah was printed in Munich for a Passover Seder for displaced Jews in 1946. Saul Touster, personal collection.

associated with the destruction of the Temple in Jerusalem in 70 C.E. For the most recent catastrophe, the term is usually rendered in English as Holocaust. The modern Hebrew word *Shoah* has also been popularized in the English language press, but Yiddish writers continue to use *khurbn*.) The commission wanted not only to gather material but also to let the world know about its findings. Its first publication was a journal, in Yiddish—*Fun letzten Khurbn*—On the Latest Destruction—edited by Israel Kaplan. Published from August 1946 to December 1948, it contained material about the ghettos and camps in Poland, White Russia, Lithuania, Latvia, Estonia, Germany, and Hungary.[33]

The commission was untiring in its efforts to collect information about the khurbn. It sought out documents not only from the Nazi period but also about life in prewar Poland, including tapes, film, and photographs. Aware of the significance of so-called folklore, they collected hundreds of songs from the ghettos and concentration camps. They took charge of an entire library of Jewish books found in a former Nazi office and made every effort to maintain a complete set of the new Jewish periodicals and newspapers appearing in Germany. They distributed a questionnaire to 4,665 Jews in the D.P. camps to gather demographic information. They even devised a questionnaire for children about their experiences in the Nazi period, and UNRRA (United Nations Relief and Rehabilitation Agency) personnel were specially prepared to talk to these children. Some 345 returns were filed, all from the Föhrenwald D.P. camp.[34] At the end of 1948, following the creation of the state of Israel, the entire archive of the Historical Commission was transferred to Yad Vashem in Jerusalem.[35]

In time, the displaced persons camps became little villages, a continuation of the old Jewish world, a last evocation in microcosm of the prewar Eastern European Jewish culture. One visitor to Waldstamm-bei-Pocking, a camp with six thousand inhabitants, reported that it seemed to him like an old shtetl. "One street," he wrote, "was named, in Hebrew, Rechov Borochov [for a Zionist leader] and on the doors of the buildings are signs indicating the offices of various Zionist parties."[36] While the overwhelmingly Zionist atmosphere was hardly typical of the prewar shtetl, the Hebrew names indicated not only the direction of popular sentiment, but also the untiring activity of the Zionist emissaries from Palestine. They sent Hebrew teachers to instruct children in the D.P. camp schools; they sent agricultural experts to help the potential immigrants who were temporarily working farms in Germany; they recruited tirelessly among the young and restless immigrants who were eager to find a new home. But ultimately it was pragmatism rather than ideology that dictated the decisions of the displaced persons, as the fluctuating poll numbers showed.

In the camp newspapers and other periodicals we find the last spontaneous expression of prewar Jewish life, with old debates carried on as if they had only just been interrupted. For the last time the liberated Jews battled for the truth of dearly held political positions, such as whether Yiddish or Hebrew was to be their national language. Secular and religious factions fought once more over the definition of *Yidishkayt*—Jewishness. The issues and passions were there in full force, and the camp elections replicated the entire range of political positions in prewar Jewish Poland. But there was also a sense that Jewish history was taking a new course. One Zionist party, urging residents of the Straubing camp to come out and vote put it succinctly: "Dos letste mol in Golus"—for the last time in the Diaspora.

But these camps were not just debating societies. With the large number of unattached young people, most longing for the security of family and home, it was no wonder that the number of marriages in the camps steadily increased. And as time went on, the feeling for ceremony also grew. In the Eschwege camp, for example, where there was only one wedding gown available, it was carefully preserved between

A Jewish wedding of displaced persons in a UNRRA camp in Berlin, October
1946. Rabbi Friedman, a displaced person himself, performed the ceremony.
United Nations Archives and Records Centre, New York.

weddings and lent out as needed. But many young women, as in our
photograph of a wedding in 1946, wore whatever clothes they had.

The not-so-secret concern shared by men and women alike was
about their fertility. Members of both sexes had been subjected to
brutal medical experiments in the camps, an experience that only
heightened their uneasiness. But even if they had not been recruited
for experiments, men were concerned about their potency, while
women who had spent months or years without menstruating because they were malnourished and underweight, wondered whether
they could even conceive a child. Added to that, the stories of Nazi
X-ray experiments to induce female infertility also left their mark as

Young mothers in the D.P. camp Landsberg, near Munich, 1948. These camps had the highest birth rate in the world. Dorit Mandelbaum, courtesy of USHMM Photo Archives.

women worried whether their bodies had been deformed in ways invisible to them. It was extraordinary, however, what a period of peace and adequate nourishment could do. As the marriages increased, so did the birthrate. By 1946 UNRRA could report: "There is an abnormally large number of pregnant women in Jewish camps in Germany, estimated to be between eight and ten thousand."[37] Their joy in their children, which was also a triumph over their persecutors, is vividly shown in the photograph taken in the Landsberg camp. In fact, by 1947 the birthrate among the Jewish displaced persons at 50.2 per thousand was among the highest in the world, and particularly dramatic when compared with the German rate of 7.6 per thousand.[38]

By 1948, when most of the Jews left the camps finally to settle abroad, their old political and cultural loyalties, based on a phantom society, dissolved in the larger world. More than that, in the United States or Israel, the private memories so fervently expressed in the poetry and essays of these intimate newspapers went underground or were overwhelmed by the task of building a new life. In their new countries of settlement, the immigrants tenaciously held onto their hometown organizations. But these were largely unpolitical centers for remembering their dead, for remembering the past, and for warming themselves in one another's company. The old causes had been put to rest, remembered with nostalgia, or muted by time so that the old political bite was gone.

As we shall see, the camps lasted far longer than anyone expected. Their residents, the occupying powers, the surrounding German population were all eager to see them disbanded, each for their own reasons, especially the Jews, who longed to begin their lives again. But the hopes of the inmates for resettlement to a permanent home met with stubborn political and social resistance.

How the D.P. camps came into being cannot be told in a single story; each camp had its own history. In fact, officially they were called not camps, but "assembly centers"—actually a more accurate term, for some of the living arrangements were not the crude barracks implied by camps. Although most were set up in former Germany army installations, others, such as Lampertheim and Zeilsheim, were houses in German towns from which the Germans had been evacuated to make room for the displaced persons. In a few places, sanatoriums were taken over to accommodate both the sick and the well. St. Ottilien, which was one of the earliest to be requisitioned for this purpose was also the site of one of the first organized celebrations of liberation. For longer or shorter periods of time, in larger or smaller groups, the Jews occupied 184 D.P. camps in the Allied zones of Germany, including West Berlin. The last camp, closed in February 1957, was Föhrenwald in the American zone. Only eleven of the D.P. camps were in the French zone, of which three were actually kibbutzim; the British administered twenty-two camps, while the Americans had 151.[39] But not all the Jewish displaced persons lived in the camps; at least a third chose to find their way in the free economy with a little municipal help in the way of requisitioned apartments.[40]

Landsberg, near Munich, which eventually became one of the largest camps, was set up by American troops when they moved into Bavaria. In their territory, they discovered that they had inherited a large population—thousands of people—who had been brought to Germany to work, against their will. When peace came, they were stranded far from home, with no funds and no more than the clothes on their back. On May 1, 1945, the American military decided to convert the former German army training camp in Landsberg into a temporary shelter for the displaced persons. Army trucks were sent to the neighboring villages to collect those who had been left hanging by the end of the hostilities: war prisoners, refugees, slave laborers. Within a few weeks some eight thousand people, representing sixteen nationalities, had been brought in. There were no children among them. For most of those brought to Landsberg, their dearest wish was to return home. By September the camp had a very different population, as all those who wanted repatriation had left. It was now made up of some 4,500 Jews for whom "home" had become an almost indefinable word.

By a stroke of fate, the American officer in charge of the camp was Maj. Irving Heymont, who came from an assimilated American Jewish family. How his relationship with the displaced persons in his charge evolved is shown in an eloquent series of letters he wrote home to his wife during his brief but significant three months in the post—September to December 1945—and later published by the American Jewish Archives. He carefully avoided letting his origins be known to anyone. "Intuitively, I knew," he wrote, "that my efforts at the camp would be handicapped, if it were known that I was Jewish. On the Army side, my actions could be subject to criticism . . . on the ground that I was prejudiced. On the other side, there would be perceptions that I should take certain actions because I was a fellow Jew."[41] In his letters we read the story of this portion of the Saving Remnant as seen though the eyes of a sympathetic and somewhat bewildered outsider.

In October 1945 Heymont faced a puzzling and troubling situation when his commanding general ordered that one thousand of the inmates of the Landsberg camp be transferred to Föhrenwald in order to relieve crowding and unsanitary conditions. Although Föhrenwald was not really a camp but a settlement that had, as Heymont wrote, "modern housing with small homes that permit normal family life," the Landsberg Jews refused to budge. He realized a few weeks later "why the people of the camp are so reluctant to move to Föhrenwald. To most of the people of the camp, the very mention of transport or move to another camp meant that many were to die. Under the Nazis, a transport usually meant gas chambers and starvation for many of those being moved. Psychologically, the people are still unprepared for any shifts of camps. They had had enough of moving and transfers in Europe. . . . Landsberg, to them, represents a form of security in Europe provided by habit, friendships formed, and participation in communal activities. This is a deep rooted inertia that I believe will disappear with time."[42]

He was right. The displaced persons in his charge did not sit still awaiting rescue from other hands. In September 1945 they had asked for and won permission to govern themselves, and the next month, they began publishing a camp newspaper. Like most other newspapers published by the displaced Jews in that period, it was written in Yiddish. Because Hebrew type was scarce, the newspaper was printed in transliteration in Latin letters, using Polish phonetic values

Street in Föhrenwald, one of the largest D.P. camps in Bavaria (the American zone) and the last to close. Its last residents left in 1957. Some camps were no more than converted army barracks. Others were established in blocks of apartment houses or, as here, in a village. American Jewish Joint Distribution Committee.

(the letter *c*, for example equaling a *ts* sound in English orthography). The newspaper was called the *Landsberger Lager Caytung*—Landsberger Camp News—and, as one realist noted, it was perhaps not so regrettable that it was obliged to use Latin letters. "In the camps," he noted, "were many hundreds or even thousands of young people from Poland, Hungary, and Romania who couldn't read Yiddish, [but who spoke it]. For them the newspapers in Latin script were the only way they could enjoy the Yiddish press."[43]

The *Landsberger Caytung* was the most important of the camp newspapers in Germany. In addition to local camp news, it contained columns about Jewish life in the "Lands of the Diaspora"—*Golus lender*—and detailed stories about Palestine, where many camp inmates wanted to settle. It reported on the American occupation forces and offered hints on immigration possibilities worldwide. It carried reports on the Zionist movement and news about Germany, but only as it related to Jewish interests. There was, of course, full coverage of the Nuremberg trials, and reports of Jewish communities elsewhere in Germany. But Germany itself—its politics, its people, its reconstruction—did not exist in the Landsberg columns.

The newspaper also became a kind of camp bulletin board, with a back page devoted to personals. At the beginning this page was almost entirely filled with appeals for information about missing family members, but as time went on the lower right-hand corner began to hold more and more announcements of weddings and births. It also carried notices of meetings of hometown associations, which had become enormously important, as we have seen, for people who had lost their families. Often these announcements were for commemorative meetings on the anniversary of the German massacre of the Jews of that town. And sometimes they were simply attempts to find and bring together whatever survivors were in Landsberg.

The newspapers did more than print the latest news. They were also in the truest sense of the word, the voice of the people. And what the people wanted to talk about was the past. *Our Hope,* a newspaper that began publication in June 1946 in the D.P. camp at Eschwege, near Kassel, was among the first to print eyewitness accounts of the death camps, including Maidenek and Treblinka. This was the immediate past. Behind that stood yet another past, bringing with it the sense of the permanent loss of everything that stood for home, for belonging, for identification with a place and a community. The survivors' sense of both parts of their past also took expression in poetry, memoirs, essays, short stories, and letters to the editor. Every statement of political views or social policy was informed by a remembrance of that shadowed past and a pervasive sense of its loss. As late as 1947, the introduction to a new picture magazine, *Jidisze Bilder*—Jewish Pictures—begins with an apology. "It must be honestly stated," the editors wrote, "that *Jidisze Bilder* is far from comparable to the former *Riga Picture Journal* which enriched and beautified Jewish life with pictures. But as the old proverb has it, 'Also this way is good.'"

From the first moment of liberation, the memories of the Jews' sufferings and losses were inextricably wound into their new lives. Zalman Grinberg, later an editor of *Undzer Weg*, spoke eloquently at a Liberation Concert in May 1945, less than three weeks after the end of the war. At the St. Ottilien Hospital, where Grinberg was serving as head doctor, he gave voice to some of the feelings of those who had just been liberated. For him, as for them, it was the immediate past that dominated thoughts and emotions:

> Four hundred twenty Jews, the last representatives of the European Jews after the most difficult period of suffering ever conceived, are now here in the hospital of St. Ottilien. These people are among the few survivors of the venerable old Jewish communities of Europe: Budapest and Prague, Warsaw, Kovno, and Saloniki. Millions of members of these same communities have been annihilated. What is the logic of fate to let us, then, live? We belong to the common graves of those shot in Kharkow, Lublin, and Kovno; we belong to the millions gassed and burnt in Auschwitz and Birkenau; we belong to the tens of thousands who died under the strain of the hardest labor; we belong to those tormented by billions

of lice, the mud, the starvation, the cold of Lodz, Kielce, Buchenwald, Dachau, Landshut, Utting, Kaufering, Landsberg, and Leonsberg. We belong to those who were gassed, hanged, tortured, starved, worked and tormented to death in the concentration camps. We belong to the army of nine million fallen under the heel of this expertly organized and cunningly prepared system of murder. We are not alive. *We are still dead.* . . . We have met here today to celebrate our liberation; but at the same time it is a day of mourning for us. Because every clear and joyful day at present or that may be in the future is overshadowed by the tragic events of the past years. . . . We are free now, but we do not know how or with what to begin our free yet unfortunate lives. It seems to us that for the present mankind does not understand what we have gone through and experienced during this period. And it seems to us that neither shall we be understood in the future. We have unlearned to laugh; we cannot cry any more; we do not understand our freedom; this is probably because we are still among our dead comrades."[44]

At this time Dr. Grinberg was thirty-three years old; he had just finished medical school when the war began. In his relative youth he was typical of the first arrivals in the D.P. camps, 90 percent of whom were between the ages of sixteen and forty-five, their careers and lives having been throttled at the moment of beginning.[45] As one veteran of the camps said drily, "You had to be young to survive." But it was just this youth, which had given the survivors the strength to endure the Nazi torments, that now propelled them to think of the future.

For them life had just begun or was about to begin anew, and the main question was where to go. The first surveys by the United Nations indicated that 90 percent wanted to go to *Eretz Israel*—the land of Israel. This was no abstract political decision but grew out of their experience of the world in the preceding six years. Paula G., who chose to go to Tel-Aviv, even leaving her family, who were bound for America, said that she never again wanted to be in a position where she could be told to go. This emotion was given even stronger expression in a speech by Jichok Grinboym, a member of the executive committee of the Landsberg camp in December 1946. He urged his listeners to "Make an end to *goles!* Become a free people in your homeland! May there never again be such a catastrophe in Jewish life!"[46] A Zionist delegate to the second Congress of the Liberated Jews in March 1947, Comrade Cholawski, spoke to the lurking fears of his listeners as he made the case for Palestine. "We should not mistake a forced resting place for a stable home. Stability is an illusion, and we should protect ourselves against it. This is just *goles* that lies in our way. Our message is: Maidenek is not a geographical place. It is rather a historical idea. Maidenek is only five kilometers from Lublin, only five kilometers from the Jewish *goles.*" Concluding to great applause, he urged the Central Committee to mobilize the Jews in the camps for "*Alija*—emigration to Palestine. Onward," he said, "to the ships!"[47]

This readiness to leave was a position that grew naturally out of a widely held feeling by the displaced Jews of total alienation from their surrounding world, in the past as well as the present, in their homelands no less than in the camps. But this early enthusiasm for Palestine modulated considerably during their long wait in the camps. Jacob Olejski, who in Lithuania had been an active member of ORT, a Jewish vocational organization, and later became an editor of *Undzer Weg*, gave it pointed expression in a speech at Landsberg in August 1945: "No, we are not Poles," he said, "even though we were born in Poland; we are not Lithuanians even though our cradles may have stood in Lithuania; we are not Romanians, although we first saw the light of day in Romania. We are Jews!"[48]

This unshakable consciousness of themselves as bound up in an eternal community was the basis for the success of *Brichah*—Flight— a brilliantly organized Zionist underground organization founded in Lublin in January 1945 by hardened fighters from the ghettos of Eastern Europe, such as Abba Kovner from Vilna and Yitzhak Zuckerman of Warsaw. The group was dedicated to spiriting the surviving Jews out of Europe and smuggling them to Palestine. This imperative was endorsed in a series of vehement statements by the United Zionist Organization of the She'erith Hapletah. At its first meeting, in October 1945, that organization's administrative board declared that "the She'erith Hapletah regards Germany after liberation as a continuation of the *Katzet* [concentration camps] and sees its life here only as a way-station on the road to Eretz Israel." For Jews in the camps or living in the German communities, the question was not whether to emigrate but only when and how. For the more adventurous, or desperate—for those who could not bear to spend one more moment on the soil of Germany or Poland—the Brichah offered immediate, if risky, help. Although the Brichah ultimately succeeded in transporting sixty-five thousand Jews from Europe to Palestine, many preferred to wait for more regular transfers, and not always to Palestine.[49] As time dragged on, whether they would leave for Palestine or the United States or Argentina, in the end was a decision that most Jews made for pragmatic rather than ideological reasons. Despite the burning rhetoric of the Zionists, many Jews in the camps had other ways of thinking about their future which led to other choices.

By 1947 surveys showed that the margin of preference for Palestine was diminishing and that half of the Jews in the camps wanted to go to the United States—for many reasons. Some, still recovering from the effects of years of wartime suffering, doubted their own abilities to cope with the hardship of living in Palestine, then an undeveloped, pioneering country engaged in an ongoing conflict with the

Arabs. Others had relatives or friends in America, and those connections took precedence over political considerations. But the hard truth was that at the war's end neither Palestine nor America was welcoming immigrants.

Great Britain, as the mandate power governing Palestine, had established a quota in 1945 permitting the immigration of 1,500 Jews a month. Aware, however, of the powerful efforts of the Zionist movement to bring Jews to Palestine by clandestine means, they also stipulated that the number of illegal arrivals who were intercepted by the British would be deducted from the quota.[50] Undeterred, the Brichah movement continued to find boats and managed to bring many refugees ashore undetected. But those who were caught were summarily consigned to detention camps, either in Palestine or on the island of Cyprus. Eventually some 51,500 Jews who had been captured by British patrols were imprisoned on Cyprus, some for as long as two years until the establishment of the State of Israel in 1948.

The United States, as it turned out, presented an even more formidable obstacle with its no less discriminatory legislation. President Truman was aroused by the plight of the displaced persons and was active in sending, first, an American investigative commission in June 1945 under Earl G. Harrison, dean of the law school at the University of Pennsylvania and the American representative on the Intergovernmental Committee on Refugees. When Truman urged the British to accept more Jews into Palestine, Prime Minister Attlee countered by proposing a joint Anglo-American commission to investigate the situation in Germany. Truman immediately accepted. Although the Anglo-American Commission recommended that 100,000 Jews be admitted to Palestine immediately and that the United States open its doors as well, neither country was prepared to act on the report. Britain remained adamant on its quota for Jews entering Palestine, and Congress did not see the displaced persons as an American problem.[51] The only way for Jews to be admitted to the United States in any significant number was through special legislation—and this turned out to be a wearying process. In a painstaking account by Leonard Dinnerstein in *America and the Survivors of the Holocaust,* we learn of the unashamed, open expression of prejudice against Jews that prevented any meaningful legislation for their relief. As Dinnerstein noted, "Most congressmen knew little about displaced persons, could not understand why they had not gone home after the war, and feared an economic depression or a glut on the labor market if a large number of immigrants started coming to the United States."[52] They also seemed unable to hear the humanitarian appeal of their president. "We are dealing with a human problem, a world tragedy," Truman wrote in a message to Congress. "Let us remember that these are fellow human beings now living under conditions which frustrate hope. . . . They live in corroding uncertainty of their future. Their fate is in our hands and must now be decided. Let us join in giving them a chance at decent and self-supporting lives."[53]

The first bill that passed—and that not until June 1948—permitted the admission of 100,000 displaced persons a year for two years, and imposed serious limitations. In order to qualify, the applicants had to have arrived in Germany, Austria, or Italy by December 22, 1945. This meant, for example, that some 200,000 Polish Jews who began to be released from the Soviet Union only in February 1946 would never be eligible for an American visa. But the Volksdeutsche, the ethnic Germans, who were expelled from the Soviet Union after the war, were given a cutoff date of July 1948. Earl Harrison, who had headed the Truman commission to Germany in 1945 to investigate the D.P. camps, responded with indignation especially to this provision, calling the Volksdeutsche "the notorious Nazi fifth column. The bill's racist character," he continued, "makes all decent Americans hang their heads in shame. [That the Volksdeutsche] should be handed special privileges over the victims of Nazi oppression is a mockery of American justice. For the first time in American history, immigrants can now be classified not by nationality, but by 'race.'" A second, more liberal bill was passed in June 1950, but the first legislation had done its job in deflecting Jewish displaced persons from the United States. By 1952, the United States had admitted some 400,000 displaced persons. Of these perhaps 80,000 were Jews; the rest were largely Balts, Ukrainians, and ethnic Germans from Czechoslovakia, Russia, and other Eastern European countries.[54]

What soon became very clear to the Jewish displaced persons was that resettlement to a permanent home was going to take time—not months, but perhaps years—and in that time these young and energetic people sought some way to feel that they were starting again. That meant finding useful and lucrative work. While various of the Jewish relief organizations set up vocational training schools and workshops in the camps, young Zionists planning for their future on a kibbutz in Palestine formed impromptu groups so that they might begin to farm, even in Germany, in preparation for their future life. In one collective the members had misgivings as to whether it was right to cultivate "this accursed soil." After a lengthy debate, as recorded by one member of the group, they eventually agreed to set up a training camp. "Our aspiration," he wrote, "is to assist in the building of a healthy Jewish society residing in its own land. . . . But since at this time we cannot get there . . . we will in the meantime find a site, . . . we will work, we will be productive."[55]

Other members of the community looked to the German economy as a place to begin. The atmosphere, however, was not entirely neutral or governed solely by market considerations. The anti-Semitism that the Nazis had fanatically promoted for the past twelve years did not die on May 8, 1945, and Jewish antipathy to the people of their murderers had hardly had a chance to subside. Nor did they wish to contribute to the rebuilding of the German economy. The mutual reluctance of Jews and Germans to engage in unnecessary contact also colored Jewish economic activity. Rather than take a job with a German firm, then, many Jews sought to strike out on their own, and that meant the establishment of small retail enterprises. In Munich, in fact, they created a new center of activity on the Möhlstrasse. As one observer described it, in addition to shops it featured "modern cafes with outdoor tables beneath bright resort umbrellas; and on the side streets luxury restaurants bearing international names: Amor, Astoria, Bristol, Trocadero."[56] Another Jew compared it to Nalewki Street, the main Jewish shopping street in Warsaw. Of even more importance for the local Munich population were the well-stocked stores that offered goods at prices below those of the established stores downtown.

How all this looked, to at least some of their customers, was explored by the novelist Wolfgang Koeppen, who projects the musings of the wife of a middle-aged bandmaster, disturbed and distressed by the changes around her:

The bandmaster, Herr Behrend, continues to conduct, only now in God knows what kind of coffee houses for Negroes, and he plays for Veronica [the singer] "When I Get to Alabama." He didn't get to Alabama. He never reached it. The time of lawlessness was over. . . . The actors had been caught and they sat out their much too mild sentences behind bars: now there were concentration camp inmates, the persecuted, deserters, swindlers who pretended to the title of doctor. The bandleader paid. . . . Everything was becoming more expensive, and once again there are all the roundabout ways that lead to the conveniences of living. Frau Behrend drinks

Nalewki Street, a busy shopping center in the Jewish quarter of interwar Warsaw. Shops were not only at street level but also on the upper floors of the building, combined with the living quarters of the shopkeepers. YIVO—Institute for Jewish Research, New York.

Maxwell-Coffee. She bought the coffee from Jews. From Jews—those were the black-haired people who spoke a broken German, unwanted, foreigners, blown here, who looked at one reproachfully out of darkly glittering, night-shrouded eyes; who wanted obviously to speak of gas and gravedigging and execution sites at dawn, pious; the rescued who did not know what else to do with their rescued lives than on the rubble of the bombed city . . .

And here Frau Behrend's thoughts suddenly swerve to that idyllic time before the war when she sat on her balcony reading the newspaper.

(And why was the city bombed, my God, and destroyed. For what sins was it punished? The thought of the five rooms in Würzburg, their home with a southern exposure, with a view over the city, over the valley, the Main River glittering, the morning sun on the balcony, "The Führer Visits the Duce," why did all this happen?) to sell goods in their hastily built shacks, goods on which they had paid neither taxes nor duties. "They don't leave us a thing," said the grocery store owner. "Nothing; they want to drive us into the ground." . . . The coffee in her store mouldered, overtaxed and its duties paid.[57]

Yet in many cases, the reality of life soon began to erode stereotypes, principles, and prejudices. One Jewish entrepreneur, who had long experience in Lodz manufacturing clothing, began again in Munich by subcontracting work to Germans. Others soon found it necessary to work with German suppliers, landlords, government officials—so that gradually they were brought into the working world of Germany, such as it was. And it was not without its ugly side. In May 1948 the Jewish owner of a shoe store in Straubing, a town near Munich, received the following unsigned note: "Jews: Your time has come. You now have your own state. Leave Straubing now and our Germany. We don't want you. Now go where you belong. We wish you luck. We don't need your shoes for 17 marks. If you don't go, you will pay for it with your life. You still have a few weeks to go. We are keeping you under watch; the day is coming."[58]

Yet in that very town of Straubing, the municipal government had set up a special commission to settle disputes involving refugees, rather than leaving the matter to a conventional court. In one landlord-tenant dispute, for example, the commissioner found in favor of the Jewish tenant, "who for years had been held by force in concentration camps because of National Socialism, and because of this there is a certain reason that one must treat such people with particular consideration." In addition, the commissioner noted that there were already laws in place that "favored racially and politically persecuted people in housing matters."

The threatening letter and the sympathetic ruling were written in the same town within a year of each other, and are perhaps symbolic of the situation that confronted the displaced persons who decided to make lives for themselves in Germany. On the one hand there was undoubtedly a deeply felt and widespread legacy of the Hitler years. For a long time, the American military government surveys found a consistent 30 percent of the German population who admitted to anti-Semitism. But the official government position, as in the Straubing housing incident, was committed not only to protecting Jewish refugees in difficulties but actually to favoring them. Whether the law was enforced in practice in this high-minded, principled way is subject to some dispute, but that it even existed gave Jews recourse before courts of law. In addition, all emblems of the Nazi Party were forbidden, as were the public expression or publication of anti-Semitic or racist remarks.

For a people in goles, this was a great deal. As we have seen, the critical difference between the Polish Jews and the Jews of Western Europe was in their expectations of civic life. For a long time, Jews in France and England and Germany had considered themselves part of the larger society in which they lived. Being a Jew was a private, religious matter, but politically and socially, in theory at least, they were the equals of their countrymen. In Eastern Europe it had been quite different; very few Jews would have called themselves Poles. By the 1930s many Jews were Polish-speaking and seemed superficially like everyone else. But they knew, and their Polish compatriots knew, that they were Jews—and that made an unending difference in a deeply nationalistic and Catholic country.

There were, of course, anti-Semitic incidents in Germany after the war, but with few exceptions these were symbolic gestures rather than actual attacks. Synagogues were sometimes marked with the swastika, and cemeteries were invaded and stones overturned or broken. But physical assaults on Jews were rare. And above all, as Jews in the Western world had long learned to cherish, under the Occupation, the rule of law prevailed.

Before the currency reform in 1948, with the mark shaky and goods scarce, what developed in Germany was essentially a barter economy. And that led inevitably to a black market. In fact, all transactions were tainted somewhere along the line. The United Nations Relief and Rehabilitation Administration (UNRRA) was the major agency active in providing supplies to the Jews in the camps, and its work was supplemented by various American Jewish agencies, notably the American Jewish Joint Distribution Committee. Among their supplies were the much-valued American cigarettes, which functioned practically as currency in Germany, as well as chocolate and canned goods of various kinds, which were great luxuries. These so-called gray-market goods were acquired legitimately but used for barter rather than consumption. It was yet another aspect of the way the German postwar economy operated.

It must also be said that there was a prevailing Jewish cynicism about the German demand for scrupulous legality in the trading of goods. Jews felt that they had witnessed and been the victims of the most appalling lawlessness of all time at the hands of Germans. They did not feel particularly obligated, as a consequence, to observe meticulously the laws of the people who had perpetrated such crimes. This attitude led inevitably to a defiant willfulness as they traded in whatever goods happened to come their way.

Jewish participation in the black market became a sore point with the German authorities and a publicly acceptable outlet for anti-Jewish statements and behavior. It confirmed the old prejudices that Jews excelled not only in trade but especially in shady transactions, and it led to bitter exchanges. In response to exaggerated charges by the county council for the area in which the large D.P. camp Föhren-wald was situated, Gen. Lucius D. Clay, the commander for the American zone, said that although barter and the black market had become a general problem, there was no evidence that the Jews were any more prominent in these transactions than any other displaced persons, or even the German population.[59]

By 1946 the German police had begun a campaign against Jewish black market activities that included raids on the D.P. camps. In March 1946, in a particularly aggressive raid in Stuttgart involving 180 German policemen with dogs, one person was arrested. As camp inmates then attempted to drive the Germans from the camp, a melee ensued in which the police fired and killed one of the bystanders. This man, Samuel Danziger, who had survived the concentration camps, had just found his wife and two children. The entire raid, as it turned out, was over some eggs. Its only positive consequence was that from then on, the German police were forbidden access to the D.P. camps.[60]

Then in November 1946, at a meeting of the German authorities with a central committee representing the Jewish residents of five major camps in the American zone, both sides attempted to discuss what could be done to regulate trade. The situation was thoroughly analyzed by Dr. Samuel Gringauz, a former judge in Memel, chairman of the camp committee at Landsberg, and president of the Central Committee of Liberated Jews in the American Zone. He maintained that the problem went far beyond the illegal activities of a few Jews. Fundamentally, he pointed out, the German farmer was reluctant to sell his produce at the official price for the essentially worthless mark and preferred to sell it more profitably on the black market. Similarly, the producers of manufactured goods preferred to sell where they could get the best price. In fact the minister president of Hesse, Karl Geiler, conceded that in many areas, as much as 75 percent of production was going to the black market. And these were transactions that German producers and buyers had managed to cover with official documents. "One cannot fight economic laws," Gringauz observed, "with police methods." He suggested, further, that the police should look at the root of the problem—the actions of the German peasants and manufacturers. "If they didn't sell on the black market," he pointed out, "there wouldn't be a black market." Although the governing committees in the five camps represented at the meeting volunteered to institute a program to combat black-market activities in the camps, these activities could not be ended as long as goods were scarce and money valueless.[61]

The participation of the Jewish displaced persons in the legitimate German economy was tentative at first. But as the wait for resettlement dragged on, what had begun as temporary ventures began to take on a more permanent character, especially as the economy stabilized. Some Jews accumulated enough capital to buy real estate, especially in Frankfurt, where some accumulated substantial holdings. A few professionals who had come through the war managed to resume their work.

In the country around them, they could form no sentimental attachment to their towns or their neighbors or the local dialect. On the contrary, everything German was associated with death and destruction. But to be independent, to be self-supporting, to be beginning life again, even in Germany, seemed superior to passing their days in the assembly centers waiting. Repeatedly, we read in the camp newspapers of the formation of new Jewish communities in neighboring towns, as more and more Jews decided to try their luck in the free economy.

They began, then, tentatively, but were swept up in the "economic miracle" that overtook Germany as its currency stabilized, its factories began to export products that were in demand on the world market, and its cities began to rebuild out of the rubble of the war. How, indeed, was a Jew to live in postwar Germany as it prospered and flourished, and simultaneously raised the fortunes of those Jews who stayed? For the many Jews who ran their businesses and started new lives, there was something unfinished here. Where were justice, retribution, revenge? It was this hunger for some response to their suffering that made the Jews in the D.P. camps follow the proceedings of the Nuremberg trials with such unwavering attention. The men in the dock had, after all, been the cause of their sufferings and they wanted to see them punished. This was less than immediate, but it was something.

The question of what constituted revenge preoccupied many of the survivors. Many remembered that after the expulsion of the Jews from Spain in 1492, the rabbis had forbidden Jews to set foot on Spanish soil or to trade with its people—for a thousand years. Should not such a ban be pronounced on Germany?

At another extreme Abba Kovner had been one of the commanders of the armed revolt in the Vilna ghetto and after the war was one of the organizers of the Brichah movement. Kovner had proposed drastic revenge on the German population. In the spring of 1945 he and a few others formed a group they called *Nakam*, the Hebrew word for revenge. Kovner's grandiose plan was to poison the water supply of Nuremberg, the site of the mass assemblies of Nazis at their party meetings. The conspirators were serious, determined men, and their plan had gotten far. One of their members had even managed to get a job in the waterworks, and all was prepared when David Ben Gurion, later head of the Israeli state, heard of the scheme and absolutely forbade the group from following through on their intention.

The group, undeterred, then turned to an alternative objective: a prison camp in the Nuremberg area that housed some twelve thousand former SS men and Nazi officials. The idea was to poison the bread served the prisoners, and again one of the members of the group managed to get a job in the camp. With two other conspirators, he painted the undersides of some one thousand loaves of bread with arsenic on the evening of April 13, 1946. The next day thousands of the inmates who ate the bread suffered terrible pains. Some went to the hospital, where they had their stomachs pumped. But all survived. The conspirators then fled to Palestine, where today they still defend their action, even as Germany seeks their extradition. Leipke Distel, the conspirator who had been employed at the prison camp maintains: "We behaved morally. The Jews had a right to revenge themselves on the Germans."[62]

At a conference on the She'erith Hapletah in 1985, one of the participants, Avraham Fuchs, who had been a resident of the displaced persons camp at Bergen-Belsen, took a different view. "Revenge did not mean only killing Germans," he said. "We had revenge when we saw the Germans acting as hewers of wood and drawers of water, when they arrived at Bergen-Belsen and were ready to sell anything for a piece of bread, when we saw them cleaning Jewish houses, the Jewish school I attended, buying cigarettes and paying for them in gold—gold that had undoubtedly been taken from Jews. We sold them bread and coffee and they gave everything they had. Revenge also meant living with German women." Yaffa Eliach, another participant at the conference, had a different response. "The sense of revenge," she said, "is not exhausted in murder and a desire to humiliate one's torturer. At the large bar mitzvah celebrations and weddings that Holocaust survivors hold, one always feels that Hitler is there and that that is their revenge. . . . Revenge is therefore a mechanism of survival and not of ideology."[63]

In the first moments of liberation, when the tables were turned in the concentration camps, some prisoners took immediate revenge by killing their guards. And sometimes the Jews turned on those among them who had collaborated. Yankel Pomerantz describes coming to Lodz in May 1945 to search for family members. "As we were arriving in the city, I watched a group of Jews converge on one man. He had been a Jewish collaborator with the Nazis in a concentration camp. He had overseen the killing of children, one man joining the group told us. Now in Lodz, Jewish survivors from the camp had recognized him. They set upon him and beat him right in the street. They delivered blow upon blow until he died."[64]

Such direct reprisals, however, were rare. Sometimes the revenge was more symbolic. Ruth Klüger described how a pair of Polish Jewish refugees were assigned an apartment in the first years after the war, when former Nazis were required to give up their apartments to "liberated Jews" arriving in the American zone. Klüger, herself a survivor of Auschwitz, at this point was living in Straubing in Bavaria. The confiscated apartment was, she said, "particularly carefully furnished. But when the young Jews moved in they discovered all kinds of objects that could only have come out of synagogues.

"Seeing this, they went about methodically breaking up into matchwood every single thing that they couldn't use. I didn't approve of this," writes Klüger, "since enough had been destroyed already, but I had to agree that the grounds for vandalism—if there were to be any—were very good in this elegant apartment that had been enriched by theft from a synagogue."[65]

Pomerantz describes another kind of indirect revenge, that of a Jew literally striking out at random at the world around him. One Polish Jew who had reached the safe haven of the American zone in Germany would from time to time be overtaken by a burst of outrage on a bus. He would then simply go down the aisle striking whoever came into range. For all those who gave vent to their feelings, however, there were many more who resisted on the ground that they would not sink to the level of their persecutors.

Jurek Becker, a novelist born in the Lodz ghetto, whose nursery was in Auschwitz, settled after the war with his father in the Soviet zone of Berlin. His work was tremendously successful and his first novel, *Jacob the Liar*, has been made into a movie both in Germany and in the United States. In his seemingly autobiographical novel *Bronsteins Kinder*—Bronstein's Children—he describes what happens when revenge is delayed. His father and several other men, all former inmates of the same concentration camp, have recognized one of their guards in East Berlin. They decide to kidnap him, take him to a secluded country house, and make him admit to his crimes. They succeed in capturing him; they bring him to the house and tie him to a bed. But their revenge has its boundaries. What they want is not his death but his confession, perhaps sweetened by the sense that now he is in *their* power.

Home—or the lack of it—was another theme that aroused the feelings of the She'erith Hapletah. What particularly incensed the Jewish refugees in the American zone was the vision of the Germans still living snugly in their intact communities—the fact that they were at home, and the Jews, after all their sufferings, were still without a place to lay their heads. Bunim Heller, in a poem published in November 1946 in the *Jidisze Caytung*, wrote:

> It's still in Europe. There are no longer any Jews.
> In peace, the tank has become a tractor.
> It has already plowed the earth above the graves
> In which a people lies buried and abandoned . . .
> The Germans stop being afraid and settle down
> It's all long since blown away and forgotten
> And they occupy their homes in peace.
> Only one still runs about there trembling
> As if under his feet, the earth is still shaking
> As if under his step, the bridge wanted to rise up.
> He seeks all his people, and he can still not believe it.[66]

Even children could feel the contrast of their deprived lives in the camps with the tranquil German world around them. Miriam Shmulewitz, who had survived the war with her parents in the Soviet Union, had moved west when they were released and found shelter in the Hindenburg camp outside of Ulm. "One summer morning," she remembers, she and a few other children started to walk to Ulm.

> On the way to town we suddenly saw a row of delightful, little houses. Just like in storybooks. The windows were hung with curtains and decorated with vases of flowers. But

in order to get to one of the houses one had to pass through a garden with trees and flowers. We were suddenly overcome with envy. We admired the quiet, the peace that lay over these houses. We children were living two families to a room in military barracks. Winter it was freezing cold, and in summer one was bathed in sweat. And here was so much beauty. We didn't say a word to one another, but every one of us wanted to play a prank on the Germans, so we ran from one little house to another and rang all the bells. All the way down the road we could hear the Germans complaining, and we enjoyed it very much.[67]

For Ruth Klüger, it was not just the permanence of the physical world that aroused her envy (and irritation). Speaking of a fellow student at the university in Regensburg, she contrasts his situation with hers. He, a native of Regensburg, "had an identity. He was at home in Germany, rooted in a particular German landscape, and he became for me the essence of a German. He knew where he was and who he was."[68]

But once again, what drove away feelings of resentment and envy was the sheer triumphant sense of being alive! In the displaced persons camps around Berlin a kind of folk ballad was created by the inmates, with verses freely added as time went on. It managed to poke fun at all the authorities in the camp—the army chaplain, the Joint officer, even their own elected camp committee. But it ended with a reflection on Berlin:

Berlin is totally destroyed
Lies buried nine ells deep
And I, a little Jew, stand and cry
His People Israel lives—Amcho Yisroel Khai.[69]

The Eastern European Jews who stayed in Germany knew that they would never be part of Germany, nor did they want to be. They were again in goles; but for the time being they were safe. In the black-and-white world of the D.P. camps, the Eastern European Jews had hardly thought of yet another Jewish population in Germany: the German Jews who had survived the war and were now attempting to rebuild their communities. But as the displaced Jews began to emigrate, and others began to enter the German economy, these two disparate elements began to meet on their common ground: in the Jewish community, the *Gemeinde*. And so in strange cities, in unfamiliar synagogues, hearing unaccustomed liturgies, the Eastern European Jews began their return to life, again anchored in the rhythms of the Sabbath and the holidays and the celebrations of the rites of passages. Among strangers, but somehow they would find their way.

CHAPTER THREE

The Last German Jews

eggendorf, a small town in southeast Bavaria, has long had a bad reputation in Jewish chronicles. In 1339 the Jews of the town were massacred, their property confiscated, and their synagogue razed because of their presumed desecration of the Host. This was a popular accusation by the medieval church, according to which the Jews pilfered the sacred wafers and then pierced them with knives, causing them to bleed—a symbolic reenactment of the Crucifixion. Then in 1348–49 the Jews were blamed for the Black Death which raged through Europe and killed off perhaps half of its population. A famous woodcut in the Nuremberg Chronicle shows the Jews of Deggendorf being burned alive in punishment. In the decades immediately following the Black Death, Jews left Germany by the thousands to start a new life in Poland. By 1910 only seventeen Jews still called Deggendorf home. The name of the town next appears during the years of Nazi rule as

The burning of the Jews of Deggendorf at the time of the Black Death, 1348–50. Jews in Europe were accused of having caused the plague by poisoning the wells. Beinecke Library, Yale University.

the site of a concentration camp with five hundred inmates, of whom four hundred were Jews.

In 1946 the camp was remade into a United Nations assembly center for displaced persons, accommodating seven hundred Jews for a few years. But relations between the displaced persons in the camp and the local population were not easy. In September 1946 a nearby farmer was robbed by six armed Polish bandits, who then disappeared. Some time later, the farmer saw a young Hasid from the displaced persons camp on the street in Deggendorf and claimed to recognize him as one of his attackers. The ensuing trial of the accused, Natek Szlamowicz, took place under American military authority. The defense lawyer, Samuel Gringauz, whom we met earlier, had taken a law degree in Heidelberg before the war and was deeply respected among the displaced Jews. In his cross-examination, Gringauz was able to dispose of the charges in short order because none of the farmer's family could agree on a single description of the invaders, and Szlamowicz was acquitted.

In spite of the flimsy case, the courtroom was packed with Jews from the D.P. camp who watched the trial with some anxiety. As it happened, the day of the verdict was Purim, the holiday in the Jewish calendar celebrating the rescue of the Jews of Persia from the efforts of the king's vizier, Haman, to have them annihilated. The resolution of the trial in favor of Szlamowicz fit perfectly with the theme of the day. Gringauz, reporting the event for a Yiddish newspaper, wrote: "Today is Purim, and today all Jews celebrate the defeat of all the great Hamans. And so do they also in Deggendorf." He described how several celebrations went on in separate rooms in one of the public buildings of the camp. In the largest room, children reenacted the Purim story, with dances and a comedian. Children perform another skit, someone sings the famous song of the Vilna ghetto. Composed during the darkest days of the Nazi occupation, its opening lines express the atmosphere of defiance in the resistance movement:

Never say you are walking your last road.
Leaden skies conceal blue days!
The hour we have longed for with
    all our longing will yet come—
Our step will beat out like a drum: we are here!

As Gringauz summed up: "Everything is so heartfelt, so joyous, so full of hope. In another room," he continued, a group of elderly people had assembled. Jews of quite another sort. A tragic gathering. Here in Deggendorf had come together all that was left of the German Jews from the concentration camps, from the once great and intelligent German Jews. All those who had managed to survive Theresienstadt. . . . The young ones had left, many for America, and some for the larger German cities. Those who remained were those who didn't have anywhere to go, or who were waiting for certificates from their children, from relatives. . . . Broken splinters from a once great, fine, splendid trunk. . . . This gathering is hushed, dignified, quiet. They are celebrating Purim, and I feel here the ceremonial of a holiday in a German Jewish temple and the silence of a faraway cemetery. In another room they are celebrating the acquittal of Szlamowitz, and in a third they are enjoying Purim. Simple people, His People—*Amcho,* people out of the folk, who have become brothers and sisters to one another, young people, without a synagogue, without any education, but with good hearts, with a sharpened intelligence and with deep Jewish feelings. Their fathers were rabbis and artisans, merchants and farmers, the pious and the ignorant, but today these differences are all obliterated.[1]

Gringauz was born in Lithuania, but having studied at a German university he knew both cultures and saw the differences between them. He may be pardoned for a certain extravagance in his account of the trial and its aftermath in view of a justifiable pessimism about its outcome. But in his vision of the two Jewish communities—the young, vital, if simple, Eastern European Jews whose Judaism was alive, versus the old German Jews with their fading Jewish culture—he was expressing widely held stereotypes that were demonstrated in the adjoining rooms in Deggendorf. Each of these groups had very little understanding of the other, but on at least one point, Gringauz's observation was correct: the German Jews who had remained in or come back to Germany *were* older than the Eastern European Jews who had survived the war. This fact was bound up with the strange legalisms of Nazi policy.

The fate of the German Jews under the Nazis was quite different from that of their Eastern European brethren. The German Jews, at least, had had some warning. In the six years between the Nazi takeover of power and the start of the Second World War, 270,000 German Jews had been able to emigrate. With the war, what had been in the first Hitler years a process of humiliation and separation from German society now escalated into the Nazi determination to "cleanse" Germany of its Jews. By 1941, as the ghettos in the East and the concentration camps were operating at full force, the Nazi government began deporting the German Jews. Few of those who went east would come out of the camps alive.

Some thousands of German Jews went underground; others, with the help of false papers, risked passing; and the members of yet another group were spared because they lived in what was called in Nazi jargon a "privileged marriage." Jews who were married to "Aryans," and who were childless or had raised their children as Christians, qualified for this category, which ultimately saved their lives. They suffered, however, all the other privations of their fellow Jews. They were allotted minimal food rations and could shop for these during only one hour in the day. They were not permitted to replace worn-out clothing or to have shoes repaired. They were forbidden to use the parks, to attend concerts, theater, or sports events, or to use public transportation. Many towns posted signs at their borders saying "Jews unwanted." After 1941 all Jews older than six years of age were required to wear a yellow Star of David sewn onto their coats. Gradually they were robbed of all property, and finally they were herded together, along with their "Aryan" spouses, into "Jew houses." When the Allied bombings began, they had to enter separate bomb shelters; they were recruited for slave labor, but they were not sent east—and that spelled life.

Many of these survivors were Jews only according to the Nazi definition. Victor Klemperer, for example, who kept a meticulous diary during the Hitler years, had converted to the Evangelical Lutheran Church in 1912, when he was thirty-one. Married to a Christian, he had made a substantial career as a professor of French literature at the Technical College in Dresden. And then suddenly in 1935, under Nazi law, as a Jew, he was dismissed from his university post and deprived of most of his pension.

Klemperer's diary describes the ever-diminishing circle of his existence as one by one all the amenities and then the essentials of life were taken away from him. Finally, he and his wife were forced out of their little house outside of Dresden and made to take up quarters in a *Judenhaus,* where they shared an apartment with total strangers. For most Jews this was the last stop before deportation, and Klemperer describes the frightful nights among his neighbors that followed the receipt of a summons to appear for a transport.

The ultimate response—not infrequent in the Klemperer experience—was suicide. This alternative, which in German is euphemistically called "free death"—*Freitod*—was one sought particularly by the elderly. Martha Liebermann, the eighty-five-year-old widow of the painter Max Liebermann, was one who chose this alternative in March 1943, rather than report for deportation. The Nazis were taking no notice of past distinction. Although Max Liebermann had an international reputation and had been president of the Berlin Academy of Art, by 1943 Nazi officials were interested only in "race," which by then had deadly consequences. Some writers have seen

Victor Klemperer, 1881–1960, a professor of
French literature at the Technical University
in Dresden, is the author of remarkable
diaries that he kept during the Nazi period
and then on into the first months of the
Communist takeover of East Germany.
Bundesarchiv Koblenz.

these suicides as a form of resistance, a last act of defiance against overwhelming power. Others have seen them as evidence of a clear and pessimistic understanding of the meaning of the summons to report for deportation. In Weissensee, the huge Jewish cemetery in Berlin, there is a section where one can still see the gravestones of the many couples and individuals who preferred to take their lives rather than subject themselves to the torment of the Nazis. In all, 1,279 Jews were buried there as suicides during those years. Although the Third Reich kept no official statistics on Jewish suicides, scholars estimate that some 3,000 Jews took their lives at the height of the deportations.[2]

Klemperer was not called up for deportation, although by 1945 even Jews in privileged marriages were being summoned. What saved his life, strangely enough, was the catastrophic Allied firebombing of Dresden in February 1945. In the ensuing chaos his wife cut the yellow star off his jacket, and they joined the anonymous ranks of those who had been bombed out. Then he registered with the authorities and signed up for regular ration cards, even a card for tobacco. Once again, he wrote, "I sat in restaurants. I traveled on the train and streetcar—everything that in the Third Reich spelled death for me."[3]

In spite of his sufferings and his survival, Klemperer had no place for theology in this thinking. Although in the twelve years since Hitler's rise he had again started to think of himself as a Jew—by descent, by history—he stopped short of joining the religious community. Yet he was troubled by his continuing membership in a Christian church and took action a few months after the end of the war. Finding it "daily ever more puzzling how people can still believe in a gracious loving God . . . after all the horrors of these years," on August 18, 1945, Klemperer and his wife both left the Evangelical Church, "which had so shamefully abandoned him."[4]

After twelve years of Nazi life, German citizens were confronted not only with Allied conquerors but also with a totally contradictory way of thinking. Rejection of Nazi ideology and conformity to the often barely understood democratic way of life nonetheless became the indispensable requirement for participation in public life, for employment by the Allied powers and for any attempt to start life again. One of the more bizarre aspects of postwar German life was the scramble for official certificates, testifying that the bearer had never been a Nazi. These certificates were popularly, and satirically, known as the *Persilschein*, after a well-known laundry powder, and their name indicated a certain skepticism as to the reliability of the official investigations. A sardonic joke of the period noted that for ten such documents one could get an "Israel" as a middle name (which the Nazis had required Jewish men to adopt), and for twenty, a red *J* in one's passport.

As these jokes suggest, the support of a surviving Jew was invaluable. When Klemperer received a request for such support from a former major in the German army, his reply showed how profoundly he had suffered and how much control he had used in the thousands of pages of his journal where he is judicious and detached. "You must have known," he writes the major,

> and all the others must have known what mad criminals they were serving, what unthinkable cruelty you protected and made possible with your faithfulness to duty. I speak only in small part out of personal bitterness. My wife and I have suffered very much: being beaten, kicked, spat upon. We suffered hunger and the permanent danger of being sent to our deaths. For me came slave labor as a street-sweeper and later in a factory. Then imprisonment and isolation cells; at the end, we eluded certain extermination only through a miracle and the unwavering bravery of my wife; the Dresden catastrophe saved me, since people took it for granted that we had been buried under the ruins of our house. And in this way, we

could flee. Yet all of this is nothing against the outrages that we experienced for years, day in and day out, all the bestiality that the Gestapo and SS people of officers' rank and uniform performed! (That is actually to give it a false name since no beast is capable of such cruelty, no beast behaves even remotely in such a fashion.) I do not speak even of the so-called warning executions that took place in Nuremberg and elsewhere, but just about the entirely ordinary daily abominations. What didn't we see with our own eyes here in the midst of cultivated Dresden (not even for once in Poland, but right here)? Didn't we see people dying around us? We became very much alone. Most of those with whom we had earlier been in contact are dead. Infrequently someone arises quite unexpectedly out of the frightful heap of corpses. We ourselves have rescued nothing except for our ruined health and a passionate will to devote the rest of our lives to making Germany human once again.[5]

We will encounter this fervent tone of voice in others who with a tough-minded clarity saw it as their task to return to Germany to foster democracy in a country that needed help. As it turned out, Klemperer and his wife were luckier than most, for they were able to repossess their little house. Although it was damaged, it was habitable, and as they moved back in June 1945, when Klemperer was already sixty-four years old, he saw within reach the restoration of his normal life— reading, writing, preparing lectures for his classes. "Once again to eat well," he mused, "to drink good wines, to take drives in our car, to go to the seashore, to sit in a movie theater. . . . No twenty-year-old can be as hungry for life. . . . And what makes me happiest is that Eva [his wife] from morning till evening can work on *her* house, on *her* garden and is thereby newly restored to life."[6] This is a zest that was not unique to Klemperer. Although at the beginning of his diaries, he was full of hypochondriacal fears that he would not live long, soon he was ready to plunge in again with reborn energy. As he noted after the Dresden bombing, neither he nor his wife mourned the loss of their property, but they cherished the fact of raw life, of simple survival.

Only some fifteen thousand German Jews came through the war alive in Germany, making up a bare 3 percent of their prewar numbers. Some had gone underground and lived in hiding, others had managed to procure false passports and lived a precarious existence hoping not to be recognized or to have their papers challenged. But most of those who survived, like Klemperer, owed their lives to their "Aryan" spouses.

There is no single story, no typical account of how people managed who went into hiding. Some found shelter with truly compassionate people who put their own lives at stake by taking in these fugitives. Others, like Walter Besser and his wife, discovered later that the couple who had given them shelter were preparing to kill them once their money had run out.

Besser and his family, who were originally from Coburg, had fled to Berlin in June 1933 after he, his father, and his brother had been arrested by the Gestapo. His brother, who was a Communist, was badly beaten. Walter and his father were released on the condition that they leave Coburg immediately. A young man in his twenties, Besser found work in Berlin and shortly after married. Then he experienced, like all Jews, the gradual closing down of his world. Until February 1943 he and his wife survived in Berlin as forced laborers, their working skills protecting them from the deportations, which had begun in 1941. By then his two brothers had long since left for Palestine. His parents, who had stayed on in Berlin, were among the first deported to Riga in 1941, and it was only after the war that Besser learned how they had been murdered. Meanwhile, he worked in a factory that made inflatable boats for the navy, while his wife was employed at a Siemens plant. In January 1943 the manager of Besser's firm advised him to go underground. Through friends, he and his wife found a couple willing to shelter them, and Besser gave them the 25,000 marks his father had hidden under the floorboards of their apartment.

Against all expectations, the Bessers were confined in a basement room of their host's house for more than two years. They spent their time staring out of a slit in the curtain that covered their window, or with Besser reading aloud while his wife knitted a long green dress. When she had finished the last stitch, she would carefully unravel the dress and start all over again. Living on the meagerest of rations, by the end Besser weighed only eighty pounds.

When they were freed by the Russians on April 27, 1945, he and his wife were interrogated—separately—for three days until their captors were convinced that their story was true. Then, although he had little education and had worked only as a machinist, Besser was put in charge of a hospital in a small town outside Berlin. What was important to the Russian commander in charge of their area was that Besser was politically "reliable." Jews in those early days, Besser notes, were very much courted in East Germany, and he was soon sent to a technical college to study economics and then assigned to the City Planning Board. The very fact that he was a Jew and thus untainted by a Nazi past brought Besser a career that far surpassed his own rather more modest aspirations, which, he said very frankly, had been to open an automobile repair shop.

Although he was not permitted to go to Israel to visit his surviving brother for forty years after the war, Besser did not mention the reason, nor did he show the slightest resentment or disappointment. A loyal bureaucrat, he did not reveal in his long interview, even in 1995, how tight a rein the German Democratic Republic kept on its citizens.

Ordinary citizens were allowed to travel only to Eastern bloc or other Communist-controlled countries, such as Cuba. Not until they became pensioners were they permitted to visit relatives in West Germany, much less travel to more distant non-Communist countries. But by that time, they would have had so many family ties in East Germany that these alone would ensure their return. From the state's point of view, as nonworkers they were no loss to the society if they defected, for they were only a drain on its resources.[7] Long after its fall, Besser remained loyal to the regime that did so much for him, either blind to the way it persecuted dissidents or still unwilling to be critical in public.

Ilselotte Themal chose the even riskier course of adopting a false identity rather than going underground. Although she had come from a protected middle-class life, where, as she said, "girls were treated like dolls," she learned quickly in the Nazi years to make important distinctions. Living underground, she pointed out in an interview, meant endangering those who sheltered her. She found this too great a burden and chose to risk living on forged papers, thus endangering only herself. She had started life happily enough in Potsdam, where her father had been a doctor. When he became an invalid, she went to work as a salesclerk in the Karstadt department store to help support the family. But on April 1, 1933, the day of the nationwide Nazi boycott of all Jewish businesses, she and all the other Jewish clerks were dismissed. Realizing that this avenue of work was now closed to her, she began an apprenticeship as a dressmaker. In 1935 her father died, and by the next year she had decided to emigrate to Palestine, where she hoped to pave the way for her mother and siblings to join her. But she never got out.

In March 1939 Ilselotte married her first husband, a musician whom she had met in the Zionist movement—and who died five months before the birth of their son, Uriel. By the time the child was born, in June 1940, Germany was at war and every able-bodied Jew was pressed into forced labor. Ilselotte notes the milestones in her history by the decrees that dramatically changed the status of the Jews. In her diary she capitalizes September 19, 1941, the day all Jews were required to wear the yellow star. Then in October 1941 the transports to the East began. In November Ilselotte's sister was sent to Lodz, and three months later her mother was also sent away. After receiving a few preprinted postcards from them, she never heard from either of them again. But she herself, as a dressmaker, was classified as a useful worker and was given huge quantities of men's jackets to sew—which she was allowed to do at home. During this time she met and married her second husband, Rolf Themal, formerly a lawyer and business-man, who, like all other able-bodied Jews, was now drafted for hard labor for the military.

The next big date for Ilselotte and her family was February 27, 1943, the day generally known as the "factory action." That was the day set by Goebbels when, as a birthday present for Hitler, Berlin was to be "cleansed of Jews." Workers were arrested at their places of employment. The aged, invalids, children were sought out at home, in hospitals—wherever they were—and deported in open trucks to collection centers. Rolf Themal was at work. Ilselotte, at home, was persuaded by her uncle not to wait to be arrested but to take her child and simply leave her room. And indeed, as she left her front door, seemingly an ordinary German housewife, with her child on her arm and a market basket in her hand, "an automobile stopped, two men jumped out and went close by me into our house, in order to take me away." Rolf also escaped being picked up at work—but from that day on, they were hunted people. For safety, they parted, and each set out on a separate illegal existence. Rolf, through friends, managed to get a set of identification papers which, as Ilselotte wrote, "seemed gen-uine and good enough, but would never have stood up to inspection by a military search unit." She undertook a more elaborate deception by pretending to be someone who had been bombed out in Hamburg and had fled to Berlin. Claiming that she had lost all her possessions, including her internal passport, she was able to play the part convincingly, affecting a Hamburg accent and giving the genuine address of a friend there. "Yes, I know that area," said the clerk issuing the new cards, "it's totally in ruins." In this way, until the end of the war, Ilselotte was able to carry official identification papers and even had ration coupons for food and clothes.

With the help of friends, she took her child and her new identity to a village in East Prussia, where she had no trouble telling a standard refugee story: that her husband was at the front, that she had been bombed out and sought safety in a small village. Once there she was enlisted by a group of Polish partisans operating in the nearby forest, to whom she had to tell her secret. In return for their protection, she was able to perform many services for them, warning them of intended raids by the German army and even helping to bring an escaped English prisoner to safety. Meanwhile, Rolf had found protection with a friend who ran a pet shop, so that, as Ilselotte wrote, "he slept among rabbits, parakeets, fish, and parrots. But he was only there evenings and at night." During the day he had to be up and about, disguising himself as a wounded veteran by walking with a stick.

As the fighting drew closer to her village, Ilselotte decided to return to Berlin with her son. With her "genuine" papers, she qualified as a refugee with a right to a furnished room. Rolf moved in with her, illegally, of course, and in this way they met the end of war together. "The second of May came," wrote Ilselotte, "and we went to stand in front of the door, carrying white sheets and cloths in our hands [as signs of surrender]. We saw the first Russians, our liberators. . . . We still could not believe it, and could not trust ourselves to tell anyone who we really were. The first Russians came and we heard of murders and rapes." Rolf, however, with great presence of mind approached the Russian soldiers as they began to enter their house and asked to speak to a Jewish officer. When the officer appeared, although there was no common language, Rolf convinced him that he was Jewish by saying "Schma Isroel," the opening words of the Jewish prayer affirming the oneness of God. The officer accepted this as a demonstration of Rolf's true identity and issued the couple Russian identification papers, at last under their real names. These became their protection for the foreseeable future.

Marcel Reich-Ranicki also survived the last years of the war in hiding. He and his wife were taken in by a Polish couple, Bolek and Genia, in a house deep in the forest in eastern Poland. He too reports the talismanic use of Hebrew words as a code of recognition between Jews at crucial moments. Caught between the German and Russian fronts, the two couples watched the Germans withdraw as the Russians moved forward. Then as they had dreaded, Reich-Ranicki wrote, someone "pounded heavily, apparently with a rifle butt, on the door. Shaking, but with his head held high, Bolek opened the door. Before him stood a tired Russian soldier who asked loudly in Russian—'Any Germans here?' . . . Bolek answered in the negative . . . and called me forward since I speak Russian. The Russian solder looked at me sharply and asked, 'Amchu'—His people?" When Reich-Ranicki indicated no comprehension of the Hebrew word, the soldier resorted to conventional Russian and asked him if he was a *Jewrey*. After Reich-Ranicki assured him that he was a Jew, the Russian, he reports, "laughed and said, 'I am also a Hebrew. My name is Fishman.'"[8] In these terrible moments, Jews of whatever nationality or depth of religious belief, felt that a common Jewish lineage was the basis for complete trust. One could ask for and receive protection from a fellow Jew wherever the front lay, whatever the barrier of language.

As Ilselotte Themal told her story many decades later, once the war was over, she could not bear the thought of remaining in Germany and returned to her original idea of emigrating to Palestine. Although her husband was most reluctant, the family actually did get three scarce immigration certificates and sailed for the Holy Land only to find that it was not the solution they had sought. Alone Ilselotte, who was younger and more adaptable than her husband, might have made a success of the change. But Rolf saw no way of using his legal training in the backward, rural Palestine of the 1940s. He found it provincial and alien and could not make a place for himself there. As a cultivated, secular European, with no strong Jewish connections, he was not willing to reconcile himself to Palestine's limitations. "To live only among Jews," he told Ilselotte, "is impossible." Within a year, they were back in Berlin and beginning to build the kind of life that they had known.[9]

Some few Jews survived in Germany by collaborating. The Gestapo in their eagerness to catch Jews in hiding had managed to blackmail a number of Berlin Jews to act as informers. The most notorious, the beautiful Stella Goldschlag, was recruited with the promise that her parents would be safe from deportation as long as she scoured the streets of Berlin and identified Jews who were trying to pass. The lives of her parents depended on her producing results: turning in friends, neighbors, acquaintances whom she recognized from earlier days. The number of her victims is unknown, but those who survived describe how she came to be seen as a veritable Angel of Death, so that even a glimpse of Stella in a cafe or a concert hall would strike terror into the hearts of Jews with dubious papers. To be recognized was an instant passport to Hell, for she traveled always with a Gestapo escort in the background. Stella survived the war, but her parents were deported to Auschwitz and killed. At the end of the war, there were still twenty Jewish informers living in a wing of the Jewish Hospital in Berlin under the eyes of the Gestapo.[10] The hospital buildings and grounds in the Iranische Strasse had been turned into an enclosed ghetto where eight hundred Jews, many of them sick, some well, were kept under Gestapo supervision. There were even some few shades who had been members of the Central Jewish Council *(Reichsvereinigung)*. Those who had the good fortune to be chronically ill survived the war in this way; others who had been carefully nursed back to health were immediately deported to be killed in the death camps in the East.[11]

Every German Jew who survived the war in Germany had seen at close hand the cruelties of the Nazi regime. But while the war lasted, as long as the Nazi regime remained in power, they were frozen into immobility and could only hope to outlast the regime. Although the Nazis saw all Jews as an undifferentiated mass, all ultimate candidates for extermination, there were considerable differences among the native German Jews. The largest surviving group, Jews in mixed marriages, were also those who were least Jewish. Often they were not members of the Gemeinde—the official Jewish community—and did not even feel themselves to be part of Jewish culture. Yet after the war, they were often propelled into leading positions in the new Jewish communities because of their command of the German language and their ability to negotiate the reefs and rocks of German bureaucracy. Many of those who had been in hiding or passing, like Inge Deutschkron (who had been a young student when the war came) found that liberation also came with new decisions. "Never before," wrote Deutschkron, "in all those years, had we ever thought of the day 'after.' We had to concentrate all our energies on the next hour, on the next day, in order to survive."[12]

A tiny number of German Jews were waiting in their havens of emigration for the opportunity to return and rebuild Germany, to "make it human again," as Victor Klemperer said. But some who had waited were disappointed that the new Germany did not actively issue invitations or attempt to recall them from their new homelands. Only a few were like the journalist Karl Marx, who had spent the war years in England and returned as soon as possible.

After the horrors of the Nazi years, Jews abroad at first thought only of how to bring those who had survived out of Germany. Even Marx reported that when he returned to Germany in 1946, "as the first Jewish civilian," his intention was "to help all the Jewish people who were still on German soil to leave this country."[13] Nonetheless, he stayed and responded to the appeals of Germans in politics like Kurt Schumacher, the leader of the Social Democratic Party, who argued that "it would not be possible to build a democratic Germany without Jews, . . . and that a Germany without Jews would only give Hitler a victory." This was the signal Marx needed. He and a fellow journalist, Hans Frey, began publication of the first German-language Jewish newspaper in the British Zone—*Jüdisches Gemeindeblatt für die Nord-Rhein Provinz und Westphalen*. Its first issue appeared in Düsseldorf on April 15, 1946.

As Marx's widow, who was somewhat younger, recalled their return from England, her husband "was persuaded that he had to go back to Germany, because there were so few surviving Jews and he felt obligated to be of help to that remnant of Jewry in Germany. . . . My husband belonged to a generation," she wrote, "that was absolutely rooted in Germany, which was one of the reasons that he could easily feel comfortable here. . . . I, who left Germany at a very young age, remained for a long time a stranger." It was probably not unimportant to his sense of rootedness that Karl Marx's family had lived for six hundred years in the Saar district.[14]

Marx's biweekly paper touched on the themes that faced every Jew who remained in or returned to Germany: the remembrance of the horrors of the Hitler years, which the editors set firmly in that long history of Jewish remembrance with its biblical roots. But the future remained murky. "We are about to celebrate Passover," the editors

JÜDISCHES GEMEINDEBLATT
FÜR DIE NORD-RHEINPROVINZ UND WESTFALEN

NUMMER 1   15. APRIL 1946   1. JAHRGANG

ZUM GELEIT

Die Militärregierung hat am 2. April 1946 die Herausgabe eines Mitteilungsblattes für die Gemeinden Rheinlands und Westfalens genehmigt.

Wir stehen vor den Pesach-Feiertagen. Unsere Gedanken gehen zurück, und wir denken an die alte Erzählung von der Befreiung aus der Knechtschaft Ägyptens. War es jemals zeitgemäßer denn heute, uns dessen zu erinnern? Haben wir nicht alle, die wir hinter den Stacheldrähten, in Gefängnissen und hinter Schicksalsmauern geschmachtet haben, die Knechtschaft Ägyptens verspürt?

Dieses Gemeindeblatt, welches noch in einem bescheidenen Umfange herauskommt, ist ein erster Schritt in die Freiheit, ein weiterer Schritt für den Wiederaufbau der jüdischen Gemeinden in Deutschland. Mein Gruß gilt nicht nur unseren treuen Glaubensgenossen des Rheinlands und Westfalens, er geht hinüber in all die Läger, in die unsere Glaubens- und Leidensgenossen heute noch – ein Jahr nach der Befreiung – gesammelt sind. – Wir kennen keinen Unterschied zwischen Ost und West. Wir haben als Juden gemeinsam gelitten, gemeinsam das Leid ertragen und haben jetzt als Juden gemeinsam dafür zu kämpfen, daß wir als vollberechtigte Bürger der Wiedergutmachung erhalten, die uns ein ordnungsgemäßes Leben gewährleistet. Gleichberechtigt wie alle, die guten Willens sind, unter der Voraussetzung der Wiedergutmachung der Zeit von 1933 bis 1945.

Wir danken der Militärregierung für die Unterstützung, die sie unseren Bestrebungen zuteil werden läßt. Wir danken dem JOINT, der JEWISH RELIEF UNIT, dem WORLD-JEWISH-CONGRESS und den übrigen jüdischen Organisationen, die uns vom Ausland aus in den letzten Monaten so tatkräftig geholfen haben. Unsere besten Grüße und unser Dank gehen an das CENTRAL COMMITTEE und insbesondere an seinen Präsidenten Herrn Josef Rosensaft, der in Amerika und mit mir gemeinsam in England für die Interessen der Juden in Deutschland in mannhafter Weise eingetreten ist. –

Möge nunmehr dieses Blatt - welches zweimal monatlich erscheinen wird - ein Bindeglied sein zwischen den Gemeindemitgliedern und ihren Gemeinden, und möge es unseren Brüdern draußen ein anschauliches Bild verleihen über unsere Aktivität in Deutschland. Wir haben für unsere Zukunft vollstes Vertrauen. Der Gott unserer Väter hat uns bis heute nicht verlassen und wird uns auch weiter beistehen.

Dr. Philipp Auerbach

Opening issue of the *Jüdisches Gemeindeblatt*—Jewish Community Paper—April 15, 1946. The first Jewish newspaper in German in the British zone.

wrote in the first issue. "Our thoughts go back, and we think of the tales of the liberation from slavery in Egypt. Was it ever more timely than now to remind ourselves of that past? Haven't we all, who have languished behind barbed wire, in prisons, behind the walls of fate, all felt the slavery of Egypt? This community newspaper . . . is a first step into freedom, and a further step toward the rebuilding of Jewish communities in Germany."

And here, with a frank recognition of old antipathies, the German-speaking Jews held out their hands to the Eastern European Jews. The editorial writer Philipp Auerbach was born into an old Hamburg Jewish family and had spent four and a half years in Nazi concentration camps. Upon his release he took an active part in recreating the Jewish community, becoming chairman of the Regional Jewish Union for the North Rhine Province. He was also the vice president of the Central Committee of Liberated Jews in the British Zone.[15] "My greeting," wrote Auerbach for the newspaper, "is directed not only to our true brothers in the faith in Rhineland and Westfalia; it goes beyond, into all the camps in which our brothers in faith and suffering are gathered, even today, one year after liberation." Then echoing the famous words of Kaiser Wilhelm, who on the outbreak of World War I had declared, "I no longer recognize any parties, I recognize only Germans," Auerbach pointed up a second important theme in the new communities.[16] "We recognize no difference between East and West," he continued. "We have suffered together as Jews, together we have borne our sorrows, and now as Jews we must fight together so that as citizens with equal rights we receive the restitution that will permit an orderly life." And at the end Auerbach touched on a third theme that troubled all those who remained in or returned to Germany: the opinion of their fellow Jews elsewhere. "May [this paper] offer our brothers abroad a clear picture of our activities in Germany."[17]

The last question that was to remain a perpetual source of reflection on both sides was the Jewish relationship to Germans. The German Jews' new wariness extended not only to the judges, administrators, and officials with whom they dealt on questions of law—but also to neighbors, shopkeepers, business associates whom they met every day. After the poisonous twelve years of the Hitler regime, every social encounter became a testing ground.

Above all, what was being reconsidered was the old basis on which the German Jews had built their lives for the previous two centuries—the premise that in some infinity the parallel lines of Jewish and German life would meet. This so-called German-Jewish symbiosis had long been scornfully dismissed by such skeptical Jews as the scholar and Zionist Gershom Scholem, who called it a "one-sided love affair." But most German Jews, before Hitler, before the war, had seen themselves firmly embedded in German society—albeit with the difference that they issued from a different history. Even a Jew who did not celebrate Passover knew that it had a resonance for him that it could not have for a German. It was part of his history, part of the history of his people, irrespective of whether he attended a Seder. But this was a difference that before the war could be invoked or not, as the occasion required. For most German Jews, whose families had long lineages in the land of their birth, this was, in fact, a difference without a distinction.

At the edge of Hitler's elevation to power German Jews were, on the whole, prosperous and *at home*. A small minority, some seven thousand out of a half-million, were members of a Zionist organization, but even they balked in 1912 when radical elements in the movement sought to extract a promise from every member that his ultimate purpose was to emigrate to the Land of Israel. In an as yet imperfect world, ordinary Jews tended to socialize among themselves, and family life was cultivated with great intensity as a way of keeping those of marriageable age within the fold. Although the level of ritual observance was not high and synagogue attendance flourished only at the major holidays, there was an unself-conscious cultivation of Jewishness at home, with regular family gatherings at the traditional times of religious observance. All of Gershom Scholem's entirely secular family, for example, quite naturally met at his uncle's house for Friday night dinner.

And while the synagogues may have been like the "best parlor," used only for ceremonial occasion, nonetheless the Jewish communities everywhere in Germany built the best and grandest they could afford. Unlike premodern times, when synagogues had been placed in back streets or carefully camouflaged to be inconspicuous, the mid-nineteenth century saw a wave of building in the extravagant "Moorish" style. Nor did the Jewish communities hesitate to set their synagogues in prominent locations. When the Jews of Berlin built their synagogue in Fasanenstrasse, its main sanctuary, crowned by three domes, had seats for 1,700 worshipers. To accommodate the more intimate atmosphere of a wedding party, the architect also included a smaller wedding salon, whose green wall tiles were specially ordered from the royal tileworks. On August 26, 1912, the day of the synagogue's inauguration, the emperor himself attended the services.

In this confusing environment of private disdain and public honor, the young did not need to be taught that special double-vision, that detachment so characteristic of their much denigrated Eastern European brethren. Jewish families simply read the newspapers differently from their Christian neighbors. Richard Lichtheim, a committed Zionist and a keen observer of well-to-do Jewish Berlin society, described the life of the smart young set around 1900—with their winters in St. Moritz, their assiduous attendance at theatres, concerts, and opera, their familiarity with the latest novels, painters, musicians. In his memoir of the period, Lichtheim described the occasion of the seventy-fifth birthday of the novelist Theodor Fontane. Celebrated as the best German writer between Goethe and Thomas Mann, he was particularly famous for his meticulous portraits of life among Prussian nobility, but noted that he received far fewer birthday congratulations from his cherished Prussians than from what he called "the prehistoric nobility"—his Jewish readers. Despite the profound immersion of the Jews in German culture, to which they had already contributed major figures, such as the philosopher Moses Mendelssohn and the poet Heinrich Heine, there remained what Lichtheim called "a glass wall that separated them . . . but through which one could not pass."[18]

What I am trying to suggest is that what may have looked from the outside like perfect mimicry had clear and precise differences for those who lived within this highly organized and stratified society. Yet far from crippling Jewish initiative and creativity, it seemed only to spur them on.

For nearly two centuries before Hitler the German Jews had been contemplating their changing place in German society. Were they merely guests in a "host" society, as the Zionists claimed? Were they second-class citizens, because they had been granted full rights only in 1871? Or were they first-class citizens who simply had to endure the seemingly intractable, often unspoken anti-Semitism that pervaded many aspects of social, business, and academic life? By the time of the Weimar Republic many German Jews had no trouble defining themselves as Germans and felt that the residual problem of anti-Semitism would in time wear away. What was more important than those apparently transitory difficulties was how much the Jews had achieved in Germany since they had begun their struggle for recognition and equality.

But by 1945 this complex old world was long gone; the brief epoch of the Weimar Republic, which had brought so many Jewish artists and political figures to prominence, had been cut short by the Nazi rise to power. The small number of German Jews who remained in Germany after the Second World War had to start from the beginning in imagining a new society and their place in it.

How tangled these relations would be is hinted at in a notice a young mother placed in the *Gemeindeblatt* in February 1947. "Seeking adoptive parents," she wrote, "for my son, one-half year old. Healthy and strong. Father of the child is a Jew."[19] She gives as an address a small town near Frankfurt. Were her reasons personal or social? Had a husband unexpectedly returned from the war? Was the community's hostility against the child's parentage too overwhelming for a single mother? Did she find herself estranged from her Jewish baby whose hair was too dark and curly, whose brown eyes were the eyes of a stranger?

Although under Jewish law the child was not a Jew, the mother was nonetheless offering her son to the Jewish community because of his, presumably vanished, Jewish father. The notice also implies that such a child would not be acceptable to "German" adoptive parents. However one imagines the situation, it is clear from the few lines of her offer that the twelve years of Hitler had dug a chasm in the popular mind between Jew and German.

In September 1947, a half-year after the *Gemeindeblatt* issued its first number, the Jewish communities in Bavaria began to publish their own newspaper, *Neue Welt*—New World. Their emphasis lay less on the past than on the future. They, too, felt a need to explain their presence in Germany to the Jews elsewhere. "May this paper," the editor wrote, "serve to sustain the ties between Jewish people in this country and abroad. May the *New World* lead to an understanding with the world around us. And finally, may it go out into the world as the intermediary for peace and reconciliation, as the carrier of our ideals and as the proclaimer of our lofty ethics. May words of intellect and culture be spoken from here by Jewish people, who, despite all their suffering, acknowledge their Jewishness with pride and dignity."[20]

Meanwhile the forces of real life, of supply and demand, were shaping the areas in which a displaced, dispossessed population could begin again. Despite the good intention of the *Gemeindeblatt* to obliterate the differences between the East and the West, the She'erith Hapletah and the German Jews settling into their restored communities had very different perspectives. Both began with the sense that they were living in temporary circumstances. Even the Jewish community in Berlin at first called itself an "emigration community."[21] But the inescapable reality for both the Saving Remnant and the German Jews was that very few were able to get out of the country. Although at first the Eastern European Jews, particularly, saw themselves only as birds of passage in Germany, waiting for a chance to emigrate, even they found their attitudes changing as time wore on. As one Hungarian Jew said, "Jews don't have roots; they have wings." But they were unable to fly, and there was a limit to what they could accomplish within the confines of the D.P. camps. ORT, the Jewish organization devoted to vocational training, ran classes to teach young people useful trades; they improvised commercial workshops making goods for sale, but all these were ephemeral and temporary. The population of the camps was largely young, unattached, and, despite their terrible losses in the war years, eager to start life again.

By 1947, at the second annual meeting of the Committee of Liberated Jews in Bavaria, the She'erith Hapletah had already begun to see that their sojourn in Germany was not going to be over soon. Nor were the quarter-million largely young Jews living in the camps or privately in the German community ready to continue indefinitely on the charity of the occupying armies or the Jewish relief organizations. By 1947, in fact, they had already begun all kinds of small businesses and were establishing themselves in the surrounding economy. The committee, ratifying what was already happening, gave the phenomenon a political twist. By adding political self-government to the already substantial economic initiative of the liberated Jews, their resolution made the gradual activity of Jews in the German economy more palatable to Zionist ideologues.

What the Congress proposed was a form of autarchy—that in the coming year thirty-six thousand Jews be employed in their own factories and workshops or on their own farms. As reported by the journalist Ernst Landau, himself an Austrian Jew and survivor of four and a half years in concentration camps, "These factories were to be exclusively for the support of the Jews living in Germany, for export, and for contracts with the American army, UNRRA, and other institutions." The ultimate purpose of the plan was the "complete spiritual transformation of the homeless Jews, moving them from being the receivers of charity in the direction of the productivization of their spiritual and material powers."[22] It was also intended to keep contact with the Germans to a minimum.

The question of "productive labor" had a long history in nineteenth-century discussions of the "Jewish question." When European society was still agrarian, the activities that fell to the Jews—banking, international commerce, retail trade, money-lending—were all decried by anti-Semites as "unproductive." What was "productive" was farming the land or making an object for use. There was no room in this model for trade and services. But the steady growth of an industrial society complicated this simple paradigm, and suddenly banks, traders, and retail and wholesale merchants were needed to facilitate the movement of goods and to provide financial support for the factories, railroad lines, roads, power, communications, and all the infrastructure of modern life.

The moral equation behind the seemingly neutral anti-Semitic discussion of "productive" and "unproductive" forces in society was incorporated into Zionist ideology, which for different reasons also wanted to see "productive" Jews. The Zionists wanted Jews not only to work in the interstices of the economy but to have a "normal" social structure, beginning with tilling the land and culminating in governing themselves. This was the logic underlying the deliberations of the Second Congress of Liberated Jews in 1947. But even the Zionists had to recognize the restiveness of the young, displaced Jews who watched months of their lives roll by without any plan or progress.

Nor could the careful language of an UNRRA report in August 1946 hide the highly charged atmosphere of the displaced persons camps. "It is recognized by all authorities," the writers noted,

> that Jewish persons after their privations . . . quickly react to any situation which reminds them of their lives under the Nazis. Incidents in the U.S. Zone in the past three months have shown that they are quickly sensitive to any form of restraint and violent repercussions result when any restraint is applied without consideration of the underlying psychological condition of the Jewish people at this time. Their emotional tensions are affected by the lack of knowledge as to whether they will be able to emigrate at an early date or not. . . .
>
> The Jewish displaced persons population is largely comprised of people under 35. Those under 25 have been completely deprived over the last ten years of normal working experience, vocational training and education. They have not had normal family life and have been living in concentrations camps or acting as partisans, living underground, etc. . . . The fact that they are living in Germany coupled with the psychological factors mentioned above presents an ever-growing possibility of security incidents.

Actually "security incidents" were remarkably rare. The tensions and anxieties of the Saving Remnant seem to have been tightly restrained rather than vented on the German population. In fact, police statistics for foreigners in Bavaria, where most of the D.P. camps were located, showed that the Jews had committed the fewest crimes. Furthermore, in 1945 and 1946 not a single Jew in Bavaria was accused of murder or attempted murder, robbery, or burglary.[23] But the Jews' high level of sensitivity is illustrated in a minor but representative incident. When a genial visiting American from a Jewish welfare organization put his arm around a young camp inmate, the response was immediate and violent: "Take your hands off me!" The American's easy and somewhat condescending bonhomie was just not acceptable to the young survivor.

The tense and highly charged atmosphere of the Jewish camps was in striking contrast to that of the other camps administered by UNRRA. These were Balts and other Eastern Europeans, people, unlike the Jews, who had not for six years daily faced the possibility of death, who had not lost their nearest family. Some had voluntarily come to Germany to work; some who had collaborated with the Germans were now seeking anonymity; some were refugees who had fled from the war zone. Others had been brought to Germany as war workers but lived under far different conditions from the Jews in their slave-labor barracks. Now they were confidently awaiting repatriation. In March 1946 no less a personage than Eleanor Roosevelt came to visit a displaced persons center in Berlin occupied by Latvians, a most gratifying social event for all the participants. "The representatives of the Baltic DPS appeared in national dress," according to the camp newspaper, "and presented Mrs. Roosevelt with a pair of hand-knitted gloves of original Latvian design."

Mrs. Roosevelt was not required to look upon emaciated bodies or tragic faces. Charming little girls handed her flowers and gifts as their elders confidently awaited suitable transportation to take them home. The account concludes with a poem of farewell in Latvian and

German conveying a rather light-hearted summer-camp atmosphere, markedly different from the searing desperation of the Jewish centers:

> In UNRRA Camp Teltower Damm
> The people often stand in line
> Seeking there to find their good fortune.
> They all dearly want to go back.
> In the camp, life is jolly
> Since every day something is going on.
> Everything is thought of
> To make the people happy. . . .
> And as the driver steers out of the gate
> Everyone, full of melancholy, thinks:
> "Good-bye Mr. Fritsch, Soumier, and Miss Deed
> We thank you all; you all were so sweet!"[24]

The Jews, by contrast, had no charming native costumes, many having reached the displaced persons centers still wearing their prisoner's clothing. Nor were they being courted like their former neighbors, the Poles. The new Communist regime in Poland, aware of the apprehension of the expatriates toward the new government, published long, soothing articles in the UNRRA *Repatriation News* appealing to the Poles' sense of patriotism and urging them to come home.[25] Such urgent invitations were exactly what was missing from Jewish life in the camps.

Although many of the German Jews and the She'erith Hapletah shared, as their first goal, the wish to leave Germany and settle elsewhere, the situation of the German Jews had a special dimension. Before the war, Germany had been their homeland. They had grown up in the German language and with German culture. Any second language would always remain exactly that—secondary, less resonant, less profound. The German landscape and German poetry had stirred their hearts. Their earliest memories were bound up with a civilization that had repudiated them and murdered their kin. But to reject that civilization was also to reject a part of themselves—and this was the sticking point for the German Jews, questions which had no meaning for the Jews from the East.

Although officially most German Jews expressed the wish to leave Germany after the war—and half of the fifteen thousand survivors did so—others knew that they would stay. Some, like Karl Marx, had a mission: to help rebuild a new and better Germany. Some hoped to regain property and businesses that would permit them to reestablish their lives. For many, however, staying was a kind of default position. They were too frightened of the uncertainties of emigration or too old or had no family abroad. Sometimes they were ill and unwanted by countries looking for strong young workers or, like the United States, unwilling to accept people with communicable diseases. A number of the survivors of the camps had contracted tuberculosis, which made them ineligible for American visas. The consequence was that not only the person who was ill but, out of solidarity, the entire family would remain behind as well.

Germany was unrelievedly "the land of Amalek" for the Eastern European Jews, but most of the German Jews who survived in Germany owed their lives to courageous Germans who had helped them, hidden them, or remained silent about their presence, even when they were not actively involved. It was said that for every German who hid or helped a Jew during the Nazi years there were another four or five who knew about it and whose silence had been as important as the active help. Hans Rosenthal, who after the war became a popular television personality in Germany, has described how a whole community had protected him by their silence. As a teenage boy in 1944 he had been taken in by a friend of his mother's in Berlin and hidden in a garden shed. In the last year of the war, as Berlin was being se-

verely bombed, his protector decided to take him into the neighborhood bomb shelter during the raids. Not only was he not betrayed, he
was treated as a good-luck talisman. "Where there is a Jew," said the
neighbors, "no bomb falls."

A number of German Jews who had worked as slave laborers in
Berlin and had been permitted to use the streetcars to get to work later
reported similar experiences on their trips. After 1941 every Jew was
highly visible, of course, because of the yellow star. Somehow in the
crush of the morning rush hour someone would manage to put some
bread or a sandwich in a coat pocket. As most Jews experienced it,
such events had a human value that went far beyond the bit of food
that came their way. Many others reported being warned by their em-
ployers to "disappear" before the fatal sweep of factories in February
1943. But all these acts are overshadowed by the heroism of the thousands of "Aryan" spouses who willingly shared the fate of the Jewish
partners and thereby saved their lives. Finally, in the first postwar
years, the German Jews who lived in the German world were out every
day, talking with their neighbors, with officials, with storekeepers,
with the business community. They could read the newspapers and
take the temperature of the country. By contrast, the She'erith Hapletah, by choice or because of the barrier of language, had very little
contact with the local population and had fewer signals to guide them.

Ernst Landau started a controversy in the summer of 1946 when
he broached the subject of the relations between Germans and Jews
in an article in the Zionist newspaper *Jüdische Rundschau*.[26] Voicing
the as yet rarely expressed assumption that Jews might actually remain in Germany, he began to speculate about Jewish relations with
their German neighbors. And he concluded by suggesting that Jews
needed to help the Germans learn how to live in a new world.

The immediate response in the D.P. press was incredulity. The
reaction of *Undzer Weg* appeared under the headline "Concentration

Camp Prisoners Should Come to an Understanding with . . . Germany!" The author, who signs himself only with the initials R.R., takes up two main themes: the old reproach of the Eastern European Jews against the assimilation of their German brethren, and the question of whether there was any possible meeting ground between Jews and Germans. In the heated language of this article we hear the voice of the Polish Jews who barely a year earlier had been freed from the concentration camps. Landau had also suffered in the camps, but he and his fellow German Jews were facing a far more complex emotional situation than the Polish Jews. Landau needed to come to terms with the fact that "a bond which had lasted for hundreds of years was torn by Hitler and his followers and cannot be put together again."[27]

R.R.'s charge of the betrayal implicit in assimilation actually has less to do with the adoption of Western civilization than with the abandonment of Jewish culture. As we have seen, by the end of the nineteenth century even the Jews in the heart of the Russian Pale knew that they could not remain forever buried in their little Jewish villages, in a timeless, disconnected existence. Yet to many Eastern European Jews, assimilation seemed a craven rejection of the Jewish past, made even more intolerable by the supercilious condescension on the part of German Jews toward the unreformed *Ostjuden*—the eastern Jews. This feeling was returned with ardor by the Eastern Europeans who condemned the German Jews and their search for social acceptance at such a great price. Any call for reconciliation with the sons of Amalek, therefore, was a vivid reminder to writers like R.R. of what they had always seen as toadying to the Germans. Even worse they perceived it as acceptance of the place in society that the Germans had blocked out for Jews, thereby fulfilling the "humanistic" role that the Germans had assigned them.

German Jews, however, saw their position in the world and in German society very differently. Far from being the humble minions of

German expectations, Jews would become the judges of the Germans. Landau comments sharply that the Germans lacked courage compared with those other West Europeans, who "took upon themselves the burden of hiding, caring for Jewish people and often sharing their last resources with the unfortunates being persecuted by a brutal system. The average German," he continued, "who doesn't miss an single opportunity to deny or diminish his complicity [with the Nazi regime], and in fact seizes every opportunity to vindicate himself in the eyes of the world, had simply neglected this humane, nothing more than humane, duty to protect his persecuted neighbor. . . . What is missing," Landau concludes, "is the inner will to think freely and individually, and not slavishly and collectively." And here is the point that so enraged R.R.—Landau's proposal that the "therapy" for this "mentality" lies in "the future education of the Germans, especially the German youth. And we must contribute to this education. That is our human duty, born out of the high ethics of the holy Scriptures of Judaism."[28]

This touched a nerve among the Eastern Europeans who could not see themselves as obligated to do anything for the Germans and regarded the reeducation of the Germans as their own responsibility. At this point, the state of the German soul was not high on the Eastern European Jews' agenda.

R.R. is blistering in his attack on Landau's position on German-Jewish contact. "Ah, the author is generous," he writes, in that he did not say

> that one should have close social relations with the Germans. Thank God at least for that! He understands that "at this point our wounds are still too fresh. But we must continually demonstrate to them by our bearing and our appearance in public that we, the sacrificial victims of National Socialist barbarism, have always been the carriers of humanism and that

we also wish to remain as such." There you have it. The goods with the well-known assimilationist trademark. The idea of our existence justified, giving us the right to live. We have to show that we are honorable "carriers of humanity." On us, on the sacrificial victims of Nazi barbarism, there still lies, according to him, the duty to show these people who gave birth to this barbarism, cultivated it, and sated themselves with it . . . that we are worthy of life. . . . And now it is sixteen or seventeen months since the liberation from the concentration camps. We live in the near neighborhood of Dachau, in the neighborhood of huge mass graves of our innocent men, women, children, and babies . . .

Even now—thousands, dazed, with their eyes filled with pain and the fear of death are remembering the eyes of our brothers and sisters packed into gas chambers, extinguished in agony. When these eyes hang over your head, day and night, they demand of the world a great and just reckoning.

The writer of these lines had no patience with Landau's careful exploration of the "mentality" of the Germans or the "humanism" of the German Jews. In a final climax of emotion, R.R. explodes: "Mentality, humanism—cursed may they be above all else, when they conceal such a base reality."[29]

These strong emotions were undoubtedly shared by many of R.R.'s readers in the year after liberation. While they sat in D.P. camps, uncertain of their future, they could see the Germans, who had brought this catastrophe on the world, snugly settling back into their homes and jobs, their domestic world intact, being wooed by the Americans, admired by the other Allies for their orderliness and cooperation. It was enough to make even an angel surly.

Landau, however, brought up in Vienna in the Western humanist tradition, and a journalist there until 1938, saw very clearly what was missing from German-speaking society, the society he had inherited and to which he still felt bound. He was ready to speak words of truth to all who would listen. "No one has ever been brought onto the right path," he wrote in the *Jüdische Rundschau*, "when he has been met with cold rejection and hatred. If we want to contribute to making the future world peaceful, then in our modest way, we must help to educate German people to understand that they must place in the foreground not the collective idea of Germany but the individual idea of humanity."[30] This was his way to repair the world.

In articles by other German Jews, we read over and over again of their sense of disappointment in the way they have been received in postwar Germany. One editorial in the *Gemeindeblatt* even recalls, by comparison, an episode three centuries earlier, when the Jews of Frankfurt had been unjustly expelled from their quarter of the city. Brought back in 1616 on orders of the emperor, they were escorted to their homes "in triumph," the editor notes, "with the beating of drums and the sounding of trumpets." By contrast, in 1947, "no one has even thought of offering the Jewish religious community the same support that other religious communities are receiving."[31]

Not only are they not received with drums and trumpets, their newspapers record a steady stream of anti-Semitic incidents, ranging from the merely hurtful remarks of passersby to the desecration of Jewish cemeteries or property. In Nuremberg a bomb was thrown into a shelter for the "racially persecuted." In Wuppertal, Jewish stores were smeared with swastikas and anti-Semitic slogans. In April 1947, under the headline, "Nothing Has Changed," the *Gemeindeblatt* published a deeply pessimistic estimation of the situation. "Imagine if Germany were not occupied," the writer begins, "the pogroms would be a daily occurrence, and once again millions would remain silent. That we are not exaggerating is borne out by a statement made by

Dr. David Treger, [the chairman of the Central Committee of Liberated Jews] in the American zone. At a press conference, he revealed that recently in Bavaria, the police were required to intervene to stop new propaganda being circulated about a ritual murder." Treger added that "according to a recent poll by the military government, 95 percent of the population admitted to being anti-Semitic."[32]

These numbers fluctuated, but that Jews felt themselves to be in a poisonous atmosphere is illustrated by two incidents reported in the German press. In Munich the *Süddeutsche Zeitung* told of a Jew who had just returned from a concentration camp, and still in his prisoner's uniform heard himself being discussed by two women who passed him on the street. "Just look," said one of the women, "once again a Jew, even though the newspapers wrote that they had burned all the Jews. And this one is already the third that has come back home."

In Berlin the tabloid *Der Kurier,* under the headline "A True Story," reported a similar incident.

> Moritz Rosenbaum is a Jew who in 1940 with his mother, father, and two sisters was deported and by some accident escaped being sent to the gas chamber. After five years of martyrdom, crippled but still alive, he was liberated with nothing but his striped uniform on his back. Returned to Berlin, he makes his way to a United Nations Relief and Rehabilitation center, where he is given a suit of clothes and some money. For the first time in many years, he is able to go like any normal person to a café to enjoy a cup of coffee. At the next table, another customer says to his companion. "Look at that dandified Jew. With them, things really never go badly."

Having come back, then, have they really come "home"? In 1947 one of the 500 Jews who returned to Berlin after spending the war years in Shanghai expressed his feelings about homecoming very succinctly: "I was perfectly clear in my own mind that one was not really returning. But far more that one was newly arriving."[33] For the Jews in Shanghai, there had been no choices. During the war they were interned by the Japanese in an improvised ghetto and allowed to practice a trade or earn money in only very limited, almost clandestine, ways. Obviously, once the war ended, they could not remain, and they returned to the only place to which they still had a right. Once in Germany, they, like the other German Jews, debated the question of staying or going.

Hans Frey, as editor of the *Gemeindeblatt,* published his reflections in November 1946. He took up all the possibilities in turn: first, he questioned the dream of Palestine, wondering whether that land could absorb so many Jews. Then he asked whether the survivors, "broken people," were really capable of undertaking the hard life in Palestine. But he was wistful about it: "When the American and the English liberated the concentration camps," he wrote, "the Belgians came and took away their countrymen, as did the French, the Dutch, the Hungarians, and all the other states. Left standing totally alone were the Jews, without rights, without protection, dependent on the grace and pity of the Allies. If we had had a Jewish state then, we would have known where to turn. Therefore we must demand a Jewish state, and the Jews of the world will all be citizens of this state." Meanwhile, Palestine remained a dream, so Frey turned to the possibility of emigrating elsewhere—America or Australia, for example. But he was dismayed by the restrictions: emigration to these countries was open only to those with close relatives, and once arrived, one was dependent on the grace and goodwill of one's sponsors. Nor did Frey delude himself about the difficulties of starting over: "In order to work there," he wrote, "one must not only command the language, one must also understand the people and the country and their way of doing things. And that one doesn't learn in one or two months."

Frey concluded:

As I see it, and I do not stand alone in this opinion, we German Jews have not only the right but also the duty to persevere here in Germany and to build up again what was taken away from us. Eight and a half billion marks worth of Jewish property was robbed from us, and since the liberation we have fought for the restitution of these damages. . . . Each person will draw his own conclusions, but he may well examine these matters and see that the world has become poorer because of this war; even countries where once milk and honey flowed are now impoverished. Only through hard work on both sides of the ocean will we be able to prevail. And we will accomplish it.[34]

It was this posture of resignation, combined with a certain tenacity, that kept some German Jews in Germany.

Landau described some of the more positive—and more powerful—feelings that kept Jews in Germany. After Landau was freed from his Nazi captors in Bavaria in May 1945, he began his postwar life in the D.P. camp of Feldafing. One day a group of American officers arrived at the camp, two of whom he recognized as fellow journalists from Vienna who had emigrated to the United States in 1938. This meeting with old friends was profoundly stirring for Landau. The effect of "this reunion with people who knew me from earlier times" was "that I felt as if I had really returned to life. Now I was once again among people with whom I had a common language. Now I could think of the future and make plans."[35] The sense of relief at recapturing ones's history, one's identity, after so many years as only a number was a very powerful inducement to stay in a community where one was known. When Landau was offered a post on a new German-Jewish newspaper in Munich, he could not ask for anything better as a journalist than to be able to work in his own language and to write for people whose concerns he shared.

Many Jews who had been hidden by Christian friends had a great sense of obligation after the war to perpetuate some of the ideals that had made such heroism possible and to repay society for the help they had received. Siegmund Weltlinger, a Berlin financier who had survived the last two years of the war in hiding, joined the executive board of the Society for Christian-Jewish Cooperation, which was founded in Berlin just after the war. The same sense of responsibility also motivated the journalist Inge Deutschkron, who went to live with her father in England after the war. She began to study and work in London but could not settle down. "In England," she wrote, "I could not free myself from the thought that I should return to Berlin and help those who had saved my life to build a democratic society. That may sound sentimental and arrogant, but I felt a certain sense of obligation to respond to the human solidarity that was shown to me during the hard war years."

But it was not quite so simple as Deutschkron had imagined. When she returned to Germany, she found that many old Nazis "sat in high places," while "those few who had risked their heads and had offered resistance, or had helped Jews who had gone underground . . . found only a conflicted kind of recognition. That they had been the silent witnesses to humanity in an inhuman time was hardly noticed. I felt very quickly that many Germans whom I met in the capital city of Bonn did not understand me or my position. For many, I was a living reproach, and became an uncomfortable and unpleasant presence."[36]

The Eastern European Jews, too, perceived and felt the antipathy or discomfort that many Germans harbored toward Jews. As the displaced Jews attempted to begin again, it was inevitable that they would be dealing with Germans. The blueprint for a separate Jewish economy, as proposed at the Second Congress of the She'erith Hap-letah, remained a paper proposal. In actuality, the working world of the displaced Jews was dominated by Germans. They were the own-ers of the buildings in the free economy where Jews lived as tenants. They were the peasants with whom the Jews bartered for produce to resell in the cities. They were the business partners with whom some Jews entered the German economy.

Eventually, in the disorderly way of ordinary day-to-day life, there were friendships, love affairs and even marriages of Jews with "the daughters of Amalek." By 1950, one thousand Jewish men among the displaced persons had married German women.[37] In part this was a result of the imbalance among the Jewish survivors: more men sur-vived than women. On the whole, however, relations between the Eastern European Jews and the Germans were wary and fragile. It would take another generation for the gap to be bridged.

Although the North Rhine–Westphalia *Gemeindeblatt* called for an end to distinctions between between East and West, between Yiddish- and German-speaking Jews, the reality of communal life was different. Unlike the United States, where each congregation is an in-dependent, self-governing financial entity, the German Jewish situa-tion is far more centralized. Because each taxpayer in Germany pays a "religion tax" to the national government, which then transmits it to the religious body of his choice, in each city the Jewish congregations are centralized into a single body—the Gemeinde—in order to re-ceive and disburse these government monies. In effect, every rabbi or priest is a government employee, supported by government taxes. The official community or Gemeinde is then responsible for adminis-tering the synagogues, schools, hospitals, and cemeteries, and for paying the personnel required to maintain these institutions. The head of the Gemeinde is thus the official spokesperson for the com-munity and can sometimes wield considerable political influence.

With so much at stake, elections to the Gemeinde governing board or to its presidency have often been hotly contested, with different political parties setting up lists of candidates representing their views. One of the thorny issues, even in prewar Germany, was the place of the Eastern European Jews in these Gemeinde councils. A number of communities adopted a rule prohibiting noncitizens from sitting on the governing board. They were allowed to be members—to pay taxes, attend the synagogue, and receive communal services—but they had no voice in making policy. This was a rule directly aimed at the Eastern European Jews, because qualifying for German citizenship was a notoriously drawn-out procedure. Jews of Polish origin who had lived for decades in Germany were sometimes not citizens.

Strangely enough, this situation was repeated in Augsburg after the war, where a group of former Augsburg Jews returned and took control of the Gemeinde. As the postwar situation became more stable, with a permanent rather than a transient community settling in Augsburg, it appeared that the old guard of the community was unwilling to recognize those "without German citizenship." By 1954 this led to an open scandal because those "without" were in the majority. As they wrote in their letter of protest to the secretariat of the Jewish communities for all of Bavaria, "At present in Augsburg there are thirty-two German Jews, sixty non-German Jews, and twenty children." And then a rather pointed comment: "Naturally our children—in contrast to the Jewish children of German background—are being raised as Jews, as far as it is possible for us as parents to accomplish this without teachers. None of our children is of the Catholic or Evangelical religion." Although the non-German Jews pay taxes, the protesters note, "the current leaders of the Augsburg community have denied us not only any possibility of membership, but also any kind of participation in the community. We are denied legal help as well as any kind of representation before German officials. In social and cultural matters we are entirely left to our own resources."[38]

In the end, the executive committee of the Gemeinde was forced to grant at least parity to the Eastern European Jews, and by 1963, their leader, Julius Spokojny, had become president of the Augsburg Gemeinde.[39] This was only the most dramatic and public of the confrontations, which occurred in other places as well. In some cases, the solution was the establishment of two separate communities. More often there was an uneasy alliance, generally with the Polish Jews predominating numerically while the German Jews occupied the leading public positions. As native speakers the German Jews were in a far better position to negotiate with the local authorities. Although many of those who survived to take these posts were men who had been saved during the war by the loyalty of their "Aryan" wives, many of the Eastern European Jews focused on the Christian rather than the heroic aspects of these unions. From time to time, a resolution would be proposed designed to prevent any person with a non-Jewish spouse from serving as an officer of a particular Jewish community. Was this revenge for earlier slights; was this fanatical intolerance and late retribution for the men who had married out of the faith? This hardly seemed like the recognition that these heroic women deserved. As late as 1974, when such a resolution was proposed in Munich, one young man stood up during the debate to appeal for humanity. "Wir sind verbrannte Kinder," he said—We have all been through the fire. "Let us not persecute one another."

In Jewish communities with strong leaders, such as Berlin, where Heinz Galinski was first elected head of the Gemeinde in 1949, there was no whisper of revolt—in Galinski's case, for the four decades he remained in office. Older members of the community called him "Our Kaiser." As the dark conscience of the Berlin City Council (Senat), he won generous privileges for the Jewish community and was always consulted on matters of Jewish policy. In smaller, more unstable communities the balance shifted as numbers changed, but for the first decades at least, the German Jews prevailed as leaders or titular heads of the communities. Nonetheless, for a long time the two groups lived apart, wary of each another and separated by language, history, and very different ways of thinking.

To complicate matters even further, the postwar Jewish communities were confronted with the descendants of the "non-Aryan Christians," who had been subject to all the disabilities of Jews, although some had been born into families that had been Christian for generations. The Nuremberg Laws of 1935 created a new category of human being, as members of this group said of themselves: "neither fish nor fowl." With five or six new Nazi classifications, based on a combination of ancestry and church affiliation, the "non-Aryans" found themselves subjected to unexpected restrictions in every aspect of life. There was not a lot of logic to what was permitted and what was forbidden. In the mad jumble of arbitrary decrees that served as law in Nazi Germany, until November 1, 1940, non-Aryans were even permitted to serve in the army.

When Hitler came to power in 1933, there were 350,000 to 400,000 people of mixed ancestry in Germany, and the new Nuremberg classifications led to immediate difficulties, for example, in the restriction on marriage. Someone with one Jewish grandparent was a "Mixed-Breed, 2d Degree"—*Mischling 2. Grades*—and was not permitted to marry another of the same classification. But he or she could apply for permission to marry a "Mixed-Breed, 1st Degree"—someone with two Jewish grandparents.[40]

A small number of these "non-Aryans" organized themselves into groups whose function was largely to keep the members informed about the latest regulations concerning their status. Their newsletters also carried personals columns through which young people attempted to meet other *Mischlinge* of the permissible rank. In Berlin they formed social clubs, ironically named *Mampe*—Half and Half—after a popular drink that was half potent brandy and half sweet liqueur.

For many Germans the discovery of this new, dangerous identity was deeply disturbing. Some were so far integrated into German society that they had shared the Nazi ideology of their neighbors; now suddenly they were in a reversed role of the hunted rather than the hunter. Neither the Protestant nor the Catholic churches were able or willing to do very much for their "non-Aryan" parishioners. In March 1940, for example, some twelve hundred Protestants of Jewish background in Stettin were notified that they were to be deported to Lublin in Poland. An official of the Evangelical Lutheran Church in Berlin attempted to raise the emergency sum of $4,400 from American Lutherans to support the deportees. But the Americans cabled their regrets and abandoned the refugees to their fate.[41] Lublin was at first intended by the Nazis as a "reservation"; Jews would be held there until after the war, when they would be sent to Madagascar. But this plan was quickly abandoned in favor of the more definitive "final solution." As one of the first historians of this period in Jewish history observed: "Out of the reservation for Jewish settlement grew labor camps, where Jews were slowly tortured to death, and out of the labor camps slowly grew extermination camps, with a highly developed, accelerated technique for mass killings."[42] The "non-Aryan Christians" from Stettin presumably did not escape the fate of the others deported to this reservation.

With few exceptions, the Protestant clergy in Germany accepted and in some cases actively supported the removal of "non-Aryans" from their communities, and as the persecution of the Jews became more and more visible, the response of the church was a general silence. An outstanding exception was Bishop Theophil Wurm of

Stuttgart, who on December 9, 1941, protested the killing of handicapped and mentally retarded persons. These victims, it should be noted, were "Aryans" from the general population. By the time Wurm's statement came out, however, 100,000 persons had already been done away with in "mercy killings." "Much has happened," he wrote, "that can only benefit enemy propaganda. We list among these actions the measures taken to eliminate the mentally ill and the increasing severity in dealing with non-Aryans, including those who are confessing Christians." But as one observer has pointed out, this rather gentle criticism referred only to appearances: "How will it seem to the outside world?"[43]

When the war ended, the Christian "non-Aryans" who survived were once again "neither fish nor fowl." Although they were not Jews in their beliefs, they felt themselves entitled to the special benefits that Jews were receiving from international agencies and from the American Jewish relief organizations. They had, after all, been exposed to all the dangers of Jews. As the postwar Jewish communities organized themselves, the claims of the "non-Aryan" Christians became one of the delicate questions they had to face.

Most troubling to the Jews who had remained behind in Germany was the attitude of the Jewish community abroad. Sharpest and most outspoken in its condemnation was the Jewish Agency. In 1949—a year after the founding of the State of Israel—when the Zionist organization closed its offices in Germany, the agency was highly critical of the Jews who remained, going so far as to deny them the right to send delegates to the forthcoming World Jewish Congress.[44] Individual Jews who had spent the war years living safely abroad reacted with horror and aversion at the thought that Jews would choose to live in Germany. Often they indulged in their powerful emotions with little knowledge and less patience for what seemed to them a profoundly wrong-headed decision. The sociologist Shalom Adler-

Rudel, for example, when interviewed in Palestine in 1946, could foresee only the darkest fate for those who stayed in Germany: "May they wait in their beloved fatherland," he said, "until their throats are also slit."[45]

There were other signals as well. The World Jewish Congress meeting in Montreux, Switzerland, in June 1948, a month after the establishment of the State of Israel, managed to express both horror at the idea of Jews living in Germany and compassion for the Jews who remained. The congress applauded "the determination of the Jewish people never again to settle on the blood-soaked German soil." At the same time it called upon the Allied nations to take measures to protect the Jews in Germany, and called upon Germany itself to recognize the Jewish displaced persons now living within its borders. "It should provide for their support and provide the means for them to rebuild their economic life."[46] These contradictory themes have remained unresolved in the minds of Jews in Israel and other parts of the world despite a half-century of postwar Jewish life in Germany.

The establishment of the Jewish state in 1948 and the recognition of West Germany by the Allies as an independent state in 1949 sharpened the question for the Jews in Germany of their status under the new legal conditions. Those in West Germany were living not under Allied protection but under a German government, the new Federal Republic, which comprised the territory of America, English, and French occupation, except for the city of Berlin. The Jewish response was prompt and realistic. By 1949 most of the D.P. camps had closed, all but twenty thousand Jews had emigrated from Germany, most to Israel or the United States, and it seemed a foregone conclusion that the postwar, postoccupation world would see only a small permanent Jewish community in Germany.

In the five years after the end of the war, Jews in the West outside the D.P. camps had reestablished the traditional communities and were embedded in the structure of German life, their institutions supported by government money. Wary as they may have been of their place in the new Germany, they were nonetheless proceeding methodically to create a permanent presence and to foster the interests of the nascent community. They began by calling a conference in June 1949 in Heidelberg to discuss the basic question: "To Stay or to Go."

This was not a private, closed meeting. Representatives of different points of view, both local and from abroad, came to discuss the future of Jewish life in Germany. Among them were the Israeli consul Eliahu Livneh; the high commissioner of the American zone, John J. McCloy; the military adviser to the American military government, Harry Greenstein; representatives of such American Jewish organizations as the American Jewish Joint Distribution Committee, the American Jewish Committee, and HIAS. Observers from ORT, the World Jewish Congress, and the Jewish Agency were also present. The argument that Jews should abandon Germany was strongly opposed by the journalist and concentration camp survivor Eugen Kogon, among others. "Permit me to say, in deepest sorrow," he stated, "that your entirely understandable position [advocating Jewish departure] means the final triumph of Hitler. What Hitler wanted to achieve would now be accomplished." His voice was inevitably the one that prevailed.

A year later, in July 1950, the Jews in Germany came together to form their own representative organization, the *Zentralrat der Juden in Deutschland*—the Central Council of Jews in Germany. It included not only the Jewish communities in West Germany but also those in the Soviet zone and the Central Committee of the Liberated Jews. It chose its first officers in January 1951, electing as general secretary a lawyer, Hendrik van Dam. The executive committee included representatives from all the zones of Germany: Norbert Wollheim for the British zone, Philipp Auerbach for the American, Julius Meyer for the Soviet, Leonhard Baer for the French. To represent Berlin, which constituted a separate entity, the committee elected Heinz Galinski, head of the Berlin Gemeinde. Even the Israeli consul, Eliahu Livneh, gave the new organization his blessing, saying, "Israel does not forget its children, wherever they may live."[47]

Then, lest any Jew be forced to seek aid from German sources, they reconstituted the prewar Central Welfare Office. On a more local level they rebuilt their synagogues and their communities. They established lodges of B'nai Brith, where they met to hear speakers on politics and the arts, but above all to socialize. Every aspect of life seemed to be covered by one or another Jewish organization, from the sports club Maccabee to the Holy Brotherhoods—*Chevrei Kadisha*—which took charge of preparing the dead for burial.

But Eliahu Livneh's generous view was not universal. The Jewish Agency in particular held an intransigent Zionist position deeply critical of the newly established Jewish community. The Jews in Germany did not need official reproaches, however, to understand the strangeness of their position. They knew that they were regarded as pariahs by many Jews in the Western world, and these Jews would not visit Germany or buy German products. Nor would many organizations, on principle, meet in Germany. Recognizing these harsh sentiments, Hendrik van Dam observed in an interview in 1963, "At the beginning, a German Jew was under greater indictment by some than a German Nazi. People criticized him for his shortsightedness in being willing to live here at all."[48] In Israel neither the Israel Symphony Orchestra nor the government radio stations would play the music of Richard Wagner. As the Jewish communities began their postwar existence, the bleak disapproval of their fellow Jews abroad did not make a difficult existence any easier.

CHAPTER FOUR

Jews Again in Berlin

The Gemeinde, the Camps

The magnetic center of the world, the goal of tens of thousands of Polish Jews after the end of the war, was Berlin, a place described by Berthold Brecht as "that heap of ruins near Potsdam." Inge Deutschkron, who had been hidden in Germany during the war, walked six hours to get from Potsdam to Berlin and confirmed Brecht's report. In July 1945, she wrote, Berlin was "a succession of piles of ruins made up of scrap-metal, stones and shredded trees. Like moles, people crawled out of these hills into the daylight. Tired and worn, they crept through the streets that had been torn up by bombs. Some stood wearily in line waiting to fill a pail of water at the street pumps, others searched despairingly through the ruins for something useful."[1] Harry Hopkins, President Roosevelt's longtime adviser, flew over Berlin in May 1945 and described it as "a second Carthage."[2] Pounded for years by Allied planes, bombarded by Russian artillery, its buildings pockmarked in street-to-street fighting, Berlin had been 85 percent destroyed. By the time peace came, the streets and the sites of former buildings were filled with rubble, while water, gas, electricity—everything needed to make a city habitable—were either intermittent or altogether unavailable. One mother of four children, still living in her old apartment, described daily life in June 1945—a month after the fighting had stopped:

> Unfortunately, the arrangements for providing the promised food have absolutely not come about. Often I have only a water-soup for the children, with a few grains of barley for thickening and a bit of green stuff. Bread is bad and scarce. I spend all day trying to prepare a little substitute spread for the bread, using the most unimaginable things. I cook my soup on an upturned clothes-iron. Electricity is available, but not gas. And I have no wood or coal for the oven. I have already chopped up various pieces of furniture that I don't really need. The ruins are thoroughly searched for anything that will burn. And by night fences are stolen. Everyone has eyes for wood, thinking of cooking a hot meal.[3]

And yet Berlin, despite its condition, was not only the center of desire for Eastern European Jews but also the center of power. The Soviets had been the first to establish their presence in May 1945. The American and the British arrived to take over their sectors on July 1, 1945, and the French on August 12.[4] Together they then proceeded to divide the city into four sectors.

At the beginning the Allies governed together through a centralized Kommandatura, but very quickly each sector began to take on its own character. Most important to the Jews coming from the East was that occupied Berlin was the first outpost of safety in what was, for them, a very dangerous postwar Europe. As the rift between the Sovi-

Women clearing the streets of rubble in Berlin, ca. 1949. Bildarchiv Preussischer Kulturbesitz, Berlin.

ets and the other Allies grew, however, the consequences of having landed in the Eastern sector of Berlin rather than in the West became substantial. Most serious was the Soviet decree in 1946 prohibiting all emigration from their zone. For the Jews from the East who had intended Berlin as only a stopping place on their way to permanent resettlement, this order was nothing less than a prison sentence. It is no accident, therefore, that no displaced persons camps were ever established in the Soviet sector. In those critical first months the native-born German Jews who were still alive in Berlin wrestled with other problems.

To the surprise of the outside world, when the fighting was over, it appeared that approximately 7,000 German Jews had survived the war in Hitler's own capital. Only a vestige of the 160,564 Jews in Berlin in 1933, but miraculous in light of the ferocious energy the Hitler government expended to track every last Jew and "cleanse" Berlin of their presence.

In more than 180 transports organized between October 1941 and February 1945, the Nazis had deported 50,535 Jews from Berlin. At the beginning of the deportations, there were still 60,000–75,000 Jews in the city. Despite the massive roundups, the emptying of the "Jew houses" where the Jews had been herded together, the arrests at workplaces, the natural deaths and the suicides, the Gestapo knew that there were still Jews at large.[5]

However few their number, it soon emerged in the summer of 1945 that there were many different kinds of Jews in Berlin, with very different histories. At the first count by the Gemeinde, there were 1,321 who had lived in hiding or had passed by using false papers; 1,628 who had returned from concentration camps; 2,126 who were married to non-Jews and had no children; and 1,995 who were married to non-Jews and had children who were being brought up as Christians.[6] These last were relatively fortunate because they had not been required to wear the Jewish star, as all the others were. Among these 7,070 survivors, then, more than half were Jews living in so-called privileged marriages, most of them between Jewish men and Christian women. These Christian partners had been responsible for the only substantial and successful act of resistance against the Nazi regime. The event was all the more remarkable because it took place in the heart of Berlin, only a few blocks from the famous Alexanderplatz.

On February 27, 1943, the Nazis were concluding their severest roundup of Jews in Berlin. Aiming this time for the definitive "cleansing," they even reached into privileged marriages and segregated two thousand of their victims in the Jewish community's former administration building in the Rosenstrasse.[7] Confiscated by the Nazis, it had been turned into stables with accommodations for the cavalry, and renamed the Hermann Goering Barracks.[8] This building was now converted into a temporary deportation center. But all these prisoners had non-Jewish wives or husbands and children. In an entirely spontaneous action, hundreds of the Christian wives of these inmates gathered in the street outside the building and demonstrated for their return, chanting: "Let our husbands go. We want our husbands back."[9] These women already had nearly a decade of resistance behind them. From the beginning, the Nazis had encouraged divorce between Jews and non-Jews—branding any sexual contact between the two as "desecration of the race." By refusing to give up their spouses, these women had demonstrated daily their steadfast opposition to the increasingly violent propaganda.

Unlike their quiet defiance at home, the action in the Rosenstrasse was not private. Although the women arrived at the deportation site separately, they took strength and courage from one another's presence. "It wasn't organized or instigated," one participant remembered. "Everyone was simply there. Exactly like me. That's what is so wonderful about it." The protesting crowd of women in the street grew from day to day until by the end of the week it had grown to six thousand. The long detention of their husbands was in itself a sign of the uncertainty at higher levels of decision making. Ordinarily, Jews were rounded up, kept for no more than two days in a detention center and then shipped off to the East. Here the tension mounted day by day, while the Nazi leaders debated how to resolve their differences. Gradually, one participant noticed, the crowd "had grown to include people who did not have imprisoned relatives . . . and it also took on a more clearly political and anti-Nazi tone."

At the end of the week, the guards in front of the Rosenstrasse building suddenly turned to force. One woman who had been in the street described how the attack began.

> Without warning the guards began setting up machine guns. Then they directed them at the crowd and shouted: "If you don't go now, we'll shoot." Automatically in that instant the movement surged backward. But then for the first time we really hollered. Now we couldn't care less. We bellowed, "You murderers" and everything else that one can holler. Now they're going to shoot in any case, so now we'll yell too, we thought. We yelled "Murderer, murderer, murderer, murderer." We didn't scream just once but again and again, until we lost our breath. Then I saw a man in the foreground open his mouth wide—as if to give a command. It was drowned out. I couldn't hear it. But then they cleared everything away. There was silence. Only an occasional swallow could be heard.[10]

On March 6 the standoff came to an end when Joseph Goebbels, whose official title, minister for propaganda and public enlightenment, hardly conveyed his malevolent mind or his power in Berlin, simply ordered those held at Rosenstrasse to be released. This was a trouble spot that the government needed to handle carefully. The defeat at Stalingrad, which the Nazis had just acknowledged, had claimed the lives of more than 300,000 German men. And Goebbels was uneasy about the effect of the deportation of thousands of Jews with non-Jewish family members: many more thousands of Germans would now have reason to be resentful, irate, or disloyal to the regime. It was clear that the Rosenstrasse demonstration was not part of an organized political movement; as one of the women said, "We acted from the heart." Afraid, however, that this example of protest might spur similar outbreaks, Goebbels wanted it ended and without giving further cause for opposition. "Why should Goebbels have had them all arrested?" his chief deputy at the Propaganda Ministry, Leopold Gutterer, asked later. "Then he would only have had even more unrest, from the relatives of those newly arrested persons."[11] Although this incident documented the differences of opinion among the various government ministries, its resolution did not halt the continuation of the "final solution," either in the killing camps in the East or the slave labor camps in Germany. In spite of their heroism in the face of a murderous regime, it was a long time before these Christian spouses won any recognition in the postwar Jewish communities.

The Jews who survived without the protection of Christian spouses were not a particularly cohesive group, nor did they have particularly strong Jewish ties. Many of the distinguished prewar leaders of the community had been deported and killed. Others had emigrated, including such important scientific and cultural figures that a half-century after the war, Germany was still feeling their loss. In 1974 a Berlin-born journalist named Bernt Engelmann made this loss tangible when he published *Germany Without Jews: An Accounting*. Field by field, he listed the notable practitioners in the arts, the sciences, and sports now lost to Germany because of their emigration or murder by the Nazis. Rabbi Leo Baeck, the universally respected head of the prewar Berlin community, had survived a two-year incarceration in the concentration camp at Theresienstadt, but in July 1945, at the age of seventy-two, he chose to emigrate to England rather than return to Germany. Most of those who remained or returned to Berlin saw themselves as living there only provisionally while they made arrangements to find permanent homes elsewhere. In the first years, therefore, the leadership of the community was unstable, with emigration and opportunity abroad taking precedence over community responsibility.

In the spirit of improvisation that characterized the first days, religious observance did not wait for formal structures. On May 6, just four days after the Soviet conquest of Berlin, Rabbi Kahane, the chief rabbi of Poland, who had arrived in Berlin with the Soviet forces, held the first religious service in a room of the Jewish hospital in Iranische Strasse. One of the patients, Bruno Blau, noted that even though the event was entirely improvised, the room could not hold the crowd. Some of those who came had to remain in the corridor or in adjoining rooms. The rabbi read first the evening prayer, and then described the situation of the Jews in Europe—that the Nazi regime had taken six million Jewish lives, of whom three million were from Poland alone. The chazan, who was also a member of the Polish army, then sang in memory of the victims the "El mole Rachamim"—Lord full of Mercy—the prayer sung at burials, which was accompanied by the sobs of the deeply affected listeners.[12]

On Friday, May 11, 1945, the preacher Martin Riesenburger held the first Sabbath service in a building at the Weissensee cemetery in the eastern part of Berlin. He had lived and worked at the cemetery during the war under Nazi command, conducting burial services for the Berlin Jews who died in those years. (It is worth noting that Riesenburger owed his survival to his "Aryan" wife. Although she had converted to Judaism, what counted for the Nazi officials was not her religion, but that she had four "Aryan" grandparents.)[13] Then, on May 17, Adolf Schwersenz, who described himself as a "Torah reader," led services in the synagogue in Levetzowstrasse, "provisionally organized," as he described it, "in the wedding chapel and regularly conducted since then."[14] (Schwersenz, too, owed his survival in Berlin to his "Aryan" wife. They emigrated to New York in March 1947.)[15]

At first, the Jews in Berlin did not attempt to reconstitute the old central Gemeinde, which had traditionally governed Jewish affairs.

Instead, four different Jewish administrations emerged in different parts of the city, each centered on the remains of a surviving synagogue. The most active was at the Levetzowstrasse Synagogue, led by Adolf Schwersenz. It carried on not only religious services—in the Liberal tradition—but also cultural programs.

Its first cultural evening took place in the synagogue on June 21, 1945—only six weeks after liberation. The many strands of Jewish and German culture that were woven into this community were represented in the programming. Bürgermeister Bachmann, the mayor of the Tiergarten section of the city, where the synagogue was located, ceremoniously opened the program, followed by Harry Dörfel, a theologian who was a member of the municipal Committee for Religious Affairs. Schwersenz himself took a leading part in the concert, singing music by Schubert, Schumann, and Giordano. One Leo Merten read in German translation a story by the Yiddish writer I. L. Peretz, "If Not Higher," about the wonder-working rabbi of Nemerov, as well as four poems by Heinrich Heine. The evening concluded with the performance of a Mozart piano trio.[16] This was a program cut perfectly to classical German Jewish taste, but with a new element—the recognition of Yiddish literature.

But this was a time when feelings ran high, and a seemingly innocuous attempt to reestablish cultural life elicited a strong letter of protest from at least one of the members of the congregation. I. Moses, an engineer, wrote that he was offended first by the removal of the Holy Ark from the synagogue so that the space could be turned into a concert hall. He was also dismayed to note that most of the ticket buyers were non-Jews and that the concert seemed to be a way of fostering Schwersenz's interrupted vocal career. (It was well known that until 1936 Schwersenz had appeared as an opera singer under the name Adi Patti. When the Nazi ban on Jewish artists had ended this profession for him, he had begun to study the cantorial liturgy. After the war, he put all his efforts into building the congregation in the old Levetzowstrasse Synagogue, attracting some three hundred members in the first months of his activity. He also organized a reception center for returnees coming from concentration camps or hiding places and needing temporary shelter.) Here Moses touched on another sensitive point, because Schwersenz was paying himself two salaries—once as cantor, and another for his community services. This practice eventually led to serious trouble.

Although the synagogue services were a first step toward normalcy, the need for restoration of the traditional Jewish community became more and more urgent as Jews appeared again and the city government began to take shape. The community's birth pangs, however, were neither simple nor painless. At stake were 3.5 million Reichsmarks, along with considerable properties, that the Nazis had confiscated from the prewar community.[17] All these assets—synagogues, schools, cemeteries, old age homes, the Jewish hospital, and so on—had been under the supervision of the *Reichsvereinigung*, the governing National Union of Jews—from 1939 until its dissolution by the Nazi regime in 1943. The question of ownership and authority was now up in the air. Which was the successor organization? And which group would now receive government support?

In the first months after the war ended, religious groups in the city were regulated by the municipal Committee on Religious Affairs, a body appointed by the governing municipal council—the *Magistrat*. The committee took a vigorous role in shaping the direction of the newly emerging Jewish life in Berlin. On June 21, 1945, it appointed a governing board of nine members to administer the affairs of what it hoped would become a unified Jewish community. Finally there were to be trustees for the property and other assets of the former Reichvereinigung. But this group, arbitrarily brought together, ran into difficulties even before it could begin functioning.

Among the nine members of the governing board was Adolf Schwersenz, who in an outspoken letter to the committee denounced two of his fellow board members as "Gestapo helpers." At the same time, other board members raised counteraccusations against him, reiterating the engineer Moses's charge that Schwersenz was paying himself two salaries out of the synagogue funds and using the synagogue services to showcase his artistic talents.

The director of the Jewish hospital in Iranische Strasse, Dr. Walter Lustig, offered further resistance, refusing to give up his autonomy. The hospital was actually a complex of seven buildings, including a synagogue as well as hospitals, a residence for nurses, and administrative buildings. In 1943 the entire operation had been taken over by the Gestapo after the dissolution of the Reichsvereinigung. As we have seen, it became in effect a ghetto in Berlin from which the Gestapo organized deportations to Theresienstadt and camps in the East. As head of the Jewish hospital, Lustig presided over this mass of wretched humanity. Placed in the unenviable position of making up Nazi deportation quotas, for a period of two years he had the power of life and death over the residents and staff of the hospital. Because many witnesses survived to recall these events, a clouded picture emerges of the role he had played.

Yet on June 6, 1945, when the Jews were encountering difficulties about being given any preference as "Victims of Fascism," Lustig wrote a strong letter in their defense to the municipal council: "A portion of the population that has been affected in such an outrageous manner by Fascism," he wrote, "in a way that has never been known in history, cannot be satisfied with a formal status of 'equality' [with other Victims of Fascism]."[18] He demanded instead that Jewish survivors be given special preference, including extra rations, and extra clothing, and that they be freed from the hard labor of clearing rubble, which was demanded of all recipients of city help.[19] The Soviets had set up a schedule that ranked sixteen different kinds of "Victims of Fascism." To be merely a "victim" rather than a "fighter" placed the applicant in a literally secondary position.[20]

When Lustig demurred on giving up his independence, the committee withdrew from its attempt to impose unity, insisting only that each of the four independent communities remain within its own boundaries. This objection soon became moot when the Soviet authorities arrested Lustig, possibly on the charge of collaborating with the Nazis or perhaps because he was becoming too troublesome. The Soviets held him for several months in a Berlin prison and then, without trial, condemned him to death. He was executed on December 31, 1945.[21]

These arbitrary arrests and disappearances became a feature of life in the Soviet zone and led to an understandable apprehension among Jewish refugees about remaining in East Berlin. The anxiety about personal safety, not confined to Jews, left a permanent wariness among residents in the Soviet zone about the government's arbitrary use of power. The poet Günter Kunert, writing about life in Berlin in the first months after the war, remembered that no pedestrian felt safe. Everyone, he wrote, ran "the danger of being snatched up by the 'Nab-Troops' of the Red Army, and then not knowing, after one had been armed with a shovel, whether one would be sent to Alexanderplatz or Novosibirsk."[22]

One woman, who as a child had been left homeless by the Allied firebombing of Dresden in February 1945, described how she and her family had then found refuge in a nearby village. After the Soviets took control of their area, she became aware of the intermittent and mysterious disappearances of neighbors and friends. When she was in bed at night, she remembered even decades later, if a car's lights shone into her room she would immediately panic, thinking that "they" had come to arrest her father.[23]

As we shall see, Lustig was not the only prominent Jew whose fate was summarily decided by the Soviets. Nonetheless, despite his arrest, the seemingly inevitable reconstruction of the unified community—the *Einheitsgemeinde*—moved toward completion. In the anxious political atmosphere that prevailed immediately after the Soviets took control of their part of Berlin, the formation of a unified Jewish community waited upon a signal from the Soviet occupier. In June 1945 Gen. Nikolai E. Bersarin, the commander of the Soviet forces, summoned Moritz Blum, a Jewish dentist living in Berlin, and entrusted him with the task of forming the new Jewish governing board.[24] What was more important was that Besarin also designated as community headquarters the historic Jewish site in Oranienburger Strasse.[25]

Here were the remains of the great New Synagogue, flanked by its administration building on one side and the former Jewish Museum on the other. Damaged though these structures were, they were still in good enough condition to provide offices and meeting rooms for the Jewish community as it struggled into existence. The beautiful New Synagogue, built in the Moorish style, had originally opened with New Year's services in 1866. That it had survived Nazi destruction on Kristallnacht was due to bold action by Wilhelm Krützfeld, the chief of Police Precinct 16. Hitler's Brown Shirts, his paramilitary reserve forces, had been turned loose on the night of November 9–10, 1938, with the task of destroying synagogues and Jewish shops and arresting selected Jewish men. On that night, as one historian described it, they had "forced their way into the synagogue and had set fire to it. But not for long, for suddenly the police chief appeared at the site with a few men and chased away the arsonists." His weapons, according to the writer, were "an extended pistol and a manila folder which held a piece of paper that placed under police protection the important artistic and cultural value of this building." At the same time, he ordered the fire department to come to the synagogue. That they came and actually extinguished the fire is all the more remarkable because elsewhere firemen simply stood by, allowing Jewish property to burn, intervening only when the flames threatened neighboring buildings owned by non-Jews.[26]

Krützfeld, who was the hero of this episode, did not get off lightly. He was reprimanded the next day by his superior officer and later was moved from post to post so that his authority was always severely limited. He was never a member of the Nazi Party, and as his son later reported, "he often said that he felt himself under watch by the Nazis."[27] In 1942 he was permitted to retire and then left Berlin. What his motives were in saving the synagogue cannot be ascertained. He never spoke about the event at home, but it is possible that as an officer of the old school, he felt a duty to protect the historical property in his care.

The building did not escape the war unscathed: the richly decorated sanctuary with seats for three thousand worshipers was badly damaged in air raids. Then in the 1950s, in an action that is still controversial, the sanctuary was taken down by the East German city administration. But the front part of the building, the entrance hall, and the rooms in the four stories above it were still usable. For Jews this was an important site of Berlin Jewish history. Only a street away was the oldest Jewish cemetery in Berlin, in which Moses Mendelssohn was buried. Backing up on the synagogue was a building that had been successively used as a Jewish orphanage, a school, a hospital, an old-age home, and finally by the Nazis as a deportation center. The very next cross street, on Artillerie Strasse, housed two rabbinical seminaries—an Orthodox one led by Rabbi Esriel Hildesheimer, and a Liberal one headed by Rabbi Leo Baeck. (Berlin Jews, punning on the street name, referred to these institutions in their heyday as the heavy and light artillery.) Rabbi Hildesheimer's seminary was

Meeting room of the Representatives' Council in the New Synagogue in Berlin as it looked in 1884. This room is in the part of the building that remained standing after the war and was restored in the reconstruction of the synagogue begun under the Honecker regime. Photographer Hermann Rückwardt, Berlinische Galerie.

located in the complex of synagogue and administrative buildings of the Orthodox Adass Israel Congregation, which, since 1869, had carried on an independent life outside the official "unified" Jewish community.[28]

After the war, the Adass Israel Congregation sank into oblivion, remembered by its former members living abroad rather than by the few Jews in East Berlin. It was not until 1986, in fact, that it once again resumed its independent existence, under the unusual circumstances that prevailed in the last years of the German Democratic Republic. What became significant for the future of Jews in postwar Berlin was that the entire neighborhood, what had been synagogues, seminaries, educational institutions was now in the Soviet sector. And the Soviets kept a close watch over the religious communities, even going so far, as we have seen, as overseeing the nominations to the first executive board of the postwar Jewish community.

By July 1945 a group of six men, with Erich Nelhans as their chairman, organized themselves as the executive committee of the new Gemeinde. The new governing group was accepted by the still-unified city government as the successor official community and was recognized as "entering again into all the rights of the Jewish community." In addition to Nelhans, the other members were Dr. Hugo Ehrlich, Dr. Leo Hirsch (a medical doctor), Arnold Peyser, Erich Mendelsohn, and Erich Zwilsky, who had been an assistant to Dr. Lustig in the Iranische Strasse Hospital.[29] There was also a supporting nineteen-member committee of representatives.

One of the first acts of the new central committee, on July 24, was to establish the principle that "there is only one Gemeinde in Berlin which incorporates all the Jews of Berlin." It further ordained that the community in the Tiergarten district—Schwersenz's congregation—would enter the official joint community. In a letter of August 10, 1945, Schwersenz was notified that he would be retained as cantor but would be paid only for these services. All other activities would have to be undertaken during his "leisure time" and on a "voluntary" basis.[30]

The city council, however, dissatisfied with the self-organized committee in Oranienburger Strasse, asked Siegmund Weltlinger to propose a new executive committee. Weltlinger, a financier, had been on the executive committee of the prewar Jewish community in Berlin and had served on the Reichsvereinigung. In 1943 he, too, had gone underground, and he had spent the remainder of the war in hiding with his wife. As the postwar city government began to be organized, he was appointed the Jewish representative on the Committee on Religious Affairs. "My particular task," he wrote in a memoir, "was to represent Jewish interests. Because the Jewish community had been totally extinguished by the Nazi government, I saw it as my special duty to see to it that the Jewish community was rebuilt along the lines of true democracy."[31] As a beginning, on September 19, 1945, he appointed his own committee of advisers. Prominent among them was Leo Löwenstein, the head of the Berlin branch of the Jewish veterans' organization—Reichsbund jüdischer Frontsoldaten—until its dissolution in 1938. Deported to Theresienstadt, Löwenstein survived and returned to Berlin, but he left in 1946 to live in Sweden.[32] Others on the committee were Dr. Kurt Werthauer, a Dr. Lichtenstein, who had served with Weltlinger on the Reichsvereinigung, and Dr. Hans-Erich Fabian, a lawyer, who had also survived Theresienstadt and returned to Berlin.

Following a conference at the end of September with the existing committee, which agreed to accept Weltlinger's authority, he nominated six men to act as the founding governing body of the restored Gemeinde. On October 12, 1945, Dr. Hans-Erich Fabian became the chairman; among his other duties, he made himself responsible for founding a community newspaper. The other members were Eric

Nelhans; Dr. Hans Münzer, a lawyer; and Carl Busch, all of whom had lived underground for the last two years of the war. Busch, who was an active member of the Liberal Pestalozzi Strasse synagogue, was interested in rebuilding religious and social life in the Gemeinde. Later he reestablished the Zionist Organization of Berlin.[33] Other members of the executive were Dr. Leo Löwenstein and Julius Meyer, a longtime member of the Communist Party. Meyer, who had spent years at forced labor under the Nazis in Berlin, had been deported to Auschwitz in 1943, together with his family. His wife and child were murdered in the camp, but he survived not only Auschwitz but also a subsequent death march. After returning to Berlin, he remarried and took up an active life in the Gemeinde.[34] (Under the postwar Communist regime in East Berlin, his Jewish activism had serious consequences for him, which we shall see in Chapter 5.) The executive committee added an advisory committee of nineteen representatives, and together these groups made up the governing framework of the community. But not until February 1, 1948, were the first democratic elections held.

By the High Holy Days in September 1945, five synagogues in Berlin were able to conduct services. None had survived undamaged, but like the Levetzowstrasse synagogue, they managed to find areas that were usable. Ernst Günter Fontheim, a student who had lived underground during the war and, like Inge Deutschkron, had walked back to Berlin from Potsdam, described the services at the Thielschufer. "Folding chairs supplied by the U.S. Army served as seating," he wrote in a memoir. "Besides us civilian worshippers there was also a fair number of soldiers of the allied armies participating. . . . The service was conducted by Rabbi Riesenburger. . . . He gave a very emotional sermon evoking the memory of all those who were no longer with us. There was hardly a dry eye in the congregation. I also remember that there were only a few talleissim available.

So one tallis was always handed to the man being called up to the Torah and then passed to the next man being called."[35]

This was the situation as it existed when Philip Skorneck, the first representative of the American Jewish Joint Distribution Committee, arrived in Berlin in November 1945. He was succeeded in spring 1946 by the second director, Eli Rock. An American, eager to see a democratic Jewish community, Rock was most uneasy about the improvised government and particularly about the caliber of its leadership. "Already," he wrote to his home office, "some of the best leaders and some of the best members have emigrated to America. In all probability, many more of the better talent in the Gemeinde will also leave. . . . Only those will remain who either feel themselves too old to begin life again in a new country or who are simply afraid to venture forth into alien lands. . . . Much the larger percentage of the Berlin Jews who remain behind," he concluded, "will be those who belong to the mixed marriage categories."[36] Coming from America at a time when Jews only rarely married out, Rock found it hard to accept the intermarriage that was the overwhelming characteristic of postwar German Jewish communities. Nor was it easy for any outsider to comprehend how the rules of conventional life had come apart during the Nazi years.

In the complexities brought on by the war and Nazi persecution, strange alliances had been forged under the dangerous circumstances of underground life. And they often did not fit the rigid categories of the prewar world. Eric Nelhans, one of the first to take responsibility in the community and appeal to the Americans for food and other help, had just emerged from two years in hiding. He had gone underground in 1943 and in that shadowy world, his path had crossed that of Gad Beck, a young Zionist, also living underground, who was responsible for a large number of other young Zionists hiding in Berlin. Beck arranged for their maintenance by using funds smuggled by couriers from the Zionist organization in Switzerland. In addition to supplying those in hiding with food and clothing, Beck took responsibility for scouting out new places for the fugitives to stay, because few had the luxury of a permanent home.

Among his most useful contacts was a Fräulein Schmidt, a Berlin woman he had come to know, then in her forties. Although born into a noble family in Prussia, she had "fallen" as a young woman and had become a streetwalker on Alexanderplatz in Berlin. She understood exactly what Beck was doing and was a main support in his efforts to find shelter for his charges. At the beginning of 1945, disaster struck when two members of Beck's group were surprised by the police during an air raid. One of them managed to escape, but the other, carrying a list identifying the members of the group, was arrested. When Fräulein Schmidt heard what had happened, she immediately got on her bicycle and without a list, working from memory, went from address to address all across northern Berlin to warn those in hiding of their danger. As Beck calculated it, she saved thirty-six lives. But he found it odd that despite her engagement in his cause, she would never allow him to visit her at home. Not until after the war did he learn why. For the last year and a half of the war, she had been hiding Eric Nelhans. In the course of time, they had become lovers, and they remained together after peace came. When Nelhans became head of the Berlin Jewish community, as Beck commented, "Our first, unofficial, first lady was a noble-born former prostitute on Alexanderplatz."[37]

As the Jews soon discovered, their way back to a normal life was not being made easier by the authorities. In a despairing letter to the American Jewish Joint Distribution Committee on July 8, 1945, Nelhans, writing on behalf of the Berlin community, begged for American help. The only ones receiving meaningful assistance from the Soviets, who then controlled Berlin, were "victims of Fascism." And these were, according to Nelhans, "nearly exclusively . . . political prisoners from the concentration camps and [those who] belonged before 1933 either to the Communist or Socialist Party. Also people of whom it can be proved that during the Nazi regime they acted against Fascism. . . . We, Jews, returning from Concentration Camps or from our hiding places receive the worst food rations. . . . We are hungry. We thought that our needs and misfortunes were over, but unhappily we still suffer from all the consequences of a still existing Anti-semitism. That is why our first cry for help is a request for food."

The American organizations were not slow to heed this request, and the American Jewish Joint Distribution Committee quickly sent in its own representatives. By September 1945 the Joint had begun a supplementary aid program in the American zones for the remaining German Jews and arriving Jewish refugees from the East. By the end of the year, it had spent more than $600,000 for food, clothing, and medicine for Jews in Germany and Austria. These provisions were brought from Switzerland, Denmark, and France on surplus trucks that the Joint had bought from the United States Army, but the bulk of the first supplies went to the D.P. camps.

When Skorneck opened the Joint offices in Berlin on November 10, 1945, he found that very little was coming through to the Ge-meinde in Berlin. He was, however, ingenious in coping with the delay. "Maybe the AJDC will surprise us," he wrote in his first report only ten days after arriving, "and keep its promise [to send food]. Meanwhile the Jewish G.I. is feeding Berlin Jewry."

A few months later, in February 1946, Skorneck reported how he had improvised on the situation in Berlin. "I met with many of the Jew-ish U.S. soldiers and U.S. civilians and they agreed to turn over to the AJDC the many packages they were receiving from home. Over 5,000 five-pound packages were received and distributed by the Joint in the first two months of my work in Berlin and this constituted the first material help the Joint was able to give to the Jewish community."[38]

But this extra help itself became the cause of a thorny problem for the Gemeinde. Although there were some seven thousand recognized Jews in Berlin, there were many others who felt that they had claims on the Gemeinde and its resources. Two groups felt that they had a particular right to expect consideration. "First," Skorneck explained, "those Protestants and Catholics who were considered Jews under the Nuremberg Laws because they were of Jewish extraction [and] suffered on account of Hitler, felt they should get some help from the Joint. The next category were the Christian spouses of Jews who had suffered . . . because they had to share their rations with their Jewish husbands and wives who did not get enough food on their 'Jude' cards [during the war]."[39] By June 1946 some 2,500 people who had left the Gemeinde before the war, some of whom had converted, some of whom had not, also sought membership. The Gemeinde on its own authority decided that those who had renounced their Judaism in an effort to save their lives would be readmitted. But the many doubtful cases awaited the arrival of a rabbi who would be able to judge them under Jewish law.

Later sizable numbers of Germans began to present themselves at the Jewish community wishing to convert to Judaism. This was a source of perplexity to the Gemeinde, which, with its motley membership, was attempting to find its way in a complicated new world. Nathan Peter Levinson, a Berlin-born rabbi who had been educated at the Liberal seminary headed by Rabbi Leo Baeck, had left for the United States in 1941. When he returned to Berlin in 1950 to serve as a rabbi, he was astonished to find himself faced with six thousand applications for conversion. Some of the applicants were, as he put it, opportunists who wanted to receive CARE packages. But one group that aroused his immediate sympathies were the German wives of Jewish men who were displaced persons. It "was absolutely understood that they should have Jewish children, and thus the women needed to convert."[40]

On March 1, 1946, the Gemeinde began to publish its first postwar newspaper, *Der Weg*—The Way—a printed letter-size paper of about eight pages. Hans-Erich Fabian, the chairman of the executive committee, was its first editor. In its opening issue, *Der Weg* raised the question that occupied every surviving German Jew—"whether it is possible to remain in this country or [whether] emigration [is] absolutely required." The editors assumed that those who had relatives abroad would surely leave. In fact, the community at first referred to itself as a *Liquidationsgemeinde*—a community bent on closing out its affairs. But the editors had doubts about whether a mass emigration would take place. First, they pointed out, more than half of the surviving Jews were married or related to Christians. In addition, most members of the community were "on the border of old age. Further, one must be clear, however bitter the fact is, that the rest of the world is not ready to welcome us with open arms. And the integration into a new way of life requires a great deal of strength and the youthful ability to adapt." Those who remained, however, would have to face a complex relationship with the Germans. Both Jews and Germans would have to take up the burden of the past. As for the Germans— "the Enlightened spirits among the German people must assume the duty to fight for a new Germany which will eliminate anti-Semitism." The article concluded somewhat gloomily with a statement made by Dr. Zalman Grinberg at the recent Congress of Liberated Jews in Munich. "One expects of us that we will help in the rebuilding of Europe, but perhaps this same Europe will once again construct crematoria for us." The most hopeful note that the editors could manage at the end was "The German people need to show us evidence of an inner change. We will be watching attentively for its every sign."[41]

This was, however, a rather despairing, default position, allowing the tide of events to wash over the survivors. A few weeks later *Der Weg* ran an article entitled "Juden in Deutschland oder Deutsche Juden"—Jews in Germany or German Jews—that firmly reiterated the traditional prewar German Jewish point of view and also reproached the editors for their default position.

"They forget," wrote W.P.C.,

> that a large number remain here quite simply because they are Germans and that does not make us worse Jews because we believe ourselves to be good and true Germans, Germans who received their education and culture in German schools, who heard God's word interpreted by rabbis in German, and further . . . are not ashamed to have Germany as their Fatherland and German as their mother-tongue. I, and those like me, remain in Germany because we do not want to leave, and because no fool, no simpleton or seducer should or could rob us of our German homeland or our sense of being German. We mean the true Germany, that of Schiller, Goethe, Kant, that is capable of thinking as a citizen of the world. This is the Germany that is developing its constructive powers in order to rebuild Europe, to construct a new, better, and more beautiful world, in which Germany would take its place as an equal and well-regarded partner. Did Germany exist then for only twelve years?[42]

This was the old idealistic voice of the Enlightenment, in which Jews who had been born in Germany saw themselves as an indissol-

DER WEG

ZEITSCHRIFT FÜR FRAGEN DES JUDENTUMS

JAHRG. 1 / NR. 27   BERLIN, 30. AUGUST 1946   PREIS 15 PFENNIG

WIR WARTEN

Carl Busch

Im Laufe unserer Geschichte haben wir Juden das Warten gelernt. Seit den Tagen unserer Väter haben wir gewartet. Und es scheint, als ob die Zeit des Wartens für uns noch nicht vorüber ist. Nachdem wir zwölf Jahre lang auf die Befreiung von dem Hitlerregime gewartet hatten, glaubten wir, daß die Zeit des Wartens für uns vorbei sei. Wir hofften, daß jetzt die Zeit der Erfüllung kommen würde, wir mußten aber feststellen, daß diese Hoffnung nicht wahr wurde, daß vielmehr eine neue Zeit des Wartens begonnen hat. Wir erwarteten, daß wir alsbald nach der Befreiung in unsere alten Rechte eingesetzt würden, daß wir unsere Wohnungen, unsere Möbel, unsere Werte zurückerhalten würden. Nichts davon wurde wahr. Noch heute ist ein großer Teil unserer Menschen ohne Wohnung. Die Wohnungen, aus denen wir vertrieben wurden, sind noch immer im Besitze derjenigen, die die Nutznießer der Juden-Verfolgungen waren. Die Möbel, die uns das Bergungsamt zum Ersatz für die verlorenen zur Verfügung stellte, werden freigegeben, und um die Wiedergutmachung ist es still geworden. So warten wir denn weiter. Wir glaubten, daß alsbald nach der Befreiung für uns die Grenzen geöffnet würden, daß wir zu unseren Angehörigen fahren könnten. Und wir stellen fest, daß von Auswanderungsmöglichkeiten nur in verschwindendem Maße die Rede ist. Lediglich aus dem US-Kontrollgebiet ist in beschränktem Umfang der Einwanderung möglich. Ein Teil der Menschen kommt aber auch aus dem US-Kontrollgebiet nicht heraus, weil sie nicht in der Zeit der Verfolgung Leiden zugezogen haben, welche die Einreise unmöglich machen. Aus den anderen Besetzungsgebieten ist eine Auswanderung praktisch nicht möglich. Und so warten wir weiter auf die Auswanderungsmöglichkeiten. Wir hofften, daß nach dem Kriege das Problem Palästina endlich gelöst würde. Und wir erleben es, daß es nur Beratungen und Konferenzen gibt. So warten wir weiter und hoffen, daß auch hier eine Lösung gefunden wird. Wir nahmen an, daß nach dem Kriege der Antisemitismus endgültig überwunden sei, und daß es kaum noch Judenhaß geben würde. Und auch hier haben uns unsere Hoffnungen getäuscht und wir warten weiter darauf, daß die Menschen zur Einsicht kommen. So warten wir, wie wir bisher gewartet haben, warten wir, wie wir auf den Messias warten. Und wenn wir nicht im Laufe der Jahrtausende das Warten gelernt hätten, wenn wir nicht durch die Schule des Wartens gegangen wären, müßten wir verzweifeln. Wir hoffen, daß unsere Wünsche sich doch noch realisieren werden und daß gibt uns die Kraft. Wir warten.

Lagerleben

1933 begann für uns Juden in Deutschland das Leben hinter Stacheldraht im Lager. Wenn auch anfangs erst wenige in die Konzentrationslager kamen, so waren doch die übrigen von einem unsichtbaren Stacheldraht umgeben, der ihr Leben von der Welt abschloß, bis auch sie in eines der Todeslager des Naziregimes verschleppt wurden.

Wir Juden haben eine schwerere Verantwortung für unser Leben und unseren Glauben als vielleicht jede andere religiöse Gemeinschaft. Suche nicht bei jeder Handlung Schutz in dem Gedanken: „Es ist meine eigene Angelegenheit". Es ist deine Angelegenheit, aber es ist auch die Angelegenheit der Gemeinschaft, noch können, wir die Welt um uns übersehen. Ein helles Licht liegt auf den Juden. Es ist eine ernste Verantwortung, ein Jude zu sein; und du kannst ihr nicht entfliehen, selbst wenn du sie ignorieren willst. In ethnischen und religiösen Dingen dürfen wir Juden niemals leichtfertig handeln. Zehn schlechte Juden können genügen um uns zu verdammen; zehn gute Juden können uns retten. Zu welchen willst du gehören?

Claude G. Montefiore, 1858—1938.

Auch heute noch, eineinhalb Jahre nach der Befreiung, gibt es Lager, und wir fragen uns, wann dieses Elend einmal ein Ende nehmen wird. Der Stacheldraht ist immer noch vorhanden, aber die beklagenswerten Menschen, die heute gezwungenermaßen ein Lagerleben führen, können sich wenigstens auch außerhalb des Stacheldrahtes bewegen. Das nennen wir Judenschicksal.

Die Jüdische Gemeinde zu Berlin war nach der Befreiung durch die Alliierten gezwungen, Lager zu errichten, die die Rückkehrer aus den Konzentrationslagern aufnahmen. Zuerst schien es, als ob diese Lager nur vorübergehend wären, als aber Tausende unserer Brüder aus dem Osten fliehen mußten, wurden sie zu ständigen Einrichtungen. Wir haben an die Hilfe der Welt geglaubt, wir haben auf die

Unterstützung der charitativen Organisationen gehofft, und doch ist es bis jetzt nicht möglich gewesen, diesem Zustand ein Ende zu bereiten und diese Menschen wieder einem normalen Leben zuzuführen. Zur Zeit unterhält die Gemeinde ein Durchgangsheim in der Iranischen Straße, das als Altersheim umgebaut wird. Daneben besteht unter Aufsicht und Betreuung der französischen UNRRA das Lager in Wittenau. Unter dem Schutz der amerikanischen UNRRA steht das Lager in Schlachtensee und das in den letzten Julitagen entstandene Lager Tempelhof.

Die Not und das Elend in dem zuletzt errichteten Lager in Tempelhof, in das die letzten Ankommenden aus dem Osten eingewiesen wurden, ist kaum zu schildern. Es befinden sich dort Menschen aller Altersstufen. Wenigstens die Kinder konnten dank der tatkräftigen Hilfe mit dem Notwendigsten versorgt werden. Trotzdem, sind alle nur notdürftig bekleidet, man kann fast sagen zerlumpt, und der größte Teil von ihnen ist ohne Schuhe. Nun warten diese unglücklichen Geschöpfe auf die Hilfe von draußen. Sie wollen auch einmal so nett gekleidet sein, wie die anderen Kinder, die sie in den Straßen Berlins spielen sehen. Und mit den Erwachsenen. steht es noch schlimmer. Trotz der Hilfe der Organisationen ist es nicht möglich, die dort untergebrachten Menschen mit dem Notwendigsten zu versehen, da es an allem fehlt. Dabei muß man bedenken, daß viele, die jetzt hierher geflohen sind, um das nackte Leben zu retten, einst als Partisanen für die Befreiung Europas gekämpft haben.

Viele dieser Menschen sind Schuster, Schneider, Tischler und würden gern für die Lagerinsassen arbeiten, aber es fehlt das Handwerkszeug, es fehlen alle Dinge, wie Material usw. Verwundert schauen sie auf die Umwelt, und mit Verbitterung im Herzen fragen sie, warum diese Zustände nicht geändert werden.

Ist es unter diesen unwürdigen Umständen verwunderlich, wenn der eine oder andere strauchelt, müssen wir da nicht die Frage nach der Schuld neu aufwerfen? Es handelt sich zumeist um junge Menschen, die heute 18 oder 19 Jahre alt sind, die sechs Jahre als Partisanen oder in einem KZ leben, die Kinder das Lagerleben begonnen, die heute wieder in einem Lager leben müssen, und die erst zu einem normalen Leben umerzogen werden müssen. Wir lesen ja auf der anderen Seite täglich in

---

An early issue of *Der Weg*. One article discusses the failure to restore property to German Jews. Another points out that one and a half years after the war's end Jews were still living behind barbed wire in D.P. camps.

uble part of their country and saw that country as one with a longer and nobler history than the shameful twelve years of Nazi rule. But it was a voice that grew fainter with the passage of time. As the headline rightly implied, the old belief in the idea of "German Jews" was rapidly fading. Even those Jews who were born in Germany and freely elected to stay out of a sense of obligation to those who had saved them, out of a wish to help rebuild *their* country, out of an unwillingness to leave a familiar, if difficult, world—even they saw those twelve years as having created a deep breach in Jewish history. After 1945 they were "Jews in Germany," and only a very rare Jew would say he was "a German."

Although the years of Nazi rule had totally separated Jews and Germans politically, the cultural and psychological dimensions were not so neatly managed. As the writer in *Der Weg* had stated, language and education had left indelible traces. Even in the 1920s idealistic young Zionists who went to Palestine had taken their Bechstein pianos with them and continued to play their Schubert and Beethoven sonatas. And how many sets of the works Heine and Goethe had accompanied the German Jews forced to flee in the 1930s? This was their culture. And for the first Passover after the war, *Der Weg* printed Heine's famous unfinished Passover story *The Rabbi of Bacherach,* a classic familiar in every German-Jewish household.

By contrast, in a displaced persons camp in Berlin, no more than a streetcar ride away, where Polish Jews were waiting to move west, the camp newspaper, written in Yiddish, drew upon an entirely different pantheon of writers. While sharing the same fate, the Polish and German Jews represented two very different worlds. That they expressed themselves in two languages that were historically related but barely comprehensible to one another was perhaps a metaphor for what was and remained for decades an uneasy relationship.

In fact, as if to affirm Jewish rootedness in German culture, *Der Weg* ran a long series of articles on Jewish notables in German literature, the arts, the sciences, and politics. The list was wide-ranging and consoling to their readers, but in the postwar world these reckonings came to seem a dated, if not a mistaken way to think about the culture of Jews in Germany.

These were among the opening maneuvers as the German Jews sought to redefine themselves in the postwar world and in its first years the columns of *Der Weg* were filled with essays reflecting on all that had happened. The feeling of unreality about being alive and free that marked so many of the statements of the Eastern European Jews appeared again in the writings of the German Jews. In an article in *Der Weg* in August 1946 Hans-Erich Fabian echoed the words of Dr. Zalman Grinberg a year earlier.

"Of course," wrote Fabian, "the threat of the SS is over, the burden that weighed on us is gone; but are we actually freed because of that? Even today we do not feel ourselves to be free. Why is that? The answer is not easy to find. We had lost our independence. We were no longer masters over ourselves. Others decided what was to become of us; others who treated us like figures in a game in which they shoved us from here to there, arousing our anxieties, persecuting us, and whose final goal was to destroy us. And as these powers were swept away, we stood there and did not know how to use our freedom. We had forgotten what the idea of freedom was."[43]

The external chaos was matched by an inner feeling among the German Jews of disorientation and uncertainty at the new world to which they had returned. And while some German Jews could slip back to the old beliefs, the old slogans, others felt that they had to rebuild themselves along with the community.

Under the prevailing circumstances of physical desolation and moral uncertainty, only one exceptional group of former Berliners was eager to return. These were the Jews who had spent the war years interned in a Japanese-controlled ghetto in Shanghai. Before the war, Shanghai had been the only place in the world that admitted foreigners without visas. Anyone who could pay for the transportation from Germany would find a haven. Ultimately some eighteen thousand Austrian and German Jews, two thousand of them from Berlin, found their way there. By 1943 Shanghai had fallen to the Japanese, who confined the Jews to the Hongkew section of the city. When the war ended, most of these refugees emigrated to Israel, the United States, or Australia. But five hundred of the Berliners chose to return to their native city. Accordingly, in the first group of Germans and Austrians who left Shanghai on July 25, 1947, there were 295 Berliners. Their three-week voyage in a former American troop ship, the *Marine Lynx,* took them through the Suez Canal to Naples. There the Berliners boarded the slow train that brought them home on August 21, 1947.[44] Some had been only children when they left. Others who had been adults returned with mixed feelings.

At the Görlitz train station in West Berlin, representatives of the Jewish community and Mayor Ferdinand Friedensburg were on hand to greet the Shanghai refugees. The mayor expressed regret that he could only meet them with empty hands. What he could offer them, however, was recognition of their status as Victims of Fascism, which guaranteed their right to better food and living conditions than most other residents and exemption from hard labor. He could also assure them that this was no longer the Germany they had left a decade earlier. If they should hear stories of anti-Semitism, the new arrivals should be skeptical. Reports in the press, he said, were often exaggerated and arose out of mere sensationalism.

But Mayor Friedensburg's words of assurance hardly lasted out the week. The next weekend, movie house newsreels showing the arrival of the Shanghai refugees elicited noisy outbursts of anti-

A Jewish man who had fled to Shanghai before the war returns to Berlin in August 1947. The passerby looks away so as not to intrude. Photographer Henry Ries. Personal collection.

Semitism from audiences all across the city. Nor did the mayor mention that their status as Victims of Fascism was valid for only a month—until October 1, 1947. At that point, as one historian of the period has written, "there began once again a paper war."[45] The new arrivals were required to fill out more forms, answer questionnaires that used hateful Nazi racial language, and appear at hearings in order to reestablish their status. As one returnee who was born in 1883 wrote in some exasperation, it must be clear to everyone that he had left Berlin in 1938 because of persecution: he could not have willingly emigrated to China at the age of fifty-five. But the paper war was not confined to refugees from Shanghai.

The most immediate problem for every Jew in Berlin was restitution: the demand for the return of property, businesses, apartments, furniture—everything that had been expropriated by the Hitler regime. The columns of *Der Weg* are filled with stories of frustrated Berlin Jews arguing their cases in court and often losing. Obviously stung by the charge that loyal Germans would not be making such demands, *Der Weg* wrote a spirited response: "We want to make it perfectly clear that restitution is not a matter of loyalty but a matter of justice. It is a justice that cannot be compromised or postponed. In any case it must be fulfilled if Germany is ever again to gain the status of a state ruled by law."[46]

Nonetheless, not until the end of 1947 did the Allied powers work out their regulations for restitution so that claims could be processed with some possibility of success. The regulations made distinctions between those who were physically present to present their claims and those who had emigrated or whose claims were being presented by the heirs because the nominal owners had been killed under Nazi persecution. Finally, there was the property of those who never returned and for whom no heirs came forward. The claims of the official Jewish community for its property, movable and immovable, its bank resources and other assets, were subject to yet another series of regulations. An English analyst estimated the value of all Jewish property losses, confiscated bank accounts, and businesses in wartime figures at twelve billion dollars.[47]

In 1948 the Jewish Restitution Successor Organization (JRSO) was established in the American zone, with parallel organizations in the British and French zones, to deal with the question of ownerless property, both private and communal. In Berlin the effect of this agreement was to place all the communal property still in use—synagogues, cemeteries, old age homes, and other institutions—in the hands of the Gemeinde. Other properties, such as unclaimed real estate, art, antiques, and bank accounts, came under the control of the JRSO. Ultimately, the Jewish community received 40 percent of the registered property, while 60 percent remained with the JRSO.

The artworks were eventually dispersed by the JRSO to Jewish museums in various parts of the world. As one anomalous result, when the Centrum Judaicum in Berlin wanted to mount an exhibition in 1992, it had to borrow from afar works by such Jewish artists as Moritz Oppenheim and Max Liebermann that before the war had belonged to the Jewish Museum in Berlin or to Berlin private collectors.

These first regulations established in the military occupation zones were narrowly conceived and dealt with the return of tangible goods that had been confiscated by the Nazis and would now be restored to their owners who were physically present to receive them. This was restitution in its most literal sense. It was not until after 1949, when two governments were established in a divided Germany, that more comprehensive legislation was drafted to include victims of Hitler who had fled abroad. This second stage of legislation involved compensation for less tangible losses, such as interrupted schooling or careers, damaged health, time spent in Nazi slave labor or concentration camps, losses incurred because of forced emigration, and fines imposed by the Nazis, as well as for confiscated property.

By 1952 both the individual German states in the West and the Federal government of Germany had passed laws to benefit those broadly defined as "victims of National Socialism." These regulations were intended to offer compensation to Jews and others who had fled abroad during the Nazi years. Legislation passed by the Berlin parliament also included "the unsung heroes"—Germans who had aided Jews during the Nazi period.[48] For those refugees who received pensions from the West German government, the payments often made the difference between want and a dignified old age. The bureaucratic processing of the applications often took years, so it was not until the end of the 1950s that many of the survivors began to receive their compensation. As of 1980 some 26,000 former Berliners were still receiving monthly pensions. With the aging of the refugees, by the year 2020, only about 1,700 are expected to be on the rolls.[49]

In 1951 the question moved to a new, international level with the initiation of negotiations for restitution between West Germany and Israel and the formation of the Conference on Jewish Material Claims against Germany. In effect, the payment to Israel for its claims became a first step in the establishment of diplomatic relations between the two countries. The third party in the negotiations, the Jewish Claims Conference, which constituted the successor organization and heir to the ownerless properties of the destroyed Jewish communities in Germany, had the stated purpose of devoting its funds to "the relief, rehabilitation, and resettlement of Jewish victims of Nazi persecution, and [of] aid[ing] in rebuilding Jewish communities and institutions which Nazi persecution had devastated."

In the final agreement, signed in Luxembourg on September 10, 1952, the West German government agreed to pay Israel nearly three billion marks in the form of material goods, agricultural products, and restitution to individuals, as well as some $115 million to the Claims Conference. The conference used nearly $7 million of this amount for the benefit of Jews in West Germany. In addition to contributing to the Jewish Central Welfare Office, which aided individual Jews who had been victims of Nazi persecution, the Claims Conference built old age homes and youth centers and set up several loan offices to help members of the community get started in various enterprises.

Particularly important to Israel in its 1952 agreement with Germany were the manufactured goods and raw materials that it so badly needed at the beginning of its life as an independent state. Felix Shinnar, who had been the deputy leader of the Israeli delegation to the conference described what these imports meant:

> Some 80 percent of the agreement was accepted in shipments of capital goods of all kinds and . . . were a visible, lasting constituent of the building up of industry in Israel during those first years. . . . Shipments under the agreement constituted 12 percent of all annual Israeli imports [between 1953 and 1965]. Under the agreement some fifty vessels, almost all freighters, were acquired; the copper smelters in King Solomon's copper mines in the south of our country, the ironworks in the north were built entirely from German shipments. In addition, about 2,000 individual enterprises, from a largish workshop to a medium-sized factory, received machinery and equipment from the shipments under the agreement, which allowed them to rationalize and modernize the operation.[50]

Both sides, however, saw the agreement not only as the occasion for "the settlement of a matter of material damages"—again Felix Shinnar—but also as "the renewed encounter of the German and Israeli people after the days of injustice and violence under Hitler." Foreign Minister Moshe Sharrett, who signed the treaty for Israel, also saw it as "something quite unprecedented, which has taken a most momentous place in the history of Israel and of Germany. This was a historic act," he continued, "that brought honour to free postwar Germany, and became for Israel a force of most important constructive aid."[51] Konrad Adenauer, signing as chancellor of the German Federal Republic, emphasized that "the dreadful things that had been done in the name of Germany rested as a heavy burden on all the political problems confronting any German government. To us Germans, the most important of political developments . . . is the fact that we were able to find the path to Israel and the Jewish people."[52]

At the same time, in the Soviet zone of Germany, the occupying power was essentially stripping the country of its industry. Whole factories and workshops were being packed up and transported to the Soviet Union, where they often lay rusting and unused in the crates in which they had been shipped. In addition the Soviets confiscated motor vehicles, railroad rolling stock, and the very rails on which the trains ran. According to the historian Henry A. Turner, estimates of Soviet expropriations ran "as high as a quarter of the total [of the industry] in their zone."[53] Under these circumstances, in the new East German government, which was dominated by Communist ideology, the very idea of the restitution of private property ran into fundamental difficulties. "Should the property of Jewish capitalists be returned to them?" was the rhetorical question claimants met when they attempted to recover what had been seized by the Nazis. From 1948 restitution became a matter that the regime preferred to discuss on ideological rather than practical grounds.

During this long process, which saw the transformation of Germany from a conquered country under occupation to a divided land with two governments, the Jewish community in Berlin was also undergoing important changes. By November 1947 it had received permission from the Allied Kommandatura to hold elections, which were set for February 1948. By this time the original feeling of the small number of Jews in Berlin that they were a *Liquidationsgemeinde* had changed to a mood of hope and energy. Now they spoke of an *Aufbaugemeinde*—a community that was to be built up.

One of the stalwart figures in the community, Erich Nelhans, however, did not figure in the results of this election. On March 13, 1948, he was arrested by the Soviets and accused of helping soldiers of the Red Army escape to the West. After a summary trial by a Soviet military tribunal he was sentenced to fifteen years at hard labor and immediately deported to a punishment camp in Vorkuta, a town in the Urals twenty-five miles north of the Arctic Circle. In 1955 many of the German prisoners of war who had been interned in that camp were released and allowed to return home. But Nelhans was not among them and was never seen again. It was assumed that he had perished during his imprisonment.[54] As we have seen, such arrests were a fact of life under Soviet rule, and the usual recourse in democracies—appeal or the right to information about the prisoner— was simply not available. The official histories of the Gemeinde note Nelhans's arrest without further comment. The Jews in the Soviet sector, where the Gemeinde offices were located, were learning to live with a capricious and arbitrary government and to take advantage of whatever areas of freedom they were permitted. Free speech was not among them.

One of the signs of the growing vitality of the Jewish Community in still unified Berlin was the immediate emergence of three lists competing in the first open election for the twenty-one seats of the Representative Committee. Their respective programs represented the community's traditional differences, which had a long prewar history. The Liberal list featured as their leading candidates Hans-Erich

Fabian, Heinz Galinski, who had been a member of the Committee of Representatives, and Jeanette Wolff. Wolff, a lifelong Social Democrat, had returned from twelve years of hardship that began with imprisonment in Germany by the Nazis followed by deportation to a concentration camp. The National Jewish Unity Group, whose candidates included Julius Meyer, Fritz Katten, Carl Busch, and Aron Saurymper, presented a Jewish national position, urging Jewish emigration from Germany and the right of every Jew to citizenship in the forthcoming Jewish state. This seemingly innocuous program actually carried a subversive message that ran counter to the long held Jewish self-definition in Germany, that the Jews were solely members of a religion. As they once again mobilized the community after the war, the new Gemeinde strenuously reasserted the Enlightenment view that Jews were neither a race, as the Nazis had claimed, nor a nation. This was the view of the Liberal list. The reiteration of the definition of the Jews as a religious minority was, in fact, the purpose of a memorandum to the Magistrat in February 1946, in which the Gemeinde in Berlin reached one hundred years into the past to establish its lineage as the legitimate successor community. "After the collapse [of the Nazi regime]," they wrote, "the term 'Jew' is again to be understood exclusively in the religious sense. According to this, Jews are to be seen as those persons who have joined the Jewish Community of Berlin," which, as the official incorporation of the Jewish community, "derives its definition from the law of 23 July 1847."[55] With this law, Prussia had for the first time recognized the Jewish community in Berlin as an official public body, calling it the Synagogue Community—*Synagogengemeinde*—and it was this historical descent with its religious definition that the new Gemeinde wanted to invoke.[56]

The Jewish Unity Party had moved on to a wider and more secular definition of what it meant to be a Jew. But this was to fly in the face of the aspirations of one hundred years of Gemeinde life in Germany, reopening the old question of "What is a Jew?" It gave the voters a serious choice.

As a sign of its broad reach—the party issued a leaflet in Yiddish calling on the "Jewish voter" to cast a ballot for List 2 because it "supports a fight for a Jewish community . . . and because its members carry with honor and pride the blue-white flag of our national liberation."[57] This leaflet was a landmark in itself, going outside the predominantly German-speaking membership to address the Yiddish-speaking Jews from Eastern Europe living in Berlin. As of April 1946 the Gemeinde counted about a thousand of its seven thousand members as being without German citizenship: that is, Jews from Poland or other countries, as well as stateless Jews. Most of these Jews were presumed to be Yiddish-speaking. At the same time, on the edges of the city were additional thousands of Polish Jews in the displaced persons camps who might one day join the community.

The smallest party, the Independent Liberals, headed by Erich Mendelsohn and Dr. Hugo Ehrlich, had as one of its main objectives the defense of the non-Jewish partners of members of the Gemeinde. It also endorsed the state of Israel, which was about to come into being, and like the other parties demanded restitution for the wrongs suffered by the Jews.

The Liberal Party, whose program seemed to embrace many of the elements endorsed by the other parties, came away from the election with ten of the twenty-one seats: the United and the Independent Liberals took six and five seats, respectively. This meant that the old definition of a Jew as a member of a religious group prevailed, albeit combined with a passionate if inconsistent endorsement of the new state of Israel. In spite of the resounding victory of the Liberal Party, the executive committee chosen after the election diplomatically included representatives of all the parties, namely Hans Erich Fabian and Heinz Galinski from the Liberals, Julius Meyer and Bernhard Wollstein from the United List, and Dr. Hugo Ehrlich from the Independents.[58] Dr. Fabian was elected head of the executive committee and remained in this post until his emigration to New York in March 1949. He was succeeded by Galinski, who as an energetic spokesman for the Jews in Germany in general and as an advocate for the rebuilding of the Berlin Gemeinde in particular, became the immovable leader of that community until his death in 1992. For more than four decades, his tenacious and single-minded perspective, in which the Nazi crimes against the Jews were always in the forefront, imprinted itself on the media as the official view of the Jewish community in Germany.

Galinski was born in 1912 in the small town of Marienburg in west Prussia—a community with only 170 Jews. His parents, who ran a dry-goods store, were active members of the Gemeinde and gave their son the conventional after-school Jewish education. But the Hitler regime had come to power as he was reaching adulthood, and the textile business where he had planned to apprentice was "aryanized" before he could begin. According to one of his biographers, it was under these circumstances that he learned to challenge every provocation from the beginning.[59]

With other Jews from small towns, Galinski moved to Berlin seeking shelter and protection in numbers. In 1938, shortly after the Kristallnacht pogrom, he married his first wife. And like other Jews who stayed past the invasion of Poland, both were drafted for forced labor in armament factories. In February 1943 Galinski and his wife were swept up in the great "factory action," which concentrated on arresting and deporting the Jews working in the Nazi war industry. Sent to Auschwitz with his wife and parents, Galinski was separated from his family and never saw them again. He was put to work at Auschwitz in the Buna plant, which made artificial rubber. As the Soviet army approached in January 1945, Galinski's unit was sent on a death march to Bergen-Belsen, where he and his fellow survivors were freed by British troops in April 1945. By August 1945 he had managed to get back to Berlin, where he firmly decided to remain, immediately taking up work in the Bureau for the Victims of Fascism, as well as in the Jewish community. At a time when so many Jews in Germany were unsure about their personal lives, even about whether there was any reason to rebuild a Jewish community there, Galinski's certainty was exceptional and assured his place at the head of the community.[60]

Preoccupied with the reconstruction of their lives in Berlin, the members of the Jewish community were also aware that since the fall of 1945, Berlin had become a transit point in the western flight of Eastern European Jews. As we have seen, the Polish Jews could not remain in their homeland, and the Western powers, after early attempts to turn away this unstoppable mass of humanity, found that they simply had to cope with the influx. Under the postwar boundaries, Berlin lay almost at the eastern edge of Germany, less than fifty miles from the Polish border. But precariously situated as an island in the midst of the Soviet Zone Berlin hardly offered to nervous Jews in flight the security of the camps under Allied control in Western Germany.

What had started in the summer of 1945 as a stream of displaced persons of many nationalities, eager to return home, changed character dramatically as winter began. By November some 120–130 Polish Jews were arriving daily at the UNRRA camp in Berlin. "These persons indicated," according to the careful language of the UNRRA reporter, "that anti-Semitism was so violent in Poland that they had been forced to leave feeling loss of their own security. . . . Whereas a few infiltrees arrived well clad with a sizable personal fortune, the greatest number came to Berlin in rags. Before long it was estimated that there were about 4,000 Polish Jewish infiltrees in the city of Berlin."[61]

H. J Fishbein, director of an UNRRA Team in Berlin, delivered a detailed report for the Anglo-American Committee of Inquiry, in which he gave more specific reasons for the flight: "The story of their experiences during the past six months," he wrote of the new arrivals, "is a monotonous one as it is repeated by all refugees coming out of Poland. They tell of letters received from a Polish organization known as 'A.K.' [Armia Krajowa] meaning Patriotic Army . . . and in opposition to the present Government of Poland. These letters threaten the Jews with outright murder if they continue to live in that locality. They are usually given a period of 24 to 48 hours to leave. These letters are further confirmed by actual terroristic acts of pillage and murder by this organization, committed as recently as several weeks ago."[62] It was a catastrophic moment to be a displaced person.

The flight out of Poland came at the beginning of one of the severest European winters in a long time. Coming on top of the destruction of war, the scanty harvest, and the dislocation of the entire infrastructure, the months ahead promised unrelieved hardship. The aim of Col. Frank Howley, chief of the Military Government in the American sector in Berlin, was very minimal—to keep the city's population alive and reasonably well nourished. He hoped to accomplish this by establishing "warming rooms" at various locations throughout the city, where people could also receive hot meals.

An untiring force in moving Jews from Poland to Berlin and then onward to the D.P. camps in West Germany was the illegal Zionist organization *Brichah*—Flight. But its efforts were not welcomed by the military commanders in charge of the Western sectors of the city. The four sectors dealt in different ways with the increasing numbers of those fleeing from the East, and their changing policies were studied by Brichah as delicately calibrated barometers of which routes they would use and when.

Philip Skorneck, the Joint representative in Berlin, worked closely with Brichah, striving to get the arriving refugees out to more permanent camps in West Germany. By the end of December 1945, when Jews were arriving at the rate of some three hundred a day, five thousand Jews had been successfully moved out under the fiction that they were German citizens returning to their homes.[63] In fact, Skorneck was able to arrive at an agreement with UNRRA for a regular means of transferring Jews out of Berlin. The trucks from the West, which UNRRA used to deliver food to Berlin, were converted on the return trip to transport the refugees.

Each of the occupying powers adopted its own solution to the inescapable refugee problem. The British blandly refused to see the Jews as anything but Polish nationals who should be repatriated. The Russians resorted to summary measures. On January 4, 1946, they informed the 2,500 Polish Jews in the transit homes in their sector that in two days they would be moved to a D.P. camp in Prenzlau, a town east of Berlin. The wary and all-too-experienced Polish Jews immediately suspected that their journey would not end at Prenzlau but much farther east, and they used the two-day grace period to escape. As the historian Yehuda Bauer noted laconically: "On January 7 no Jews were left in the Russian sector."[64] Most fled to the French or American sectors in Berlin, while 250 left on illegal papers for the British zone in West Germany. In the French sector, "already overcrowded with Polish Jewish infiltrees," according to the eyewitness Joint report, "the flight of the Jews from the Russian sector created almost impossible conditions." Through the intervention of Philip Skorneck, the French authorities opened a block of apartment houses in their sector, in Wittenau, for these new refugees.[65] While the

French began by accepting 500 people, the camp was very soon accommodating 2,400.

Meanwhile, in the American sector, the military government was proving reluctant to accept any more newcomers. A particularly acute situation involved some 200 women, wives of men who had escaped from the Russian sector and who were waiting for them in a house that had been placed at their disposal by a Jewish Berliner. Many of these women were in the late stages of pregnancy, others had small children with them. It was under these desperate circumstances that the Americans relented in their policy of denying admission to "infiltrees."

Within days of the crisis, Colonel Howley moved an infantry division out of their barracks in the Schlachtensee area of Berlin and made the space (called Düppel Center) available to the displaced persons. In their new quarters, they were housed military style, according to the UNRRA report, "four persons in a room in two storey wooden barracks." But even this was not enough to accommodate all the new arrivals, and a second displaced persons center was opened, again in a vacated troop barracks, in the suburb of Mariendorf, with room for 4,000 persons.[66]

Between the end of 1945 and September 1946, the flight of Jews out of Poland through Berlin to the West reached its peak, with some 25,000 Jews passing through the D.P. centers in Berlin to the Allied zones. But by winter 1946 the hectic movement had gradually subsided, and Jews who had landed in Berlin, like their fellow Jews in the West, decided to wait out their future where they were. The two main D.P. centers then took on a more stable character, developing the institutions that we have already seen in the camps in the West: synagogues, schools for children and for vocational training, wide-ranging cultural activities, and sports. By spring 1947 the Schlachtensee camp had a population of some 3,300, and Mariendorf 2,500.[67]

As the U.S. Army and UNRRA administrators in other areas had already learned, the Jewish displaced persons were notoriously "troublesome" (in official language) and impatient with any outside authority. By fall 1946 they had organized their own Central Committee of Liberated Jews in Berlin, with representatives from the centers in Schlachtensee and Mariendorf. One of their main objectives was to administer the camps themselves, and because UNRRA was then cutting its personnel, it soon turned over much of the operation of the camps to the resident Jews.

This was hardly a homogeneous community, but was, rather, an agglomeration of Jews of varied backgrounds, ages, experiences and languages. Most, however, were bound together by the lingua franca of this and all other camps—Yiddish. In August 1946 the camp newspaper *Undzer Lebn* was founded—written in Yiddish and, unlike most of the Yiddish newspapers in the West, printed in Hebrew letters. The political parties that competed in the elections for the camp administration reflected the shades of Zionist opinion that had existed before the war, from religious Zionism to the labor left. In spite of the parties' commitment to Hebrew as the Jewish national language, the debates were carried on in Yiddish.

The editors of the camp newspaper freely admitted that Yiddish was no longer the only, the natural language of the Jews, but they passionately advocated its continuance. It was already the language of instruction in the schools. The camp at Schlachtensee differed from the camps in the West, which were populated largely by young unmarried people. In Berlin the camp population included a relatively large number of families with children who had lived in remote parts of the Soviet Union during the war and had then been released. These children became the object of a tug of war between the Yiddishists and the Zionists who advocated Hebrew. There was also a third language.

"The adults speak Polish," the editors of the newspaper wrote with regret, "but one educates children in the language of the Cultural Office [Yiddish]. The school should work on the children so that they speak at home and in the street in the same language as in the school. The theatre needs to show the best of Yiddish creations. The public that runs to German and Polish plays needs to be shown a good production in Yiddish . . . so that they may be persuaded that this is not an impoverished language."

Another more vehement article attacks the subject with all the sarcasm that was the trademark of the Yiddish press. "One has escaped from Poland, left everything behind in the cursed land," wrote the engineer D. Kohn, "where even now our brothers are being killed. But one has carried along the Polish language as a 'precious souvenir' across all borders and to part with this 'beloved' language is impossible. There is a sense that it is more 'aristocratic' to speak Polish. Some Jews would rather speak bad Polish than good Yiddish." Kohn has a solution: "The camp administration can become the supporter of the Yiddish language by making it the only official language."[68] As indeed it was.

Despite these apprehensions *Undzer Lebn* revealed in its pages the wit and energy of its young community of readers. It featured a center spread of cartoons satirically commenting on politics abroad and the idiosyncracies of camp life. It carried poems and stories, and, continued through several issues, a delicious parody of the Sholem Aleichem character Menachem Mendl.

This figure, who is featured in the cycle of Tevya stories, is a ne'er-do-well who has left his wife, Shayne Shayndl, and their children behind in Kasrilevka while he goes off to Odessa to make their fortune. His chosen highway to success is speculation in stocks and currency and in one episode he even extracts some money from Tevya to "invest" for him. We hear of his adventures through his letters to Shayne Shayndl, where he is always trembling on the verge of some huge success, which, as the next letter reports, invariably collapses. In Shayne Shayndel's replies, she is always the soul of common sense, urging him to give up his futile dreams. Instead, he ought to come home and care for his wife and children and earn a living at some conventional honest trade.

In *Undzer Lebn,* Menachem Mendl makes a triumphant reappearance (with the help of a David Kohn) under the title "Menachem Mendl in Berlin." As usual, he writes to Shayne Shayndl about his latest currency dealings, this time in American dollars. He also comments wryly on the excessive religiosity of camp life. "Since you ask me where I live," he tells her, "you should know that I live at UNRRA and with me a lot of other Jews. We have a synagogue, also a religious committee, a kosher kitchen, and we are well supplied with Jewishness, blessed be the Name of the Lord, even over our heads!"

"The dollars," he writes her "have moved up to 100 points but it doesn't pay me to sell them because everyone says that they will rise and rise. It's like being on fire since [the currency market in] Frankfurt has also thrown itself into these goods." And then Menachem Mendl, in the old way, loses himself in his fantasies. "I will buy you a Persian lamb coat trimmed with silver fox and little boots, because all the aristocratic women here are dressed that way."

Shayne Shayndl responds in her usual acerbic style: "I did indeed regard you as a madman when I read in your letter how you were dealing in currency. . . . Listen to me, Mendl, I don't like the sound of the whole thing. I was not accustomed to hear from my father about such airy business. And as my mother says (May she live long!), 'From air one only catches a cold.' . . . And I can't understand what you write about UNRRA. Is that the name of a woman, and if it is, you have brought black sorrows on my head. That's all that's missing from my life! You should immediately leave that place instead of turning me into an abandoned woman with three small children."

Mendl reassures her about UNRRA: "I can tell you," he writes, "that it is neither man nor woman but an office with a director and all its usual joys. They've taken us Jews and fenced us in with barbed wire and it's called a camp. There we receive food three times a day without cost and, also without cost, clothing. Apart from that we are honored by the whole world. They call us D.P.s, and they reassure us that with God's will at some time we will be able to travel on. We would like to, but when nobody here knows."

As usual Shayne Shayndl has the last word. "I cannot understand," she writes, "why they are keeping you there locked up behind barbed wire like some kind of thieves and robbers. What kind of crime is involved here?" Finally, she asks, "How long will you wander about in the world doing the old airy business? It is time, Mendl, to think about the true way and not only for yourself, but also for all of the people of Israel."[69]

Opinions about the "true way"—how to live in the postwar world—filled the columns of the camp newspaper. While officers of the occupying armies and the officials of relief organizations coped with the very real problems of food and shelter for thousands of displaced Jews, the Jews themselves reflected about how they were to continue their lives outside the resonant culture they had known before the war. The cultural office in the camp was not a mere center of entertainment but a place to consider how Jewish cultural identity was to be defined in the future. "While before the war, we had a unified society made up of people who followed an orderly life, today we have a varied community. We have children who have experienced more than grown-ups, children torn far away from any Jewishness, children who speak many different languages; adults who have experienced ghettos, concentration camps, and the partisan life. People who disguised themselves and passed as Aryans. . . . After seven hard years, when the She'erit Hapletah began to restore itself on the cursed German soil, there emerged a new variation of a community, the quite self-aware camp community, independently organized."[70]

When the Düppel camp was organized in 1946, the population included eight hundred children, most of them orphans. A report by the child welfare officer of UNRRA, however, spells out the experiences of these children. "They had been in concentration camps," wrote the officer, "had lost their parents and for many years had lived by their wits: cheating, stealing, homosexuality and evasion of the law were behavior problems presented by this group which required expert treatment in order for the children to have a chance to live normally again."[71] For both the children and the adults in charge, a communal life in a kibbutz in Palestine seemed an ideal solution—at one stroke providing them with a substitute family and an opportunity for a productive life. In September 1946, when 750 children left for Palestine, the interviews with them published in *Undzer Lebn* reveal eight- and nine-year olds, grave and responsible beyond their years. Invariably they talk of learning a profession so that they can be helpful to others, as if even at that early age, they no longer expect joy for themselves.

Far more serious was the question of reintegration into society of some of the older boys who had become almost feral creatures in the six years of war. Some twenty prisoners abandoned by their guards on a death march set up the nucleus of the camp in Feldafing. A Hungarian schoolteacher nicknamed Baatchi took it upon himself to work with the young boys who arrived with him and a group of men who had just been set free. "Along with the men," reported Baatchi,

> were a number of young boys ranging in age from fourteen to seventeen. The youngsters were not only in better physical condition than the rest of us, they were tough, fearless, to-

tally unscrupulous and seemingly devoid of emotion. Despised and feared even by older and stronger men, they could survive the hardships of the camps despite their youth primarily because of their physical fitness and the special attention they had received from the "Kapos" and other privileged prisoners who kept them as mascots and mates for their sexual perversions. In some camps the German had singled out young boys and appointed them "Kapos" and block leaders, knowing that the youngsters would not hesitate to turn against their comrades once given preferential treatment and power.

"Though Baatchi has tried to organize various activities and to teach them the rudimentary rules of social behavior," wrote his fellow D.P. Simon Schochet, "he is hardly able to get through to them. They form bands and steal not only among themselves, but from other blocks as well, although they have enough to eat and wear. Terrible battles range among the boys, and some of them simply disappear. Homosexuality is another great problem."[72]

Typical of these young hoodlums was Samuel Pisar, who at the age of twelve had been deported with his family from Bialystok. Although his family perished, he found two boys of his own age in the camps. They quickly became family for one another and survived the war together. Sixteen at the end of the war, his family murdered, Samuel reflected on what to do next. "Peace had come to Europe," he wrote in his memoir. "I could go where I pleased. Where could I find a place called home?" He and his friends knew that there were no Jewish survivors in Bialystok, and they dared not go back because the city was now under Soviet control. "We were," he wrote, "three lost souls groping along, unsure of our footing—but stirred and stimulated by the heady air of a brand-new world in which everything was possible and everything was permitted. We thrived in the midst of chaos and destruction. . . . [But] the viciousness of camp life and the amoral jumble of the postwar scene had badly impaired my sense of right and wrong. It could hardly have been otherwise. Today, when I marvel at my escape from the Holocaust, I thank providence not only for sparing my life but for saving me from the spiritual debasement toward which I was headed, a kind of postwar juvenile delinquency."

What saved him was not only providence but an unknown uncle—his mother's brother—who discovered that the boy was alive and traveled from Australia to take him home. For this feral child, as Samuel wrote, family life was "much too tranquil for my taste." But even he understood that "after six years living as an animal, aware only of the physical and the immediate, cut off from the nourishment of the mind," he needed to catch up. "My life, I now understood, had been at a dead end. Physically I had escaped. I was breathing, but Hitler had programmed my mental and moral destruction from his grave. The struggle for survival was going on once more, survival through study. It had to be waged with the same determination, the same fury."[73] Samuel Pisar was lucky. He had a loving and determined family to watch over him and help him rebuild his life. The fate of those like him, but without family or friends, was much harder.

Although the groups described by Schochet represented the extreme element among the thousands of orphaned children who survived the war, the others, too, needed more than the conventional schoolroom education. Those too young to remember an orderly world, a coherent society, needed to be taught the rudiments of social behavior, although for many the emotional damage could never be repaired. The adults who ran the newspapers, founded the theatres, and restarted the political parties, reaffirming deeply felt ideas, were all part of a bridge between the raw present and the rich history-laden past, conveying in every poem, song, or story links to a complex Jewish history. In the vocabulary of both Yiddish and Hebrew were imprinted powerful historical references. History, language, and people were bound into one. The fourteen-year-old boy, ignorant of Yiddish or Hebrew, who spoke only the rough Polish or German of his jailer needed to be brought back to his place in Jewish society, in Jewish history.

An early editorial of the camp newspaper *Undzer Lebn* stressed independence while acknowledging the physical help offered by UNRRA. But, continues the editor, M. Chait, "it is not up to the outside organizations to rebuild us intellectually. We alone must be the initiators and must be the ones to realize this enterprise . . . the most important element in the order of the day in the restoration of life to our people."[74]

In the Berlin D.P. camps, as in the D.P. camps elsewhere in Germany, artists, musicians, actors, writers, and political thinkers were able to express themselves before their natural audience for almost the last time. Once they left, they would be dispersed into other cultures. In their new countries of settlement, they would truly be "remnants" trying to find a place in already established Jewish communities. That sense of being alone among themselves, perhaps for a last unique moment fostered the rather heated tone of writers to the newspaper. One compared the situation in Berlin to that crucial moment after the destruction of the Temple when "the Jewish people were faced with the threat of forgetting." Then the remedy was to establish an academy in Jabneh, a town on the sea coast of Judea. With a sense of the seamlessness of Jewish history, the writer assigned to Jabneh in 70 C.E. and Berlin nearly two thousand years later the same objective: to rescue Jewish learning. The definition of Jewish learning, of course, was the source of instant debate, because many cultural traditions were struggling for supremacy. While the secular Yiddishists seemed to prevail in the schools, in the theatre, and in publications, the Zionists dominated the imagination of the displaced Jews, many of whom hoped to emigrate one day to the Land of Israel. The newspaper, as a consequence, was filled with stories about Palestine.

At the same time, the advocates of secular Jewish culture (in Yiddish) were critical of the narrower Zionist, Hebraist approach, claiming that "Peretz and Sholem Aleichem are as dear to us as [the Hebrew poet] Bialik. There are strong connections," the writer continued, "between our national culture and the treasure house of the culture of humanity. The Song of Songs, the Wisdom of Solomon have been the inspiration for generations of poets, just as Cervantes and Shakespeare have educated our Yiddish writers."[75] What was at stake here was more than language; it was the way Jews were defining themselves in the modern world. For a hundred years in Eastern Europe, since the Enlightenment and secularism had broken through, in the fifty years since Zionism had become a tangible goal, Jews had seized these alternatives to the traditional enclosed religious life. This debate was no less urgent in the postwar world. Whether a school was run in Yiddish or Hebrew was a commitment not only to a language but to an entire worldview.

The advocates of traditional Jewish religious schools established a yeshiva at the small Tempelhof camp in Berlin, as well as a primary school for children, and a special seminar for religious women. They had a pervasive influence, as well, on day-to-day camp life, as Menachem Mendl complained, by attempting to enforce the Sabbath and insisting on kosher food.

In the camps the creators of Jewish culture were well aware, however, of its transitory nature. A theatre troupe calling itself *Baderech*— On the Way—was organized in June 1946 in Berlin, drawing upon the musicians and actors in the Düppel camp. The company signaled its temporary nature in its choice of name and then bravely proceeded to improvise without adequate scenery, costumes, or even texts. In fact, while preparing the ever-popular Sholem Aleichem play *The Big Win,* the actors had to put the script together from memory. But the personnel of the company sometimes suffered drastic changes. In one week at the end of 1946, for example, all the musicians emigrated, so that the company could afterward offer only dramatic productions.

The camp population was not entirely dependent on the resources within its confines, and excursions were organized to take those who understood German to theatres in Berlin. As a follow-up to a viewing of Schiller's *The Robbers* in December 1946, for example, the cultural office sponsored a lecture on "*The Robbers* and Its Epoch." Three hundred people turned out for this event, where the speaker was Elijahu Yones, a member of the editorial board of the newspaper.

In October 1947 the usually quarrelsome camp suddenly united in resistance to attending a concert given by Yehudi Menuhin in Berlin. Despite his name, Menuhin had been raised by his Hebrew-speaking parents in a strongly anti-Zionist atmosphere. It was at the same time a rather unworldly household, and although both parents were originally from Russia, they lived quite apart from the surrounding Jewish community in San Francisco, where Menuhin's father earned his living as a Hebrew teacher. Educating their children at home, the parents devoted themselves to fostering the musical careers of their two astonishingly gifted eldest children, Yehudi and Hephzibah.

At the end of September 1947, when Menuhin was thirty-one years old, he gave a concert in Berlin for the benefit of a German children's charity. The program was conducted by Wilhelm Furt-wängler, whose career had been tarnished because he had continued to hold his post as a conductor in Berlin under the Nazis. By 1947 Furtwängler had been cleared of outright collaboration and, as Menuhin wrote, "was back in the place of honor. As I had imagined," Menuhin continued, "to play the greatest German music with this greatest of German conductors was an experience of almost religious intensity. I came down from the clouds to find myself a traitor."[76]

What had happened was that he had agreed to a proposal of the American military government to give a concert for the Jews in Düppel Center on the day following his benefit concert. Because there was no adequate concert hall at the camp, the Tivoli, a former movie theatre in Berlin, with seats for two thousand, was rented for the occasion, and trucks were provided to carry the Jews to the concert. At the appointed hour, Menuhin discovered that only some fifteen people had turned up. An article by Elijahu Yones in the camp newspaper explained the displeasure of the Jews in Düppel. Yones, himself a survivor of the Lemberg ghetto and subsequent deportation, referred to this experience in an open letter to Menuhin, written in the familiar slashing style of Yiddish journalism: "When I read of your 'humanitarian deeds' toward 'distressed German youth' and of how your new worshippers applauded you, I knew that in your audience there must have sat those two passionate lovers of music, Eppel and Kempke—SS men from the Jurewitz camp near Lemberg, who liked to have us sing while they shot our brothers down. . . . Wherever you travel, our newspaper will follow you like a curse until your conscience awakes."[77]

Menuhin decided to confront his critics, and the day after the failed concert he and his wife visited the Düppel camp. The pair seem to have been oblivious to the intensity of the feelings of the people they were meeting; when they arrived, Munuhin related, they were "immediately surrounded by an unsmiling crowd." His wife offered her hand to the nearest man and greeted him: "Guten Morgen." She clearly had no understanding of how a German greeting would fall upon such ears. "He stared and hesitated," Menuhin wrote in all innocence, "but she kept her hand out until he was forced to take it."

יהודי מנוחין האָם לעצמן זונטיק נעגעבן אַ קאָנצערם אין בערלין. די הכנסה איז איבערגעגעבן געוואָרן פאַר דייטשע
פראָיעקט און ציבגונג און 14־יעריקן קינסטלער, שמואל באַק.   קינדער (ס.ע.ס.ס.ר.)

A cartoon drawn by fourteen-year-old Shmuel Bak following Yehudi Menuhin's
concert in October 1947. Bak lived with his mother in the Landsberg D.P.
camp. The sign next to Menuhin reads: "Yehudi Menuhin, der berühmte
Geiger"—the famous violinist. The children hold a sign that says "Deutsche
Hitler Jugend"—German Hitler Youth with "Hitler" crossed out. The caption
in Yiddish reads: "Last Sunday Yehudi Menuhin gave a concert in Berlin.
The proceeds were passed on to a German project as shown in the drawing."
The cartoon was published in the nationally distributed *Jidisze Caytung*—
Yiddish Newspaper—of October 3, 1947.

This time the entire camp population turned out, filling the meeting hall, "sallow-faced men and women in threadbare suits and
babushkas," as Menuhin described them, "who felt themselves out-
lawed among outlaws, lost in the interstices of real nations, the condemned who had not quite died."[78] These "sallow-faced men and
women" were, however, people full of feeling, with powerful ideas of
right and wrong. By common consent, Eliajahu Yones was pushed
forward as spokesman. Only a year older than Menuhin, he had experienced the horrors of German persecution and the murder of his

entire family during the war. In his remarks he attempted to awaken Menuhin to the state of mind of his listeners. Speaking in Yiddish he said: "Mr. Menuhin, we the people, and you have no language in common. Therefore, instead of talking to each other, let us imagine ourselves walking down the streets of Berlin. When you, the artist, observe the ruins you will say: 'What a pity that so much that was beautiful was destroyed.' When we who lost our families see the same ruins, we will say: 'What a pity that so much remains standing.'"[79] In the end the meeting concluded on a note of reconciliation, but it was not until a few days later, when Judge Louis E. Levinthal, the U.S. Army adviser on Jewish affairs, took Menuhin to visit the Reichsbank in Frankfurt, that he began to confront at least one aspect of the Nazi terror. As one historian reported this event, Levinthal "showed him vaults bulging with heaps of wedding bands, earrings, bracelets, gold teeth, children's lockets and other gold jewelry that the Germans had removed from the Jews who perished in the concentration camps as well as stacks of gold bars melted down from similar items. At the sight of this Menuhin blanched and was momentarily speechless. In the end he turned to Levinthal and said: 'Now I understand what they told me in Berlin.'"[80]

Across town, the Gemeinde newspaper *Der Weg* seemed unaware of the passionate feelings unleashed by Menuhin's appearance, and covered the Furtwängler benefit concert by reviewing the music and Menuhin's performance. The article opened, however, with a paragraph devoted to Furtwängler, "who, as is well known," the editors write, "stood by many Jews in hard times."[81]

These contradictory views of events were swept away nine months later, in June 1948, as not only Berlin but the whole world confronted a new international crisis. In the unstable four-power alliance that occupied Germany, Berlin was always a source of anxiety and weakness to the Western Allies. Lying deep within the Soviet zone and without even a neutral land corridor from the city to any of the Allied areas, it was totally at the mercy of Soviet caprice. Border guards might suddenly close a checkpoint, keeping traffic waiting for hours, or even days, until they decided to reopen it. At the entrance to the Soviet sector within Berlin, the control was even more rigorous, as Western visitors were prohibited from bringing in cameras, books, maps, or even calendars. But all this was only a reflection of much larger world politics as the honeymoon of wartime cooperation faded and the Cold War set in. Berlin lived then in a permanently precarious state, for its supplies were brought in by land over roads that ran through Soviet-controlled territory.

Under the increasingly difficult circumstances, as early as May 1947 Col. William B. Stinson, the head of the Displaced Persons Section of the American Military Government, earnestly recommended that the D.P. camps be closed as of August. His main purpose was to eliminate the burden of transporting all the supplies for the camps from the U.S. zone in West Germany. Furthermore, many of the Jews in the Berlin camps had relatives in the West whom they wanted to join. And finally, the supporting voluntary organizations also preferred to have the displaced persons in the West, where they could be integrated into the existing facilities. The displaced Jews themselves had no brief for Berlin, which for them was only a stopping place on their way west.

Colonel Stinson's proposal was not put into effect, but in that summer of 1947 the Soviets embarked on a systematic program to interfere with the orderly movement of people and supplies into and out of Berlin. Beginning in January 1948 there were increasing numbers of traffic stoppages due to "technical difficulties." Then in March, Marshal Sokolowskij, the Soviet representative to the four-power Administrative Council of Berlin, stepped down, in effect ending whatever cooperation still existed among the occupying powers. In June 1948

General Clay, the American military commander, sought the aid of the Jewish agency to organize the schedule of trains that would take the refugees to the American zone.

This tidy plan was forestalled by the Soviets. On June 24, 1948, they declared a total land and water blockade of Berlin, in effect placing the city under a state of siege. The Allies were at a great military disadvantage in Germany. General Clay had sixty-five hundred troops in Berlin, while the Soviets had four hundred thousand men within striking distance of the city. The additional sixty-thousand American troops scattered across the rest of Europe did not begin to make up the balance. In any case, the Americans were not prepared to start a war, but they were prepared to resist. Assured by the mayor of Berlin, Ernst Reuter, that the people of Berlin were ready to endure any hardship rather than capitulate, General Clay began the first steps toward instituting what became a formidable airlift. The first plane with relief supplies arrived on June 26, two days after the blockade began. The blockade lasted nearly a year, until May 12, 1949, when the Soviets agreed to end it, conditional upon a meeting of the foreign ministers of all four powers to discuss the state of Berlin. In that time, the Americans flew in nearly 2½ million tons of supplies, in a day-and-night stream of planes landing at the rate of one every sixty-two seconds.[82]

But long before the blockade ended, the D.P. camps at Schlachtensee and Mariendorf had been emptied. A month after the blockade began, General Clay decided to evacuate all those displaced persons who wanted to leave. In part, he hoped to reduce, even by a few thousand, the number of people in Berlin who needed to be supplied. Beginning on July 23, 1948, he authorized the planes that flew in carrying provisions from the American zone, to carry displaced persons out as passengers. For many it was the first airplane flight of their lives. In the course of the next ten days, 5,536 persons were flown from Berlin to Frankfurt, and then transported by train to some twenty different Jewish D.P. camps in the American zone. About 150 Jews in the America sector, however, chose to remain behind. A few had an invincible fear of flying. Others had already started small businesses in Berlin and were not ready to give up the toehold they had in the postwar world.

In the French sector, where there were only 180 Jews in the Wittenau camp and some forty living privately, the evacuation was delayed until mid-September, when the Jews were flown out, again in American supply planes, to Frankfurt.

When the Berlin blockade ended, the displaced Jews were gone, except for the small number who had chosen to stay behind. The Gemeinde, unlike Jewish communities elsewhere in Germany, was overwhelmingly made up of native Jews. But politically it was in an anomalous position. Around it, the world had grown tense. The demarcations among sectors in Berlin grew more visible. People moved freely enough from one sector to another, working in one and living in another, but the city was now much more closely controlled. Although it had seemed natural enough for the Gemeinde to make its headquarters in the great synagogue in the East, now its members were steadily moving into the Western sectors. The totalitarian whiffs of the new system led most Jews in the East to seek a more democratic alternative—except, of course, for those who were ideologically committed to Communism. Those who fled, however, were proved to be right, as the rising tide of anti-Semitism in the Soviet Union soon broke on the heads of the Jews in its satellite countries.

CHAPTER FIVE

Jews in East Berlin

ith the end of the airlift in May 1949, it was no longer possible to ignore the very real differences between the eastern and western sectors of Berlin. The early unwillingness of officials in the Russian sector to recognize the Jews as "fighters" against fascism now became symbolic of their general denigration of the Jews in the Soviet zone of occupation. Classifying Jews as merely "victims" placed them in a lesser category than "fighters." We have already seen how Jewish claims for restitution of property or businesses were rejected as unacceptable capitalist demands in a socialist society. But the harsh reality that followed on this principle was that the Jews were doubly expropriated: first by the Nazis and then by the Communist regime. In 1951, when the recently founded state of Israel asked the two Germanies for help in the resettlement of the war refugees who were now flocking to its shores, the West German government responded with a complex formula of goods and funds. The East German government, however, refused to provide funds on the ground that to do so would only strengthen "Israel as a center of aggression against the Arabic national liberation movement using the cover of 'restitution.'" At the same time, the East Germans denounced West Germany's willingness to work with Israel as "a resumption of its colonial politics."[1]

Unlike West Germany, the East had the sympathies of a special group of Jews: those who had been Communist Party members in the past or who saw the postwar period as an opportunity to live in a new Communist state. But these were not Jews who had any connection to Jewish life. On the contrary, they had returned to their homeland to build socialism, not the Jewish community. But they far outnumbered those who simply hoped to resume their prewar life. By 1955 fewer than three hundred of those who had returned to the East belonged to the Gemeinde. At the same time, some three thousand Jews who came back regarded themselves as atheists, without any religious or ethnic ties, and certainly with no connection to the Gemeinde.[2] Above all they identified themselves as German Communists, returning with renewed idealism. A number of distinguished names were among the Communist faithful who had spent the Hitler years abroad, many in Mexico. Some of the best known were the novelist Arnold Zweig, the poet Anna Seghers, and the writer Stefan Heym, who had returned after serving in the U.S. Army during the war. Prominent Jews with Communist convictions who returned to East Germany were received with honor and privilege, which meant apartments, jobs, and subsidies for their artistic enterprises.

Many more would have returned to Soviet-ruled Germany but were barred by an increasingly suspicious government. The East Germans had adopted the Russian fear of contamination from the West. The writer Helmut Eschwege, who had been born in 1913 in Hamburg, did manage to return, but he grew keenly aware of the growing ugliness of the atmosphere. He had emigrated to Palestine in 1934 as a member of the left-wing Hashomer Hatzair Zionist movement. Still a steadfast Communist at the end of the war, he wanted to return to the Soviet zone of Germany. In 1946 he started back, stopping first in Prague, where he got a letter vouching for his political reliability from the well-known journalist Egon Erwin Kisch. He also carried with him a list of equally idealistic friends in Palestine who hoped that he could help them return to Communist Germany. After he was allowed to take up residence in Dresden in 1947, he presented this list of potential immigrants to the appropriate government office in Berlin. Although he traveled to Berlin every two weeks to check on the progress of their applications, he came to realize after a while that his friends would never be admitted. "We later discovered," he wrote in his memoirs, "that already at this early date, a murky ideology prevailed, according to which emigrants from the West all arrived with firm contracts from the imperialist powers to foil the development of socialism wherever they were admitted. Therefore, the authorities sought to allow as few of these Western agents as possible to enter the Soviet Occupation Zone."[3]

Other Jews who were in the Soviet zone at the end of the war were, as in West Germany, those who had managed to survive by hiding or passing or, like Victor Klemperer, by having an "Aryan" spouse. A small number had returned from concentration camps or forced labor and had naturally gone back to the home from which they had started. How long they stayed then depended on a variety of factors, not least of which was their attitude toward the Soviet Union and its puppet government in East Germany.

It was the Blockade of Berlin that definitively broke apart the loose four-power postwar alliance that had governed Berlin. In June 1948, just as the blockade began, the Allied powers introduced the new German mark (the Deutsche mark) and thereby put an end to the illegal and marginal trading that had characterized the first post-war years. It was widely acknowledged that the only way to stop the black market and the irregular barter system in Germany was a stable currency. The Russians, however, would not accept the new mark in their zone and thereby opened a permanent economic gap between the two sectors, especially as the Deutsche mark developed into one of the most solid of the postwar international currencies. Very quickly, people living in East Berlin found it advantageous to work in the West and earn hard currency rather than in the poorly paid, state-operated "Peoples' Own Enterprises" of the East, where the money had no value outside the borders of the state. "Our money" said one worker, "is really no more than scrip."

The change in money in the West was matched by the equally momentous change in political control in the East. In the first years after the war, a variety of political parties competed in the East. Anton Ackermann, a member of the officially favored Socialist Unity Party (Sozialistische Einheitspartei Deutschlands, SED), had sought to make a distinction between what was happening in Germany and Stalinism in Russia. He even proposed "a special German way to Communism." But at the thirteenth meeting of the SED Executive Committee, in September 1948, all deviations, even Ackermann's mildly patriotic formulation, were sharply criticized.[4] Under the influence of Moscow, the party transformed itself from a popular mass organization with all its attendant variations and dissension, to a strictly organized instrument dominated by a disciplined cadre of indoctrinated party members. By January 1949 the new centralized SED forbade the formation of any factions or groups with political differences within the party.

The Jews in the Soviet-bloc states had long lived with the rigidly enforced policy of the Communist parties on matters large and small. What they were not prepared for after the war ended was an outbreak of virulent, organized anti-Semitism. Directed centrally from Moscow, it spread to every Communist satellite in Eastern Europe. It had its origins in the paranoid mind of Stalin, who had begun to see a hostile Jewish conspiracy around him, but it was supported by a long-standing popular prejudice. The Eastern bloc nations were assiduous in following Stalin's hints and began to remove longtime, loyal Communists of Jewish origin from their posts. The newly acquired Soviet Zone of Germany was no exception.

As early as 1947 the Soviet Union had begun a press campaign against "cosmopolitanism," which was universally understood as a code word for Jews. This was followed even more unmistakably in 1948 by a campaign against "Jewish bourgeois nationalism." And because the well-known bourgeois desire for creature comforts was in direct opposition to the Communist regime's inability to provide these comforts, it was quite clear what the politically correct position had to be. But the campaign was not allowed to rest on these theoretical grounds and soon began to escalate, as Jewish party members were accused of disloyalty to the regime. The Jews were not, however, the only targets. The East German Communists were also eager to rid themselves of any competing socialist parties.

Using strong-arm methods, the Socialist Unity Party, the single party ultimately permitted by the Soviets in the East, literally drove the Social Democrats and other non-Communists from the Berlin city hall. In September 1948 the democratic parties, led by Ernst Reuter, seceded to the West, where they set up a new city government. In November the Soviets recognized the rump government in East Berlin, but in December the democratic elections in the Western sector brought out an overwhelming 86 percent of the voters, who chose a Social Democratic government for their part of the city. It was this government, with Reuter as mayor, that resolutely held the Western sector of the city together during the blockade. On May 23, 1949, two weeks after the end of the blockade, the German Federal Republic came into being, with a population of some 49 million people. A few weeks later, the German Democratic Republic (GDR), with a population of 16 million, was solemnly called into existence in the East by a People's Congress, making official the de facto division of the country into two separate economic and political zones.[5]

One of the first public demonstrations of the internal "cleansing" of the SED in Berlin was the arrest in June 1949 of Bernhard Steinberger, a Jew whose wife was Hungarian. A few weeks earlier she had been jailed in Budapest in connection with the arrest of Laszlo Rajk, the Minister of the Interior and Foreign Affairs, and this was enough to place Steinberger in the midst of a web of suspicion. Rajk's arrest was the beginning of a sweep through the Hungarian government in which thirty-eight officials were arrested, twenty-seven of them Jews. At his trial, which began in September 1949, Rajk and two Jewish codefendants, who were actually Communist Party functionaries, were accused of being "accomplices of the Zionist movement which was well known as a servant of capitalist imperialism against the people's democracy all over the world." After a brief trial, all three were convicted, sentenced to death and hanged immediately.[6]

Rajk's was the first of the Stalinist show trials of the postwar period, not only ending in death sentences for the principals, but also extending in ever-widening circles to those who had had some contact with the accused. Steinberger's crime was not only his presumed contact with Rajk, through his wife, but the fact that he had survived the Nazi period by escaping to Italy and then Switzerland. According to a new directive issued by Gen. Ivan Serov, the head of the Military Bureau for Internal Affairs in the Soviet zone, the SED was required "to remove all those who had been contaminated by the West during the war. Among these are comrades who for a considerable period of time were prisoners of war in Yugoslavia or had emigrated to the West and were thus possibly wooed to be agents by Imperialists or Titoists."[7]

After a summary trial, Steinberger, like Erich Nelhans of the first Berlin Gemeinde, was sentenced to serve an indeterminate sentence in the labor camp at Vorkuta. But unlike Nelhans, he survived, was released in 1955 and was permitted to return to the German Democratic Republic. Steinberger was only the first of many victims. Serov's directive was taken up by the Central Committee of the Party and led to a systematic witch hunt for all those contaminated by contact with American secret agencies. By Soviet definition this included the Zionist movement, followed by the Jewish relief organizations, such as the Joint and HIAS (Hebrew Immigrant Aid Society), defined by the party as the "Trotskyist Jewish movement." Leon Trotsky, Stalin's archenemy, was Jewish and had been driven into exile in Mexico, where he was murdered by Soviet agents in 1940. He remained forever after the permanent symbol of dissidence. His was the blackest of names. Zionism was just entering the Stalinist vocabulary at this time as a pejorative code word. Later the party defined it more precisely as a "nationalist, imperialist movement" and required members of the Soviet bloc to attack Israel and defend the Palestinians as the victims of Israeli imperialism.

Amid all these changes, the Jews in Berlin were caught in an anomalous position because their headquarters, in the synagogue in Oranienburger Strasse, was in the East, while the members were living in both the Soviet and Allied sectors. With the official position in the East distinctly cooling toward them, the Jews in the Soviet zone soon came to realize that they were living in a separate country from their fellow Jews in the Allied zones. Yet Berlin—as a city divided among four powers—remained for a long time a physical bridge between the two Jewish communities.

In time the Jews in the East began to learn of the isolating effect of the accident of geography. As early as July 1946 the major Jewish congregations in the East had formed the Union of Jewish Communities in the Russian occupation zone. Included in the new union were the eight surviving Jewish communities in the Soviet zone, the largest being those of Dresden and Leipzig. (Berlin was not among the founding members.) The founders hoped that this umbrella organization would coordinate their own activities and also would be their voice in dealing with the Soviet occupying power. As their first president they elected Julius Meyer, a loyal Communist Party member who lived in East Berlin and also served on the executive committee of the Berlin Gemeinde.[8] But in 1950, when the Central council of the Jews in Germany was founded in Düsseldorf, in the West, the East German government did not permit the members of the union to join their fellow Jews in a single unified organization.

The Jewish communities in Berlin lived under a double pressure: both from the Soviet-directed East German government and from the Jews in the outside world who continued to find any Jewish presence in Germany unacceptable. Nathan Peter Levinson, a Berliner who had been a student in the Liberal seminary for the Science of Judaism until his emigration in 1941, returned to serve as a rabbi in the community in 1950. As an outsider, he could see with particular clarity the effect of the anxiety under which the community operated. He described how the tension rose when a new order arrived from the city government or Soviet authorities to pass a political resolution according to their requirements. Then, he wrote in his memoirs, "dramatic scenes played themselves out at the meetings of the principal governing committee, as the members screamed at one another, as they debated the requirement that they condemn [for example] the 'the vengeful spirit of the Federal Republic' and 'its prevailing Fascism.'"

At the same time they could only absorb with sorrow the external Jewish disapproval. "Whether one wished it or not," wrote Levinson, "whether it suited the Jewish organizations outside of Germany or not, there were once again—or still—Jews in Germany who needed to resume the use of the instruments of their Jewish identity."[9] But there were few left who were qualified to lead these "instruments": the schools, synagogues, scholarly institutes, celebrations of festivals. As Levinson observed, "the government of the Jewish Community in the first years after the war had to be improvised."

Although there were five synagogues functioning in Berlin, Levinson was the only rabbi and had to make do with the help of three "preachers" who had not been ordained but who could conduct services and teach school. One of these preachers was Martin Riesenburger. Levinson, like others, was extremely skeptical about Riesenburger's qualifications, noting that he could not read an unpointed Hebrew text.[10] In Hebrew the vowels appear as diacritical marks (points) under the consonants which make up the letters of the Hebrew alphabet. Because an experienced reader does not require the points to read the text, this failing was a serious handicap in conducting services. When the Torah (the scroll of the Scripture) was removed from the Ark and unrolled on the reader's desk in the synagogue, Riesenburger would not have been able to read the text directly from the scroll, because it is unpointed.

In 1950, when Levinson arrived, the internal affairs of the Jewish communities in the East were particularly troubled because of their need to satisfy an exigent government and by their diminishing numbers. Yet they were only at the beginning of a serious period of crisis. The first intimations of what lay ahead came from abroad as the purge that began with Laszlo Rayk continued.

Czechoslovakia had been a model Communist state, banning Zionist organizations as early as 1948, nationalizing the resources of Jewish charities and jailing members of the community who had worked with such foreign Jewish relief organizations as the Joint. In

1951–52 the Czech Communist Party expelled its Jewish members. But the fiercest retribution against Jews erupted in the trial of Rudolf Slansky in Prague in November 1952. Slansky, a lifelong Communist, had spent the war years in Moscow and returned to his native Prague in 1945 to become secretary general of the ruling Communist Party. A member of the Politburo as well, he occupied a powerful place in the emerging Eastern Bloc.

On November 28, 1951, he was arrested and charged with being an agent of American imperialism and Zionism. After a year in prison, on November 20, 1952, he and thirteen other high party members, some occupying important government posts, were brought to trial. Eleven of the fourteen defendants were Jews, and the tale of a Jewish world conspiracy used so effectively by the Nazis was once again aired, this time by a Communist government. During the trial, each of the defendants "confessed" in highly stylized language to the "crimes" of which he had been accused. Slansky himself began by blaming his bourgeois and Jewish background. He then went on to call himself a "careerist, opportunist, and hypocrite, a coward who had betrayed his comrades to the police," and finally a "traitor, murderer, and spy." The trial ended on November 27 when Slansky and eleven other defendants were sentenced to death and the remaining three to life imprisonment. Without delay, the twelve condemned defendants were hanged on December 3, 1952.[11]

Much closer to home was the case of Paul Merker in Berlin, a non-Jew, who before the war had been a member of the German Communist Party's Politburo and had fled to Mexico City to escape the Nazis. He returned to Germany after the war and on November 30, 1952, just three days before Slansky's execution, was arrested in Berlin because of two major deviations from the Communist Party line. Both in his writings while in Mexico and afterward, Merker had seen anti-Semitism as the centerpiece of Nazi ideology. When he returned to East Berlin in 1946, he opposed the distinction made by the Victims of Fascism organization that classified the Jews as only "victims" and therefore not eligible for the same help as the "antifascist resistance fighters." In opposition to the official party line, Merker also advocated financial restitution to German Jewish survivors. As the historian Jeffrey Herf has noted, the party's rejection of these views "constituted a decisive blow against hopes for a distinctively East German Communist confrontation with the Jewish catastrophe."[12] These differences led to Paul Merker's downfall.

Merker's deviations from the party line were simply too much dissidence for the hierarchy to tolerate. In 1950 he had been expelled from the party, and in 1952 he was arrested and charged with having conspired with Slansky and two of his codefendents to destroy Communism in Eastern and Central Europe. Merker survived this accusation although he was held in prison until 1955, when he was finally cleared of espionage. But his advocacy of Jewish causes had made him permanently unreliable to the party, and he never again held an official position.

These developments were watched with alarm by the tiny Jewish community in East Germany. A week after the Slansky executions, the Jews in East Germany began their flight into West Berlin. To knowing observers of politics in the East, it was clear that the press and other state agencies were escalating the tempo of their attacks against the Jews. On January 4, 1953, a month after Slansky's execution, *Neues Deutschland,* the official party newspaper in East Germany, published an article titled "Lessons from the Trial of the Slansky Conspiracy." The writer condemned the "destructive nature of Judaism" and attacked Zionism as a movement "controlled, directed, and governed" by American imperialism and working in the interest of Jewish capitalists. Two days later the Central Party Control Commission (ZPKK) detained Julius Meyer, a longtime party member who also had been prominent in the government of the Berlin Jewish community. The ZPKK interrogated him for two days, seeking to establish that the Joint, as an international Jewish organization, was part of the Slansky conspiracy. Upon his release Meyer immediately drove south to Erfurt, Leipzig, and Dresden to warn the Jewish communities there of the arrests that might lie in store for them and to urge vulnerable members to escape while they could. Within a week, the leaders of the Jewish communities in Dresden, Leipzig, Erfurt, Halle, Eisenach, and Magdeburg had abandoned everything and arranged to take their families to Berlin.[13] With much of the border between East and West Germany already closed, the one easy opening to the West was in Berlin, where a subway ride carried a passenger from one zone to the next and a private car could cross the American Checkpoint Charlie. Finally, there was the Friedrichstrasse train station with its famous waiting room, the "Palace of Tears," where members of divided families took leave of one another. In January alone, five hundred Jews fled from all parts of the Soviet zone to West Berlin. On the day after the Slansky execution, a third of the 163 Jews in Dresden left for the West. Helmut Eschwege, who lived in Dresden, described the growing state of panic: "The anxiety among the Jews took on dangerous forms. Not only the heads of the communities, but also Jewish officials in the party and even Jews who were members of no party fled abroad. Those Jews who remained behind, whether members of the Gemeinde or not, remained without leaders."[14]

On January 14 Rabbi Levinson invited Heinz Galinski, the chairman of the Berlin Gemeinde, to join him in a press conference to urge the Jews of East Germany to get out of the country as soon as possible. Galinski and the other members of the executive committee refused, referring scornfully to Levinson's action as "American politics." But Levinson had already heard that the state security police had searched the Gemeinde offices and confiscated official documents. He had also received reports that community members were being arrested and interrogated. Addressing the press alone, he called attention to the official anti-Semitism and its threat to the Jewish communities. He then urged all Jews in the Soviet zone to leave for the West. Having himself escaped from Hitler in 1941, his message was simple. As he wrote in his memoirs: "I told them all: 'You should vanish. I have already experienced this once before.'"[15]

Galinski, who was known for his autocratic style of management, had threatened to fire Levinson immediately if he spoke to the press. When Levinson persisted, Galinski followed through and dismissed him from his post as rabbi in Berlin. But Levinson's open declaration of the dangerous situation of the Jews forced the executive committee of the Gemeinde to take a stand and make its own public statement.[16]

The next day, *Neues Deutschland,* the official regime newspaper, carried the news of the arrest in Moscow of the Jewish doctors who had been attending Stalin. The Soviet press, which was copied verbatim in East Germany, described the doctors as agents of the Joint, "the international Jewish bourgeois nationalistic terror organization." They were accused of having already murdered many high Soviet functionaries and had been prevented just in time from killing Stalin. The Jewish community in Berlin did not wait any longer. Galinski called another press conference and essentially repeated the points made by Rabbi Levinson the day before. On January 16, the day after the announcement of the "Doctors' Plot," the Gemeinde closed its offices in East Berlin and moved to the West. On the same day, both the president of the Union of Jewish Communities in Hungary and the Joint representative in Budapest were arrested.[17]

The East German regime did not waste any time either. Two days later, it established a new Jewish community for "Greater Berlin," which moved into the offices in Oranienburger Strasse just vacated by the original Gemeinde. A new executive committee and subsidiary governing board were quickly appointed by the city government. Predictably, almost all of the new functionaries were reliable members of the Socialist Unity Party (SED). Among them were informers who reported regularly to the STASI, the state security service, which kept a tight watch over what seemed to a Communist state an intrinsically suspect group. The only officer of the former Jewish community to remain behind was the preacher Martin Riesenburger.[18] On January 19 he joined two members of the newly appointed executive committee in a statement published in *Neues Deutschland*. There, lest there be any doubt about the loyalty of the Jews to the state, they praised the "spirit of friendship among peoples and the proletarian internationalism in the East German republic, a state," they continued, "where anti-Semitism is not tolerated."[19]

The response of the East German government to the escape of the Jewish leaders took a violent form in language, if not in deed. Using as its mouthpiece the VVN (Association of those Persecuted by the Nazi Regime), the regime published an inflammatory explanation of their departure two days later, on January 21, 1953, in the newspaper *Neue Zeit:* "Once they [the escaped leaders] realized that their double role in the VVN had been seen through, they departed to settle in West Berlin, the city that has become the El Dorado of the fascist bands of murderers, of the executioners of millions of Jewish people, and sought shelter in the headquarters of the central American agencies. They lie in the bosom of the organizers of the mass extermination camps of Auschwitz, Maidenek, and Treblinka; they have fled to the instigators of the barbaric mass murder and the destruction of Lidice and Oradour." And more in this vein.[20]

The destiny of the two Berlin Jewish communities is vividly illustrated in the way they were housed in the years after the break. On moving west, the founding Berlin Gemeinde took up temporary quar-

Representatives of the Jewish Community after it had fled to West Berlin.
The picture shows Willy Brandt, second from left, visiting the Berlin Gemeinde
upon taking office as mayor of the Allied Sector in 1957. With Brandt is
Heinz Galinski, the head of the community, flanked by Jeannette Wolff
and Siegfried Cohn, members of the Representatives' Council.

ters in Joachimstaler Strasse—the site of an Orthodox synagogue
with additional rooms that the Gemeinde used as offices. Only a few
blocks away were the ruins of the synagogue in Fasanenstrasse.
Opened with great pomp in 1912, it had been vandalized and desecrated by the Nazis on Kristallnacht, November 9–10, 1938. Though
untouched by the air raids during the war, by the 1950s its deteriora-
tion was judged to be beyond the powers of restoration. An arrangement was made between the Gemeinde and the Berlin Senate about
the future use of the valuable site, in the center of the new West Berlin.
It was agreed that the Gemeinde would demolish the ruins and the

The headquarters of the Jewish Community in West Berlin, completed in 1959. It stands on the site of the destroyed Fasanenstrasse Synagogue. Both the entrance portal and the ornamental column at the left were salvaged from the ruins of the old building. Landesarchiv Berlin.

Senate would pay for removal of the rubble and the construction of a new community center that would house not only administrative offices but also a small synagogue, a restaurant, meeting rooms, classrooms, and a library. The negotiations and construction took time, but in 1959 the new Gemeinde home, built in a bare modern style, was ready. The architects had managed to rescue and reuse the portal of the old synagogue as the main entrance and had also saved an interior column to further decorate the facade. It bore the verse from Leviticus 19:18, "Thou shalt love thy neighbor as thyself."

One of the ornaments of the new Gemeinde house was the library assembled under the direction of Jürgen Landeck. Originally from Magdeburg, Landeck had been sent to Palestine for safety in 1939 by his parents when he was fifteen. His parents perished, but Landeck returned after the war on the invitation of the Berlin community.[21] By the 1980s he had assembled a choice library of more than sixty thousand volumes of Judaica, with an especially strong section on German Jewish local history. As he ruefully noted, many of the old volumes that he bought from dealers, at auction, or from private individuals still carried on their flyleaf the stamp of the Jewish community library to which the books had belonged before they were confiscated by the Nazi regime—a silent commentary on their own history.

In East Berlin the magnificent sanctuary of the New Synagogue had been damaged during the war by Allied bombs, and its continuing presence, a reminder of former glory, became an irritant to the ruling powers. In 1958, in a still controversial move, the East German Gemeinde gave the government permission to tear down the damaged sanctuary as a "traffic hazard." As one member of the contemporary Orthodox community points out, it actually fronted on no street but took up the area of a city block behind the turreted facade that was left standing.[22] Originally ornamented with three splendid domes—a large central one flanked by two of smaller size—the synagogue retained its main dome but had been shorn of one of its smaller domes in the bombing. The shabby, lopsided remains of the entrance portion of the building became the home of the new East Berlin Gemeinde and continued as its headquarters—unchanged and unrepaired—for the next four decades.

After Stalin's death in March 1953 and Khruschev's spectacular denunciation of Stalinism at the Twentieth Party Congress in 1956, the situation for the Jews still remaining in the Soviet Zone eased somewhat. As Michael Brenner has pointed out, "In the post-Stalin era the leadership of the German Democratic Republic showed an in-

The New Synagogue in Oranienburger Strasse, East Berlin, as it appeared during the forty years of Communist rule. Note that one cupola is missing. This picture was taken in 1984. Landesarchiv Berlin.

creasing interest in the existence of the small Jewish community and began to offer it official state support. The few hundred Jews who were still enrolled on the books of the Jewish communities were protected like the last surviving representatives of a dying species. Also it would hardly make a good impression in the world press if precisely under the anti-fascist successors to the Third Reich, their part of Germany were 'cleansed' of Jews."[23]

This double policy led to a certain confusion among the Jews in Berlin. At the same time that the government was hounding and arresting its leaders, it also decided to restore the synagogue in Rykestrasse as a showplace of worship. Located in northeastern Berlin, it had been designed for a Liberal congregation in 1904 and incorporated in its original complex a school for five hundred students on the street front. The synagogue itself, with seats for two thousand people, was approached through an archway from the street and faced an inner courtyard. Unlike the popular Moorish style which had dominated late–nineteenth century synagogue building, such as the New Synagogue, the Rykestrasse synagogue reverted to classical North German architecture based on vitrified brick, gables and tile roofs. In November 1952 the city council allocated 300,000 marks for its restoration, and under a new name, the Peace Temple, it was reopened for the New Year holidays in September 1953, with Martin Riesenburger presiding.[24] Without enough men for a daily minyan— the quorum of ten required for formal services—the synagogue was used only on the Sabbath and holidays. As an imposing setting, it became a showplace used by the government for selected ceremonies.

The government not only designated the official Berlin synagogue but also appointed its rabbi, bestowing this title on the preacher Riesenburger in 1953. With this act, he was being recognized for his loyalty to the regime rather than for his training. He had had only a sketchy Jewish education, having studied religious philosophy for two years at the Liberal College for the Science of Judaism and then an additional year at the Orthodox Rabbinical Seminary, but he had never been formally ordained. Himself aware of the discrepancy between his activities and his actual qualifications, as late as 1950 he titled himself "Preacher" on his letterhead.[25]

Despite his lack of academic qualifications, Riesenburger had begun his career by conducting services and preaching in the synagogue of the Jewish Old Age Home in Berlin in 1933 and had stayed until 1942, when its residents were deported and the home was closed. In 1943 the central German Jewish organization, the *Kultusvereinigung*, which had its offices in Berlin in Oranienburger Strasse, assigned him to preside over services at the Levetzowstrasse Synagogue, which was then being used as an assembly center for Jews about to be deported East. But as Riesenburger reported, he conducted no services at Levetzowstrasse. Then in June 1943 he was transferred to the cemetery at Weissensee, where he was to preside over burials and assist in the management of the cemetery.[26]

As a good speaker and as a loyal follower of the party line, Riesenburger was indispensable to the government. Known as "the Red Rabbi" he was repeatedly asked to expound on government policy at large public events.[27] In a move reminiscent of the old German institution of the *Judenbischof*—bishop of the Jews—he was even promoted to *Landesrabbiner*, regional rabbi, in 1961. In the Middle Ages, the rulers of the small states that had made up the German lands had appointed their "Jewish bishops" to act as intermediaries between the state and the Jewish community. As men with divided loyalties, they were never popular among their fellow Jews. And like his predecessors, Riesenburger was also regarded with a certain suspicion, certainly among the Orthodox Jews remaining in the Berlin Gemeinde.

The contradictory messages sent by the government did not clear the air for the Jews remaining in the country; the old prejudices con-

tinued to live on undisturbed by either ideology or reality. Salomea
Genin, who was born in Berlin in 1933, emigrated with her parents
to Australia to escape Hitler. Growing up, she became a dedicated
Communist, and in 1963 returned to East Berlin. While at the university there, she began to discover her colleagues' attitudes toward Jews.
She describes a conversation with a friend about a sociology conference in Uppsala, Sweden. What caught her eye in the program was
the name of a convener, Sven Levy. She asked her friend whether she
thought Levy was a Jew? "With frightened eyes, she looked at me,"
writes Genin. "'I would never ask that.' 'Why not?' I asked her, astonished. With her next sentence, she stuttered. 'Why then . . . why
then I would have somehow had the feeling as if I had asked someone if he were a thief or whether he had tuberculosis.' . . . Suddenly,
I understood why in the GDR press and literature there were no 'Jews'
but only 'Jewish people' or 'Jewish fellow-citizens.' They still found it
an insulting word. But, after all, that is anti-Semitism!"[28] Salomea
Genin wrestled with her doubts until May 1989, when she finally left
the party.[29]

The steady movement of the Jewish population from East to
West is perhaps the clearest evidence both of the growing suspicion
and hostility toward Jews and of Jewish skepticism toward slogans
about "brotherhood" and "tolerance" that surfaced again and again in
the German Democratic Republic. In 1948–49 there were 3,800 Jews
in the entire Soviet zone and two-thirds, 2,625, were in East Berlin.[30]
Of the 316 Jews in Leipzig in 1950, for example, 54 left, as stated in official language, "for address unknown." Their fellow Jews—and
everyone else—knew that they had fled to the Federal Republic. By
1956 only 1,900 Jews were left in East Germany. This quiet hemor-
rhaging of the Jewish population went unhindered until the government closed off all movement in 1961. But the Jewish communities felt

the change keenly even before then, as they lost their active members and their youth.

The statistics after the great flight at the beginning of 1953 showed a skewed population. Even before 1953 more than half the Gemeinde members in East Germany were over forty-five years of age. This tendency only sharpened with time, and by 1974, ninety percent of the Jewish Community members in East Germany were between fifty-five and ninety years old. Eight hundred Jews remained in the country, of whom 450 were in East Berlin. Only eighteen of these Berliners were younger than twenty-one years of age.[31] When the Berlin wall fell in 1989 and the East German regime collapsed, there were 377 Jews left in the entire German Democratic Republic. As the size of the Jewish communities dwindled, and as the few remaining members were well beyond child-bearing age, the resulting atmosphere was one of decline and decay. A birth or a bar-mitzvah was celebrated not only by the family but as a signal event in the community. Yet inevitably, there were fewer and fewer of these festivals of renewal.

Like all statistics emanating from a totalitarian regime, these figures both reveal and conceal a great deal of information. One of the first questions is how the Jew was classified in this atheistic Communist state. In the German Democratic Republic, the category was as narrow as possible. The Jew was defined only religiously, with no reference to any historical, ethnic, or social background. It was also not wise to be known as a Jew if one hoped to make a career in government, in the university, or in any other visible position, such as publishing, theatre, or music. In 1950, when the ruling Socialist Unity Party undertook a purge of its undesirable members, the journalist Bodo Uhse was asked to write an article for the official party newspaper describing the unmistakable characteristics of the "undesirables." These were, in his account, which echoed all the anti-Semitic cliches, "the stateless, rootless cosmopolitans; the bearded, hook-nosed enemies of national independence, the international infiltrators into a genuine people's culture." Some 150,000 members of the party were expelled, mostly former Social Democrats and many Jews. As Inge Deutschkron commented, to be excluded from the party was the equivalent of economic ruin because "no government agency, no institution or organization would hire someone who had been dismissed."[32]

During this period, Helmut Eschwege, always a stormy petrel, tested the definition of a Jew in answering a party questionnaire. "Under the rubric 'Nationality,'" he recalled in his memoirs, "I entered 'Jew' since after all that I had experienced, I felt like one. At that time, however, the party expected Jews to write in 'German.'" The designation Jewish was applied strictly to religious affiliation. For this transgression Eschwege was tried before a party tribunal in 1953 for deviation on the "nationality question." In a society where proof texts were as powerful as in any religious sect, Eschwege defended his choice by citing a speech by Stalin in 1920 accepting the idea of various nationalities coexisting in one state. But he was trumped, as he wrote, by yet another citation: "On the question of Jewish nationality," his trial judges ruled, "we in the GDR base ourselves on Stalin's writing on the national question from the year 1913."[33] In that essay, much quoted in certain limited circles, Stalin had defined the Jews out of nationhood. "A nation," he wrote, "is a historically constituted stable community of people, formed on the basis of a common language, territory, economic life and psychological makeup manifested in a common culture. . . . Among the Jews there is no large and stable stratum connected with the land which would naturally rivet the nation together."[34] Hence the Jews were not a nation.

Although the number of Jews, thus narrowly defined, had dwindled to fewer than four hundred by the end of the GDR, the actual number of people who thought of themselves as Jews without belonging to the official community was probably ten times as high. But in those early years, so marked with danger and terror, few who were not already inscribed in the books of the Gemeinde would step forward to add their names.

One consequence of the narrow definition of the Jew was to cut off, for a long time, all possibility of Jewish activities beyond synagogue services or burials. The teaching of Hebrew or Yiddish, lectures on Jewish history and literature, concerts of Jewish music, except for liturgical music, were all unacceptable within the strict limits of the Communist definition. But there was a paradox. Although the Jews in East Germany were classified as a religion, they were treated as a nationality. Government policy toward stamping out Jewish learning and Jewish culture exactly mimicked that of the Soviet Union, where the Jews were, in fact, classified as a nationality.

In East Germany, this conflict between reality and theory became particularly acute with the founding of the State of Israel. As we have seen, the Soviet Union had been among the first to recognize the new Israeli state. It had, however, quickly changed course when it realized that Israel was not ready to join the Eastern Bloc and was turning instead to the West in its search for allies. As a consequence the propaganda machine in the East could only condemn the "Zionist imperialist" oppressors of the Palestinians. In this period of the Cold War, Israel, as part of the Western camp, became the target of the same attacks being leveled at other "capitalist," "imperialist" powers. While the Jews in West Germany were able to express their enthusiasm for Israel freely, the Jews in the Soviet zone literally had to withdraw all signs of connection. At first, as Helmut Eschwege noted in his memoir, "on every holiday, the Jewish flag would be flown from the windows of the Jewish community offices. But after 1952, they were well hidden."[35] Whatever their feelings, the Jewish communities maintained a discreet silence as their government showered invective on Israel at every point in its young history. As a religious minority and as loyal citizens of a totalitarian regime, the Jews could only endorse the foreign policy of their state.

Another consequence of this restricted definition was that the Jews were deprived of recognition of their sufferings under the Nazi regime. In the state-sponsored memorials to those who died in the concentration camps at Buchenwald and Sachsenhausen, the Jews were not even mentioned. As a "religious minority" they were subsumed under the nationality of their country of origin; thus they served to swell the numbers of Poles, Hungarians, and Germans who were commemorated. When Felix Bergmann, an Israeli scientist who had fled from Germany in 1933, visited Buchenwald in 1960, he was outraged at this omission and wrote a furious letter to Otto Grotewohl, the president of the GDR. The official reply written on behalf of Grotewohl by the head of the Committee of Antifascist Resistance Fighters blandly reiterated the official line. Bergmann wrote again even more pointedly, calling the official policy of the GDR "a frightful distortion of the facts. . . . The Jews came into the camps," he insisted, "as 'Jews,' as members of the Jewish people, and within the camps were fenced into special sub-camps, separated from the 'Aryans' of all the other lands and all the other peoples. And they were tortured to death with especially bestial methods and by being given especially low hunger rations. . . . Don't you know," he asked, "that in the extermination camps and in the gas chambers, side by side with the sons of your people, Poles, Ukrainians, and others were also active [in killing Jews]? It is truly a mockery of my people when you now declare that the 'Jews were deported and exterminated in the camps as Polish, Russian, Hungarian . . . German citizens.'" The GDR policy, he continued, "which refused to recognize the [Jews in the GDR as part of] Jewish nation" was a continuation of this historical misreading" and in Bergmann's judgment was "only a new form of brutality."[36]

Bergmann's protest had no effect on the party line, of course, and the communities continued their moribund existence. Two years later, when Peter Lust, a Canadian writer for a German-language newspaper, visited East Germany, his account of his visit to Buchenwald, where he had been guided by a Communist former inmate, confirmed Bergmann's fears. Lust writes about the heroic deaths at Buchenwald of Polish and Soviet resistance fighters. He also tells the legend of a four-year-old Jewish boy smuggled into the camp and saved by the inmates. But not a word about the tens of thousands of Jews from Germany, the Netherlands, Hungary, Romania, and elsewhere who died there or who, after 1942, were sent to certain death in Auschwitz. What he saw and was told was, of course, identical to what countless East German schoolchildren heard on their obligatory tours. Like Lust, these young East Germans came away with the heroism of the Communists under Nazi persecution confirmed and with no knowledge that Jews had been killed in these camps.

Lust remained throughout his visit a gullible journalist. He praised the efforts of the government to support the Jewish community: for example, its payment of modest pensions to the Jewish "victims of Fascism," after the age of sixty. This is enough, he wrote, parroting his guides, for them "to live simply." And that should be enough, he implied, for anyone in a Socialist state. Lust also noted that the government paid for the upkeep of the Jewish cemeteries and "took great care to rebuild temples and synagogues wherever the existence of a Jewish group made it feasible." He observed only in passing, however, in reporting a conversation with an old man, that the Jews could not get out of their country: "Israel?" says the man. "I would love to go there and finish my days in the Holy Land. But please don't write about it and if you do, don't give my name." His son adds, "How do we ever get there? We cannot even get to West Germany!" But Lust did not explore the implications of these restrictions. Ever the good guest, he concluded: "The religious congregations, far from being persecuted by the Government, are treated like rare specimens. . . . They are museum pieces, and the GDR government would like to keep them in existence as long as possible to prove to the outside world that it is indeed the most anti-Nazi government in Europe."[37]

In the cramped life of the Jews in the GDR, the East Berlin Jewish community was particularly hard-pressed in its search for legitimacy. Although it was the largest and the most visible of the Jewish communities, the East German Union of Jewish Communities refused to grant it admission because its executive committee had been hand-picked by the party. In fact, the East Berlin community was not admitted to the union until 1961—when a new chairman, Helmut Aris, himself an SED member, arranged for them to be taken in.[38] Tightly supervised by the government, the community could do little but offer its sycophantic congratulations to the regime on all notable anniversaries and to endorse its policies unquestioningly.

The control from the center affected every aspect of Jewish life in the East. As of January 1953 the Jewish community newspaper the *Allgemeine Jüdische Wochenzeitung*, which had originally circulated in all the occupied zones, suspended publication in the East in order not to endanger its subscribers. Just as in the Soviet Union, all books, newspapers, and periodicals from the West were forbidden. For a while the East Berlin community published a local bulletin, but it was superseded in 1961 when the central union began to issue a national quarterly magazine, the *Nachrichtenblatt*. The publication's cheerful and uplifting accounts of news made it suitable even for distribution abroad, and six hundred of the twenty-five hundred copies printed were sent to selected individuals and institution outside the GDR. Although it offered bulletins on Jewish life in other Eastern Bloc countries, it never published any news about Jewish communities in the West.[39] But its content was too banal even for East Germany. The minister of religious affairs protested at one point that the paper had to have more content than simply greetings and birthday congratulations. And even Peter Kirchner, the head of the Berlin community after 1971, echoed this complaint, adding that he had heard both from members of the community and from those abroad that "It travels unread immediately into the wastepaper basket. . . . Are we not responsible to our readers," he asked, "no matter where they live, for a little more?"[40]

The hand of the government was everywhere in Jewish life, not only in managing the affairs of the Berlin Gemeinde. In 1956, for example, the central union proposed to send eighteen children between the ages of six and fourteen to a vacation camp in Bavaria that had been organized by the Jewish Central Welfare Office in the West. This first application was denied by a brusque telephone call from the Ministry for Interior Affairs. In 1958 the communities applied again with a different plan: to establish a Jewish vacation camp within the German Democratic Republic. The government rejected this proposal as well, preferring to send the Jewish children to one of their own youth camps for Young Pioneers—the training ground for future Communist Party members. There the Jewish children would be permitted to organize a separate unit, but under the central supervision of the camp directorate.[41] By 1959 the Union gave up on its hope to send its children west. As the officers learned, the Central Committee of the Party was denying the application to send the children away in order to protect them "from the rising Fascism and anti-Semitism in West Germany." Realizing that even children were prisoners in their own country, the Jewish communities in East Germany then began organizing a vacation camp within the boundaries of the GDR, finally settling on Rügen, an island in the Baltic Sea, as its site. The program, which was acceptable to the regime because it followed the guidelines of the Young Pioneer camps, was permitted to add a Sabbath observance on Friday nights, as well as some instruction in Hebrew and the elements of Judaism.[42]

Until 1971 the Berlin community was directed by a government-appointed executive committee, headed by Heinz Schenk. Upon Schenk's death, Peter Kirchner, a longtime member of the Gemeinde, succeeded him. A doctor specializing in neurology and psychiatry, Kirchner was not a full-time administrator, but he did have the good fortune to arrive at a time when the political climate was changing and he could permit some modest enrichment to the dismal structure of Jewish life in East Berlin. It was not until 1976, however, that the first democratic elections were held in the East Berlin Gemeinde to choose an independent executive committee. Kirchner was elected chairman of the community—a post that he held until January 1991, when the long divided parts of the Berlin Jewish community were united after a separation of nearly four decades.[43] But when he took office in 1971, Kirchner felt that he was presiding over a literally dying community, with its 450 elderly members; by 1983 there were only 200. "I must concede," he said in an interview then, "that in view of the aging of our community, and the fact that there are few new-comers, in a few years we will have only a hundred members."[44]

Nonetheless, he was able to expand the activities of the Ge-meinde beyond religious services to offer a series of lectures on Jew-ish literature and history, as well as concerts of synagogue and folk music, in the crumbling Oranienburger Strasse headquarters. His wife, Renate, took charge of starting a Jewish library, which opened in 1977 with a stock of sixteen hundred books that gradually increased over the next decade to some five thousand.[45]

What is striking is how much of the conflict and anguish in the community's early history was elided in the reports for consumption abroad. In 1988 Kirchner, as head of the Gemeinde in East Berlin, contributed an essay on his community to a book about Jewish life in Berlin. Written just a year before the fall of the Berlin wall, it carries all the hallmarks of official party-line writing. The German Democratic Republic is still the best of all possible worlds, where only good things happen in a problem-free atmosphere.

In his account of the facilities for children, Kirchner writes blandly: "Every year the Union of Jewish Communities arranges a vacation camp for children during the summer months on the island of Rügen. This camp enjoys great popularity and at the same time permits contact among the youngest members of the communities in our land." Not a word here about the enforced origin of this camp or its bitter prehistory. He concludes his essay on a triumphant note: "Jewish people [N.B., not "Jews"!] who live in the GDR feel that in all matters they are citizens with equal rights in a state in which they live free of every possible anti-Semitic persecution and hostility, and where they can follow their religious desires. In accord with the religious freedom guaranteed by the Constitution, they are constrained by no restrictions."[46]

Yet in an interview a few years earlier, Kirchner glided over a major restriction in the lives of East German Jews. In response to a question about the relation of the Gemeinde to Israel, he replied as if he were reporting a privilege: "A number of members of our Gemeinde have relatives in Israel whom they may visit when they have reached the age of a pensioner." [47] The grief this ruling caused many East German Jews can be imagined. Helmut Eschwege, for example, received permission to visit his aged mother before he reached retirement age, but it came a week after she died. Eugen Gollomb, the head of the Gemeinde in Leipzig, whose parents, wife, and child, as well as seventy relatives, had been killed by the Nazis, longed to visit his only surviving brother in Israel. Impassioned letters to the authorities eventually brought him a visa—several weeks after his brother's death.[48] And these are only the stories of prominent members of the Jewish community. Peter Kirchner claimed not to be a member of the SED, but he could not have been a more faithful follower of its principles.

In its last decades, the Berlin community hardly presented a welcoming front to newcomers. It was a time when the search for "roots" had pierced even the Iron Curtain. Many young Jews or part Jews who had been brought up in ignorance of their ancestry by parents rigidly loyal to the party line were intrigued when they discovered this new dimension to their lives. But as Thomas Eckert, who came from such a family, described his attempt to join the Berlin Gemeinde, it was a discouraging experience. "I always knew," he said, "that there was a Jewish Gemeinde in East Berlin. I often went by the synagogue. But the Jewish Gemeinde in East Berlin . . . awakens the impression that here is a community that lives behind closed doors. It is extraordinarily complicated to be accepted by them. Sometimes one has the impression that they are a frozen, closed association because they have only very few members, all of whom have known one another for decades. For a young person, it is very hard to become part of this group."[49]

But Eckert was on his way out of the GDR, anyway, having submitted a formal application to leave. Others, who were staying, were more energetic in their efforts to bring some life into the ossified community. One of these was Heinz Rothholz, who carried on a remarkably free-wheeling life in the highly regulated world of the GDR. He had managed to become an independent entrepreneur, opening first a toy shop and then a craft shop, which he turned into a private art gallery. As a member of the executive committee of the Gemeinde, he wanted to arouse the interest of young people by offering cultural programs in connection with the Friday evening services. One of his most daring efforts was to sponsor the first slide show about Israel. "We did not allow our evenings to be disturbed," he said, "by the anti-Zionism, even when the Gemeinde at that time [in the 1970s] was very much against Israel."[50]

The changing cultural climate in the 1970s first became apparent in the churches. In the nearly twenty years since the revolutionary rigor of the Slansky period, a new generation had come to the fore. In the churches there was now an interest in "Christian-Jewish dialogue," and ministers and priests found it instructive to take their confirmation students to visit synagogues and acquaint them with Jewish religious practices. In addition a group of young activists based in the West named Action for Atonement enlisted many idealists who freely gave their time and labor to work on Jewish sites. In atonement for the sins of the Nazi generation, their projects included work on neglected Jewish cemeteries in the East—restoring headstones, clearing weeds and brush, and so on. These somewhat stylized encounters nonetheless broke the isolation of the Jewish communities, bringing them into contact with some of the less rigidly orthodox members of the Communist state, as well as with outsiders. It was also a time when religious groups began to take independent action.

Helmut Eschwege in Dresden, one of the earliest participants in the movement for Christian-Jewish friendship, was much in demand as a lecturer on Jewish history. He was part of the group Encounter with Judaism that was founded in Dresden by leaders of the Evangelical and Catholic churches. In Leipzig a group named Church and Judaism met annually; most of its fifty participants were theologians, priests, ministers, or interested students. The explorations by these groups of religious and historical themes took a political turn in November 1975, when the United Nations Assembly voted to endorse a resolution sponsored by the Eastern Bloc and the Arab states. The notorious resolution, which was actually a veiled attack on Israel, condemned Zionism as a form of racism. But in the GDR, it was promptly denounced by the Evangelical-Lutheran churches, a brave step in a country not accustomed to opposition.[51]

By this time, when both Jews and Judaism were practically extinct in the GDR, it became safe to revive Jewish culture. Eastern European folk musicians appeared, some of them not even Jewish, to play klezmer music before non-Jewish audiences. What gave these performances an eerie quality was that this was the music not of the German Jews but of the Jews from Russia, Poland, and Romania. Yet to non-Jewish German minds it filled the stereotype of Jewish folk music, which many Germans had never heard. These performances attracted large audiences of non-Jews, at once reverent, enthusiastic, and ignorant. At a festival celebrating Jewish life in the Ukraine, one in an annual series that began in 1982, the attentive audience, composed almost entirely of German-speaking Berliners, listened to a long speech in Yiddish by the editor of a Yiddish literary magazine in Kiev. It was grammatically flawless, but it might as well have been in Esperanto. It was as antiseptic as if he had rehearsed it from a phonetic transcription. The characteristic inflections, the music of Yiddish, its very soul, were gone. But he, too, was a museum object and was enthusiastically applauded.

One of the most successful of the new performers was Jalda Rebling, whose Dutch Jewish mother, a singer, and German father, both committed Communists, had survived the war in hiding in the Netherlands. Rebling was born in East Berlin in 1952 after her parents had settled in the GDR. Trained in the theatre, she later began to sing the Yiddish songs that had been in her mother's professional repertoire. Her work was officially fostered, and she reciprocated the support in her loyalty to the regime. In 1983 the Canadian sociologist Robin Ostow interviewed her in Berlin. Noting that Rebling's concerts of Yiddish music were often sold out months in advance, Ostow asked her who this audience was. Rebling's answer was totally irrelevant but totally correct politically. "Very many were very young, but there were also a number of elderly people. . . . Many of the young people were perhaps drawn to our performances in reaction to the revival of neo-Fascism, particularly in West Germany, in France, and in the USA." Her comments on a concert trip to Israel follow the same closed ideological pattern, describing a binary world securely divided between good and evil, the proletariat and the imperialists. "For us," she reports, "it was also important that we could tell the Israelis something about the GDR and in turn had the opportunity to report to our friends here something about Israel." But her political training has taught her to understand why the Arabs and the Israelis cannot live peacefully together. "That there is no peace there," she says firmly," is the consequence of the *divide et impera* [divide and conquer] politics of the colonial powers."[52]

Rebling was no less loyal to the Soviet Union, praising Birobidzhan, a province cynically established in 1928 by Stalin as a "Jewish homeland." There, she reported, on the basis of a report in the Soviet newspaper *Soviet Homeland*, "Yiddish is still a living language, [where] it is still taught and where Yiddish songs and books continue to be written."[53] But this was a fairy tale. The settlement of Birobidzhan began with the arrival of some 35,000–40,000 Jews in its first decade. The settlers were quickly disillusioned by their situation, and by 1939 only 18,000 Jews were left. By 1970 the number had dropped to 11,452. What Rebling could not know from the controlled press in the GDR was that the during the Stalinist purges of the 1950s many of the Jewish cultural leaders in Birobidzhan were attacked as "lackeys of Western bourgeois culture," the Jewish Museum was closed, its artifacts were dispersed, and thirty thousand Jewish books that had been in the public library were burned. Those who were arrested were beaten and jailed, and some were executed. By the time of the thaw in the 1960s there was very little in the way of Jewish culture or of a Jewish population to produce works of any meaning.[54]

But even in a totalitarian state the party line is not for forever. The GDR had broken off diplomatic relations with Israel in 1967, following the example of the Soviet Union, but this ultimately became a symbol of the GDR's self-isolation.[55] In his final years Erich Honecker, the last president of the GDR, cherished international dreams for himself and for East Germany. He began to tire of his subordinate role, which confined his foreign travels and grand receptions to other Eastern Bloc states. What he hoped for was to establish an independent place in the world for the German Democratic Republic and to emerge from his position as the head of a minor satellite state. He also hoped to expand the GDR economically by breaking out of the closed trade circle of the Warsaw Pact nations. This meant achieving recognition from the formerly vilified powers in the West. In particular, Honecker wanted a "most favored nation" status for East Germany as a trading partner with the United States and hoped that he himself would be invited to the White House. To that end, in January 1986 he played host to an eleven member visiting committee of the U.S. Congress. But despite several diplomatic conversations, matters proceeded no further.[56]

Although it may have suited the East German regime ideologically to allow the Jewish community to continue its museumlike existence in synagogues too large for their tiny numbers, it also began to emerge that if the government had international ambitions, it would have to change its treatment of its Jewish minority. What satisfied party orthodoxy only created mistrust in the West. The rationale for the tight travel restrictions, for example, as protecting GDR citizens from "neo-Fascism" were slogans that fooled no one in the West. What Westerners saw was that East Germans were kept closely confined and only rarely and arbitrarily accorded permission to travel abroad. When Helmut Aris, the head of the Union of Jewish Communities, was permitted to go to a meeting of the World Jewish Congress in New York, he complained that American Jews were extremely unfriendly to him assuming that if he had been allowed out, he must be a party functionary there to do its bidding.

As early as 1974 the U.S. Congress in dealing with the Soviet Union had tied the "most favored nation" trading clause to the demand that Soviet Jews be allowed to emigrate freely. Although emigration was not an issue (yet) in the GDR, it was clear to the ruling powers that now was the time to play "the Jewish card."[57]

Unfortunately, the government was trapped by its own propaganda and could only begin a quiet campaign of rapprochement. In 1980 the GDR began to normalize its relations with Israel, cautiously at first, with cultural and scholarly visits. In addition to the harmless exchange of dance and dramatic companies and literary readings, archivists and historians from Israel were even given access to selected archives in the GDR. One of the key events signaling the change in the party line was the invitation to Edgar Bronfman, the president of the World Jewish Congress and the head of the international corporation Seagram's, to visit the GDR in October 1988. With this contact, the regime hoped that Bronfman would smooth its way into trade with the West. As part of the festivities, Honecker presented Bronfman with the Great Star of Peoples' Friendship in gold. It was awarded, according to the citation, "in recognition of his great merits for the defense of justice in the world in the spirit of humanity and anti-fascism, for peace, friendship, and cooperation between peoples." In meetings following the awards ceremony, Oskar Fischer, the foreign minister, once again opened the question of trade with the United States and won from Bronfman a promise to use his influence for the East German cause.[58]

Erich Honecker, right, presents the Great Star to Edgar M. Bronfman. At left is
Israel Singer, general secretary of the World Jewish Congress. October 1988.
Bundesarchiv Koblenz.

While the government continued in its slow attempt to gain a place for itself on the international scene, it also began to pay attention to the remnant of a Jewish community still in East Germany. What animated this sudden interest was the belief that few as they were in number, the Jews in East Germany had wide international contacts— friends and relatives all over the world, some of whom exerted great power. Winning them over to the East German cause became a high priority. This idea, which had a very ugly resonance, particularly after the all-too-recent Nazi epoch, was nonetheless embraced by Honecker and his cronies. It may help to explain many otherwise inexplicable events relating to Jews in the last years of the German Democratic Republic.

One of the strangest of these events was the revival with government help of an Orthodox community. The revival began in the 1980s, when the "community" consisted of just two resident members, the father and son Offenberg. This community, which had been founded in 1869, had had a distinguished history in the seven decades of its existence. Beginning as a minority within a minority, the Adass Israel—the Congregation of Israel—had shared the frustrations of other Orthodox congregations in nineteenth-century Germany as the Liberal movement gained the upper hand in Jewish religious life, dominating the unified communities to which all Jews were required to belong.

The traditional practice of Judaism that had characterized German Jewish life for centuries was disturbed in the nineteenth century as Jews with a modern education, and especially those who were adherents of the Enlightenment, began to question the traditional liturgy and many Orthodox practices. They were motivated in part by a desire to reform Judaism by freeing the Law that governed every aspect of Jewish life from its later rabbinical excrescences. But they also wanted to modernize Jewish services according to a more Western

European model. By midcentury, the two thousand Jewish communities in Germany were largely dominated by this religiously Liberal outlook, which created serious problems for dissidents. But this was no private matter because the government preferred not to recognize these differences.

Even before the unification of Germany in 1871, the hegemony of Prussia spread over more and more of the previously independent German states. In its drive toward centralization, Prussia sought to regulate the internal life of its various religious communities. According to a law passed in 1847, all Jews in any given city were required to belong to the single Jewish community organized there and to pay taxes to support it.[59] Any attempt to leave the Gemeinde was interpreted as also leaving the religion.[60] This law was troubling to a small but vocal number of Jews at opposite extremes of Jewish practice. At one end were the members of the Reform movement, a group that held more radical views than the Liberals. In Berlin, for example, the small Reform congregation held its services on Sunday and disputed the need for circumcision.

At the other end of the spectrum were the Orthodox Jews, who were relatively few in number but strong in feeling. By 1914, in fact, only 10-20 percent of German Jews were enrolled in their ranks.[61] In the unified, overwhelmingly Liberal communities, the Orthodox felt not only that their special needs were not being met, but their taxes were being used to support activities of which they did not approve, such as building an organ in a synagogue. In Frankfurt, the birthplace of neo-Orthodoxy under the leadership of Rabbi Samson Raphael Hirsch, his followers preserved their independence by paying taxes in both the officially recognized community and in their own Orthodox congregation. Despite their shrinking numbers, the Orthodox saw themselves as the true standard bearers of Judaism, and immediately after the law of 1847 was passed, they began the struggle to achieve government recognition for their communities.

In 1876 they achieved their long-sought goal when the German national legislature passed the Secession Law, which permitted the Orthodox to leave the unified communities and carry on their religious and cultural life as they chose.[62] The life-giving aspect of this change was that they were also guaranteed a proportional government subsidy for the maintenance of their own institutions. Adass Israel in Berlin aspired to be just such a "secession community," but it achieved full government recognition of this status only in 1885, sixteen years after its actual separation from the unified Berlin Gemeinde.[63]

In the constellation of some one hundred synagogues in Berlin, Adass Israel maintained a unique and independent place. Beginning modestly with a small synagogue in the Gipsstrasse, in 1873 it founded the distinguished Rabbinical Seminary under Rabbi Esriel Hildesheimer. In 1904 the congregation moved to a new community complex in the Artilleriestrasse built to its own specifications, with the synagogue as the centerpiece of this grouping. It continued the old tradition of placing the reader's desk (the Bimah) in the center of the synagogue, with the ark for the Holy Scrolls on the east wall. There were 450 seats for men on the main floor and an additional 350 seats for women in a balcony that was faced with an iron latticework. The new complex also housed the rabbinical seminary, with its own small synagogue, a ritual bath, and apartments for the rabbi and several other administrators, as well as community offices. Although it was small compared to the Unified Gemeinde, with not more than 500 members at its height in 1913, it was nonetheless an intensely active community with a deeply committed membership. For its members Adass Israel provided not merely a place of worship

but also the daily support that observant Jews needed—such as en-
suring the supply of kosher meat, bread, and milk products, and even
a kosher food store. One former member of the community, Dr. Jacob
Levy, who had escaped to Palestine in the 1930s, wrote in his memoir
about the atmosphere in the synagogue. As a child he had felt how the
dignity and devotion of the congregation were heightened at holiday
services by the requirement of formal dress. "At that time," he recalled, "it was customary on ceremonial occasions to wear a top hat,
and indeed it made a solemn impression on the Sabbath when the
whole Gemeinde stood up and the rays of the sun, somewhat dimmed
by the stained glass windows, were reflected in the silky gleam of the
top hats."[64]

The congregation included among its leaders at that time not
only men of great learning in the Jewish religious tradition but also
some who had simultaneously entered the secular world. Prominent
among them was Abraham Berliner, head of the Adass Israel Gemeinde. He was a scholar whose work ranged from learned treatises
on Rashi and Onkeles to studies of Jewish life in the Middle Ages, a
monograph on the Jews of Rome, and biographies of important Jewish figures. Joseph Wohlgemuth, the founder of the Orthodox peri-
odical *Jeshurun,* who taught homiletics at the rabbinical seminary,
was also the author of many religious and secular works.

Dr. Esra Munk, who became the last rabbi of Adass Israel, took
up his post in 1899. But with the first Nazi boycott of Jewish businesses on April 1, 1933, he foresaw the desperate consequences of the
new regime and did not fail to let his congregation know. He took the
text for his sermon on that April day from the words of the Hebrew
hymn: "Let us return to the old ways." "My devoted listeners," he said
to his congregation, "let us not give ourselves over to illusions. The
times of old when we lived in tranquility and peace, and could carry
through our days in a secure society—these days will not return. For

us 'Return to the old ways' can only mean: Return to our old, original Jewish doctrine."[65] These pious words did not help in the face of the Nazi program, and the last synagogue service was held in the summer of 1941.

In addition to the formal members of the Adass Israel community, some 2,500 Jews on its periphery attended its functions and used its facilities on special occasions. In fact, during the interwar years, the synagogue in Artilleriestrasse was so crowded on the High Holidays with Jews newly arrived from Poland that its main aisle was called the "Polish corridor"—a reference to the strip of land taken from Germany and awarded to Poland by the Treaty of Versailles to give Poland access to the Baltic Sea. In 1930 the community opened a new group of schools in the elegant Hansa district of Berlin, including a primary school and separate high schools for boys and girls. A synagogue was also built into this new complex, which soon became a new residential center for the Orthodox Jews in Berlin who were members of Adass Israel. By the time the Nazis came to power in 1933, the community owned three synagogues, a ritual bath, its schools in the Hansa district, a cemetery, and a hospital. On the night of November 9–10, 1938, when most of the synagogues in Germany were torched, the two main synagogues of Adass Israel in the Artilleriestrasse and in Siegmundshof were untouched.[66] But the community did not escape: on November 10 the Nazis rounded up the teachers for deportation to concentration camps.

In 1939 all the Adass Israel property was confiscated by the Nazi government, and then after 1945 these holdings became the property of the successor government, the German Democratic Republic. In time the GDR turned the synagogue's property over to the Berlin Jewish Gemeinde (East), though this was largely a paper transaction, because the community had no use for what remained of these facilities. In fact, the old Adass Israel synagogue was remodeled into offices for a variety of GDR businesses, and the hospital was converted for use as the headquarters of the Deutsche Reichsbahn—the German railroad.

For four decades after the end of the war the community seemed to be extinguished, remembered only by its widely dispersed former members. The reemergence of a legally recognized Adass Israel in the last years before the collapse of the GDR owed its existence to the will of two men with wildly divergent purposes: Erich Honecker, the head of the state, and Mario Offenberg, a descendant of an Adass Israel family, who had grown up in Israel but moved to West Berlin to complete his education. How Offenberg became the beneficiary of Honecker's ambitions, assuming the leadership of a phantom Gemeinde, richly supported by the GDR, still remains in many ways unexplained.

In 1975 Offenberg completed his studies at the Free University in Berlin and presented his doctoral dissertation, titled "Communism in Palestine: Nation and Class in the Anticolonial Revolution." The anti-Zionist thesis proposed a union of Arabs and Jews against imperialism. For the next three years, Offenberg worked as a documentary filmmaker, screening his films about the conflict between Arabs and Jews in Israel at Leipzig film festivals. In 1977 the Palestine Liberation Organization gave him an award for his documentary *The Struggle for Land, or Palestine in Israel.*[67]

A decade later a very different Mario Offenberg appeared in East Berlin, now intent on reviving Adass Israel. Whatever old Adassianers still survived in East Berlin were well hidden. The result was that Mario Offenberg and his father, Ari, constituted the entire resident Gemeinde. But this was a crucial moment, for a portion of the old Adass Israel cemetery in Wittlicher Strasse was in danger of being used for a new building for the STASI. Although the cemetery was nominally in the hands of the Jewish Gemeinde (East), it had been neglected since 1974, when its single caretaker retired. Because the rear portion of the cemetery was not fenced in and the rest of the walls were crumbling, it had become easy prey for vandals. It was this seemingly unused rear portion that the Gemeinde in December 1982 sold to the Ministry for State Security, which planned to build offices and apartments there. In November 1985 Mario Offenberg claimed that during the war this area had been used for illegal Jewish burials and was therefore hallowed ground. His trump card in approaching Honecker, however, was the news that he had invited Adassianers from all over the world to come to a reunion in Berlin in June 1986. What Honecker did not want at this point was the report abroad of a neglected and vandalized Jewish cemetery.

What happened next was astonishing. In January 1986, by Honecker's order, the best resources in Berlin were galvanized to work on the cemetery. During a hard winter the craftsmen even brought in special warming devices to make possible the fine restoration work on the stone. By June the walls had been rebuilt, the gravestones righted, the brush cleared. When one hundred Adassianers arrived from abroad to visit their family graves, they saw only a well-tended cemetery, which was solemnly rededicated in their presence.[68] During this visit the surviving Adassianers and their descendants formed a new Society for the Advancement of Adass Israel in Berlin, whose purpose was the reestablishment of the Gemeinde and the reclamation of all its property.[69] They also gave Mario Offenberg their proxies authorizing him to continue his work.

But neither the West Berlin city government nor the Gemeinde in the West was willing to recognize the legitimacy of the Offenbergs or to acknowledge that *their* Adass Israel was the successor to the Gemeinde extinguished by the Nazis in 1939. After Offenberg's first brilliant coup in restoring the Wittlicher Strasse cemetery, the East German regime became more cautious about offering support. The Offenbergs retained a lawyer, Lothar de Mazière, to present their cause to the government. There was division, however, at the highest levels. While State Secretary Klaus Gysi wanted to recognize the new Adass Israel as the successor to the prewar Gemeinde, the Central Committee of the Party was unwilling to restore the "People's" property to private hands. In addition, the heads of the established Gemeinden, both East and West—Peter Kirchner and Heinz Galinski, respectively—made no secret of their view that Offenberg was an interloper and that the property of the old Adass Israel should not be turned over to his committee.

But all the principals were overtaken by history. On November 9, 1989, the Berlin wall fell and a new provisional government came into power in East Germany. By a great stroke of fortune, the new minister for religious affairs was none other than Lothar de Mazière. With a friend in a high place in the government, things began to go rather better for the Offenbergs. On December 14, 1989, the Council of Ministers of the newly formed government voted to restore all rights to the Adass Israel Gemeinde and offered it all necessary government help.[70] The following March, the council voted to support the Adass Israel Gemeinde with a budget of 810,000 marks for the year, including salaries for fifteen employees—among them three caretakers for the cemetery, a librarian, a Hebrew teacher, a rabbi, and a kosher slaughterer. Mario Offenberg retained the position of executive director.[71]

At this point two of the rooms in the old Artilleriestrasse complex (renamed Tucholskystrasse by the GDR) had been cleared and placed at the disposal of the new Gemeinde. Eventually the entire building was returned to Adass Israel, which reestablished the synagogue, restored the ritual bath, and began to build its communal life, hoping to attract Orthodox Jews from both East and West. The most significant source of new members were the Russian Jews who began arriving in increasing numbers as a consequence of the rising anti-Semitism and governmental chaos at home. When the East German

Entrance to the courtyard of Adass Israel, ca. 1987. The portal remains from the old building complex of 1904. Photographer Nicola Galliner, Berlin. Personal collection.

government in the spring of 1990 passed a resolution "to offer asylum to persecuted Jews," it encouraged them to pack up and leave. By February 1991 some four thousand had taken advantage of this offer.[72] Actively seeking out the newcomers, by the end of 1990 Adass Israel claimed two hundred members, most of them Russian immigrants.[73] As newcomers to the West, they needed an introduction into two cultures: the new German world in which they hoped to live and the old Jewish tradition, which many were discovering for the first time. Whether they would remain with the rigors of Orthodoxy as practiced by Adass Israel once they were established in Germany was something that would be resolved in the future.

Whether the current Adass Israel is finally determined to be the legal successor to the institution founded in 1869, there is no doubt that the modern congregation is of a very different order from the original, which was composed of scholars and those committed to the wholehearted practice of Orthodox Judaism; the new congregation is largely made up of those trying to find their way, and of newcomers to Judaism, learning its basic precepts.

The strained relations of Adass Israel with the Gemeinde of Berlin were resolved only in 1997, with the election of Andreas Nechama as head of the unified Berlin Gemeinde. Heinz Galinski, the head of the Gemeinde since 1949 and the implacable opponent of Adass Israel, had died in 1992. The change in leadership cleared the way for real changes to take place. In July 1997 the leaders of the two communities met and issued a statement of assurance that "in the future their relationship would rest on a basis of mutual respect, equality, and cooperation. . . . With this acknowledgment of Jewish pluralism," they continued, "may Jewish life in Berlin be strengthened in its religious, cultural and social spheres, and may it contribute to the enrichment of the spiritual and communal life in the German capital." This declaration was greeted with pleasure by old Adass members all over the world, and as Rabbi Lord Jacobovits, head of the Conference of European Rabbis, wrote from London, "This agreement will bring considerable relief to Jewish communities everywhere."[74]

After four decades of repression of Jewish life, the final and most extravagant gesture toward the Jewish community in East Germany by the Honecker regime was its reconstruction of the great New Synagogue in Oranienburger Strasse in all its former gilt and glory. The impetus was the approaching fiftieth anniversary of the Nazi pogroms of November 9–10, 1938. As a gesture to the past scholarship at Oranienburger Strasse, but also as a statement to the world affirming the honored place of Jews in the German Democratic Republic, in July 1988 the government established the Stiftung Neue Synagogue Berlin—Centrum Judaicum. Hermann Simon, vice chairman of the Berlin Gemeinde (East) was appointed the first director of this new research and archival center.[75] Among the treasures in the Centrum Judaicum is its portion of the old Central Jewish Archive. This archive, which began in 1904, collected papers documenting the history of Jewish communities all over Germany. After the end of the war, they were deposited in the Central Archives of the East German government. In 1950 one part was given to the Gemeinde in Berlin, and it eventually came to the Centrum Judaicum. Nearly four hundred communities are represented in the holdings of the Centrum Judaicum. Another portion was sent to the Central Archives for the History of the Jewish People in Jerusalem, and a small part to the Leo Baeck Institute in New York.[76]

The most expensive part of the restoration was the rebuilding of the facade and the entrance area of the synagogue. With the utmost care, bricks, stones, and carvings were rescued from the still-standing ruins and painstakingly numbered. Old plans, photographs, and architectural drawings were consulted, and ultimately the government

New Synagogue in Oranienburger Strasse, Berlin. In 1992 after its restoration.
Photographer Klaus Lehnartz. Landesarchiv Berlin.

invested some 85 million marks in the project.[77] Although the work had hardly begun, the rededication ceremonies took place on the fiftieth anniversary of Kristallnacht with the unveiling of a new tablet mounted on the wall of the synagogue. It read: "Fifty years after the desecration of THIS SYNAGOGUE and forty-five years after its destruction, it will rise anew, by our will, and with the support of many friends in our country and across the world. Jüdische Gemeinde Berlin. 9 November 1988."

The first reward of the careful sifting of the rubble came almost a year later. On October 19, 1989, workmen at the synagogue found the original Eternal Light that had hung in front of the Ark. A delicate silver lamp, first installed in 1866, it had been presumed destroyed with the rest of the synagogue. Malvin Warshauer, the former rabbi of the congregation echoed the prevailing feeling of wonder, seeing the discovery "as practically a modern Hanukkah."[78] The building was finally finished in December 1994, becoming once again a landmark of Berlin, with its three domes gleaming over the city in turquoise and gold. In the meantime, Honecker, the man who had started this project—for all the wrong reasons—had fled to Chile and had seen his government dismantled and his country united with West Germany. The German Democratic Republic was no more.

CHAPTER SIX

New Generations in Germany

ermany a half-century after the end of World War II is filled with echoes. Voices, images, languages ricochet across time, arousing unexpected and profound feelings. When the Jews in Germany look back on that half-century, they find it hard to recognize their earlier, displaced, anxious selves in the confident, well-organized community they have built. Yet at the start of the twenty-first century, they also face unexpected problems as Germany's economy faltered and its social fabric revealed some serious and ugly problems.

As we have seen, the Eastern European Jews, the remnant of the Saving Remnant, who decided to remain in the late 1940s, had a most tentative attitude toward their newly chosen home. That uncertainty, combined with an almost physical resistance to meeting Germans, determined a life with very clear social boundaries. As they said, they were living on their packed suitcases. In actuality, this metaphor meant that they were living as they had long been accustomed to live in Eastern Europe—among themselves. A few lines from the nineteenth-century writer, Max Hermann Friedländer, wonderfully convey this atmosphere. "They had learned by experience," he wrote, "the great art of living and existing without land or property, without house and home, without rights and freedom, without light and air."[1]

Two things had changed in that old equation: "rights" and "land." In postwar Germany the Jews were living in a state governed by law and not by the whim of a tyrannical ruler, and since 1948 the Jews, like every other people, had a land of their own—the State of Israel—to which every Jew had the "right of return." These factors were the basis on which the postwar Eastern European Jewish community in Germany could contemplate an existence in the most unimaginable of countries. Social integration with their neighbors was certainly the last thing they wanted. And the long ghetto experience of a life lived apart returned in Germany as natural and desirable. For these survivors, their sense of separateness was heightened as they felt themselves isolated even from their fellow Jews abroad who condemned them as pariahs.

What they had seen and experienced at the hands of the Germans dominated their dreams and their thoughts. But for the longest time the outside world did not want to hear about it. True unspoken comradeship and understanding, they discovered, could be found only among those who had shared their losses, their terrors, and their history.

It was not a sad world that the Eastern European Jews built in postwar Germany, but it was a shadowed one. They were absorbed in building lives and family. The shadows fell on their children. The parent generation knew very well how to live in *goles*—in exile. In many ways they were more comfortable in their new environment than their children were. They built a world inhabited by friends, relatives, and countrymen who spoke their language. And in this small world, they gathered together for protection and for the social comfort of community.

The younger generation had to invent a new way to be a Jew in Germany. The old prewar model, with acculturation as its ideal, was no longer appropriate. And even for the remaining German Jews the spell had been broken. Although they might still enjoy reading the German classics and might still live by the social mores of times gone by, their relationship with other Germans was now permanently edgy and problematic.

By 1950 the twenty thousand Jews securely settled in postwar Germany began to build a structure around themselves. As we have seen, two-thirds of these Jews were of Eastern European origin, and one-third were German-born Jews. But proportions differed from city to city. In Munich, for example, 90 percent of the members of the postwar Gemeinde were Eastern Europeans. In Berlin, where most of the Eastern European Jews had opted to be flown out of the D.P. camps during the airlift in 1948, the remaining settlement was made up largely of German Jews. Each community carried its own atmosphere, its own emphases depending on which element dominated. And these differences sometimes led to fierce struggles. In Cologne, when the first executive committee was elected after the war, the Eastern European Jews, who actually held a numerical majority, protested the results bitterly. The new executive could not "enjoy their confidence," they said, "because: no women were in the committee; no one was elected who had been in a concentration camp; not a single member of the committee was married to a Jew."[2] By 1950, under the pressure of court action, the community abandoned the old rules excluding noncitizens from voting rights and from holding office. By 1963 Julius Spokojny, a concentration camp survivor who had been born in Poland, was elected head of the community.

Outside their own carefully constructed world, Israel dominated the survivors' imagination. Its miraculous emergence as a nation, having been only a dream for millennia, was the great Jewish triumph in the postwar world. Many Jews in Germany harbored the thought that one day, when they felt financially secure enough, they would finally unpack their suitcases there. As time went on, families sent their children to Israel for a year of study, to serve in the army, or to work on a kibbutz, but also with the barely concealed hope that they would find Jewish mates. In the meantime they spent countless evenings listening to emissaries or newly returned travelers describing the wonders of the Holy Land. In the synagogue schools, the children were taught Hebrew and Israeli geography, as if to prepare them for future emigration.[3] And fund-raising balls, bazaars, and other events all ensured a steady flow of contributions for Israeli causes.

This little postwar world was very different from the complex society of a half-million Jews that had preceded it in Germany. Over the centuries this vanished community had built the synagogues and institutions that the new arrivals were now restoring. Although the ruins of this lost civilization were all around them, the remnant of Eastern European Jews had other preoccupations, other ways of being Jews. What was achingly missing in the first postwar decades were the intellectuals, both those who had ornamented Eastern European life at home and those from the German Jewish world who had been such striking figures in Jewish learning and on the German cultural scene. A few surviving journalists came back, among them Hans Habe, Karl Marx, Ernst Landau. The Marxist sociologists Max Horkheimer and Theodor Adorno returned to their institute in Frankfurt; actors and writers for whom the language was indispensable also returned. But most of these intellectuals did not enroll in the Jewish community. When the community in Hamburg built a new Jewish hospital in 1960, there were not enough Jewish doctors or nurses to staff it.[4]

Although the first generation of She'erith Hapletah had few professionals, it was an absence that was hardly noted. Starting over again in an essentially hostile atmosphere, the displaced Jews in postwar Germany counted themselves lucky to have found a safe base from which to earn a livelihood. They ran small factories or retail and wholesale businesses. Some were craftsmen, a handful resumed their professions as doctors or lawyers, and some, who became highly visible, speculated in real estate. Many hundreds had positions as functionaries in the reviving Jewish community centers. As early as 1946 the Berlin Gemeinde employed 540 people, of whom half worked in the community hospital.[5] For their social lives, Jews in postwar Germany expected to depend on one another. They lived alongside their German neighbors, but under social systems that were mutually incomprehensible.

Lea Fleischmann, who was born in 1947 in the D.P. camp Föhrenwald, became more and more aware, as she grew up in Germany, of the fundamental differences that marked even everyday happenings. In a memoir she compared the reactions of German and Jewish mothers to the commonplace event of a child falling. In response to the child's tears, writes Fleischmann, the German mother scolds her child: "Pull yourself together," she says, "and stop screaming." This "pull-yourself-together pedagogy," continues Fleischmann, "was alien to me. . . . If I fell and cried, then I was picked up and kissed from top to toe, hugged and consoled. The idea of toughening as a form of child rearing was unknown to my parents." Many Jewish mothers in Germany had lost their children in the death camps; it was no wonder, then, that they saw their postwar children as "tender plants," in Fleischmann's words, "to be coddled and protected."[6]

There is no question that Jews born to Eastern European parents in Germany after the war had more questions about their identity, about where they belonged, than did their parents, who by birth, language, and history, whether secular or religious, were indelibly members of Eastern European Jewish culture. Some of them had been snatched from it as children, but nonetheless it was the center from which every other identification flowed. Until the 1970s, in fact, they continued to publish a Yiddish newspaper in Munich which was distributed nationally. Where they made up the majority in the synagogues—as in Reichenbachstrasse in Munich and in Joachimstalerstrasse in Berlin—the old Eastern European melodies and order of service prevailed: no organs, none of the nineteenth-century Louis Lewandowski synagogue music so dear to the hearts of the prewar German Jews.

For their children born in the German Federal Republic, life began with a question. Were they Germans or Jews or German Jews or Jewish Germans? What had been enough for the first generation, for the Saving Remnant—the unshakable sense of self in a clearly defined universe—only left the second generation of Jews in Germany uneasy. They, too, were in goles, but exile had a different quality for them. They had absorbed German culture; they spoke the language; and ultimately 70 percent of them married Germans. The closed world of their parents, where Germans made rare appearances, was not for them.[7]

Yet few would claim to be, like the political scientist Michael Wolffsohn, "a German-Jewish patriot." Knowing very well how provocative such a formula is, Wolffsohn explained it very clearly. "What I mean by it is above all the citizens' pledge to support the general good of the Federal Republic—because it is a democratic German republic. Due to an aversion to the word 'patriot,'" he notes with a certain irony, "many people prefer 'citoyen.' Then it's French and above suspicion."[8]

Rafael Seligmann, a writer with a parallel history to Wolffsohn's, was also born in Israel to parents who had fled from Germany, and he returned in 1957 when he was ten. During a talk show in 1990 he asserted that he felt himself to be a German "and certainly a better German than people like Herr Schönhuber and his consorts."[9] "The reaction," writes Seligmann, "was divided. The audience applauded, but one of the Jewish members of the panel responded: 'With such a statement you are identifying yourself with twelve years of Nazism.'" Reflecting on this statement, Seligmann concluded that it illuminates "our dilemma as postwar Jews: the anxiety that by identifying with Germany we are denying our own Judaism and thus out of opportunism placing ourselves on the side of the perpetrator."[10]

There are still German Jews of the older generation who insist on the prewar formula that they are "German citizens of the Jewish faith." But in the tense and prickly Jewish community, these are few and fading voices, except for one. The most distinguished and surprising figure to lay claim to this old expression was Ignatz Bubis, the head of the Central Council of Jews in Germany from 1992 until his death in 1999—surprising, because Bubis was not clinging to a long-held German-Jewish tradition. Bubis was born in 1927 in Breslau (then part of Germany) to Russian Jewish parents. In 1935 the family moved to Poland, to the town of Deblin to escape the rising anti-Semitism in Germany. But the war overtook them, and Bubis was the only member of his family to survive. Because of the anti-Semitism in postwar Poland he moved to Berlin, where he began his new and successful life. In a book-length interview in 1993, he explained what he meant by invoking the old formula. He had used it, but with an expansion that gave it an entirely novel emphasis. "We are German citizens," he began, then adding a few important words, "with all their rights and duties and of the Jewish faith."[11]

All these varied formulations are actually alike in emphasizing the need for Jews to live in a state governed by law. But their citizenship and their obligation to defend this law did not affect their abiding identification as Jews. Bubis, a consummate politician, knew that very well when he took up the nineteenth-century slogan. He not only evoked the central intent of the major German Jewish defense organization but also reminded his readers of the age of the Enlightenment, when the Jews wanted nothing more than the right to be equal citizens with others in the country of their birth.

For most young Jews, however, the question of identity could not be resolved with a political or legal response. Unlike Jews born in Germany before Hitler, the children of the Surviving Remnant had no fond associations with the landscape, with the city streets they crossed every day on the way to school. Proverbs or nursery rhymes recited by their teachers did not arouse a warm sense of recognition. More often than not they were puzzling to children who heard different proverbs, different rhymes in a different language at home. When they passed the synagogue they were not reminded that this was where their parents or grandparents were married. Most of them, in fact, had never known their grandparents. And the tombstones in the cemetery did not carry the names of their ancestors or near relatives. At every turn they were reminded that their relatives were buried in unmarked graves, if they had been given the dignity of a burial at all.

The strange sense of not being part of the world where they had grown up led to a constant examination of the questions of home, of belonging, of language. Nor was this a silent generation. In essays, books, periodicals, and films, they not only examined their own feelings but also scrutinized with the eyes of the outsider the Germans among whom they lived. This time it was not, as the philosopher Gershom Scholem had said of his contemporaries—a disappointed, one-sided love affair. There had been no love affair, but only a wary watchfulness of the Other, together with a critical examination of the Self. "I benefit from the death of my people," wrote Richard Chaim Schneider, a young filmmaker, in his book on the Holocaust. "Is that right?

I have sought out this theme and it is [also] forced on me. By ancestry and birth. By reflection and observation. Everything is Holocaust."[12]

The feelings stirred up by the Holocaust were undoubtedly the main reason for the aversion in Jews abroad to the very thought of a Jewish community in Germany. When in 1985 the International Psychoanalytic Association met in Hamburg, for the first time on German soil, the organization treated this decision as a signal moment of reconciliation. In an article in the winter 1985 *Newsletter* of the association, Mortimer Ostow, a New York psychoanalyst, canvassed the situation under the question "What Should Our Attitude Be?" Ostow had already visited Germany and was able to speak from some experience. But he began at the beginning. "Since I was not a victim," he wrote, "I am not in a position to forgive. Nor," he added firmly, "can I forget." But Ostow understood his fellow Americans, especially the Jews among them: "A cost-free self-righteousness," he admonished, "is not a very helpful position." And that, of course, was exactly the position that too many American Jews had assumed on the rare occasions that they came to Germany.

Three years after the psychoanalysts met in Hamburg, Cynthia Ozick, an often controversial writer, published an article in *Harper's* magazine pugnaciously taking as her title the widely held view among American Jews: "Why I won't go to Germany." Like Ostow she also felt that she could not "stand in for the murdered Jews of Europe." And yet, of course, it is just this identification with the murdered Jews and the rejection of the living that prevented her from going to Germany and learning something from the survivors who had chosen to live there.

It was not, in fact, until 1993 that the first delegation of American Jews representing the United Jewish Appeal came to visit Berlin—and then only as a stopover on the way to Israel. Among their escorts was Geoffrey Hartman, then a professor of Comparative Literature at

Yale University. Born in Frankfurt, he had been saved because his mother sent him away to England on a children's transport in 1938. In preparing these very apprehensive visitors for Berlin, Hartman knew that they had been paralyzed by the images of the Holocaust. But he sought to move them forward. "We have come in hope," he said: "or rather to choose hope: to give a clear sign of our solidarity with the Jewish community in Berlin as well as in Germany as a whole, and to forge a stronger link between it, the UJA, and Israel. When I say we have made an important choice, I allude to the fact that this first, official mission to Germany comes very late. For there are still many in America . . . who are convinced they should not set foot in Germany, that even at this date reconciliation is premature."

And this was nearly fifty years after the end of the war. But Hartman understood that this trip to Berlin portended a real change of mood, a willingness on the part of American Jews to move beyond their own feelings to a consideration of the outside world. The UJA participants had not come to Germany to visit cemeteries or scenes of horror. Rather, "in coming to Germany," Hartman stressed, "our focus is on the Jews who are present, and very much alive."[13]

These were brave words, and undoubtedly moved those who heard them. But meanwhile, the glacier of worldwide Jewish distaste for the idea of a Jewish community in Germany has not even begun to melt. Unexamined and unexplained, it remains immovably part of the received opinion of world Jewry. It gained resounding confirmation in January 1996, when Ezer Weizman, the president of Israel, paid a state visit to Germany. In an interview with an Israeli newspaper during his visit, he declared that he could not understand how Jews could live in Germany and that they all belonged in Israel. Ignatz Bubis and other officials of the Jewish community responded to this affront, of course, but perhaps the sharpest reply came from one of President Weizman's own countrymen, who pointed out in the news-per *Ha'aretz* that Weizman had a lot in common with the right-wing extremists in Germany who were also demanding that the Jews leave. And finally, the writer reminded Weizman that although he was the president of all the Israelis, he was certainly not the president of all the Jews.[14]

Growing up, the second generation could not escape the knowledge that their fellow Jews abroad saw them with mixed emotions ranging from curiosity to condemnation, but simple understanding was in very short supply. At home, they were no less adrift. The world so carefully prepared by their parents twenty years earlier did not really fit. What was their Jewish culture when they no longer read Yiddish? What was their synagogue service when the practices of the shtetl seemed alien to them? One of the great weaknesses of the postwar community, in fact, was its lack of rabbis and the tradition of learning. The old rabbinical seminaries in Germany had long since vanished, and the communities were forced in their first years to import their rabbis from abroad, largely German Jews who had fled during the Hitler years. In a few cases where there were cohesive settlements of Polish Jews, they sought out rabbis who had been trained in the traditional Polish yeshivot. While it was true that attendance at Sabbath services in postwar Germany was low, counting only 4-5 percent of the Gemeinde members, the communities sought rabbis to fill more than the minimal role of leading services. They were needed at all the life-cycle events: births, deaths, weddings, bar mitzvahs. And even more important in those postwar years was the question of who was a Jew, compounded by the many applications from would-be converts. All these needed rabbinical adjudication. Yet as late as 1960 there were only seven rabbis in all of West Germany with Western academic training, and another four or five who were graduates of Eastern yeshivot.[15]

In 1979 the Central Council of the Jews in Germany took a first step toward solving this problem by establishing an institute for Jewish studies—the Hochschule fur Jüdische Studien—in Heidelberg. Although it did not offer a rabbinical degree, the Hochschule did train people to work in the Jewish community as social workers or teachers. For a rabbinical degree, students had to go abroad to a seminary of their chosen denomination. Unexpectedly, however, the school became a magnet for many non-Jews interested in Jewish life and culture so that Jews have became a minority of those enrolled. Of the 120 students in the year 2000, 40 were Jewish—at that, a proportion that was higher than in December 1992, when only 20 of the 125 students were Jews.[16]

The special summer courses at Heidelberg had a more intensely Jewish character than during the academic year, as Sonja Schmidt from Dresden discovered. The daughter of Helmut Eschwege, she had grown up without any Jewish religious training and had studied biblical Hebrew under the auspices of the Evangelical church. In 1989, after much bureaucratic delay, the state secretary for church affairs in East Germany granted her permission to attend the Hochschule for a two-week summer course which drew many Jewish students from abroad. "I was startled to discover," she reported, "how far removed I was from the Jewish identity that the others brought with them as a matter of course. I was particularly moved . . . by the relationship to the teachers. At the Technical University [in Dresden] I had experienced an authoritarian relationship between the teachers and the students. The freedom of the students there [in Heidelberg]—and also that one could discuss every everything with one's teachers—that was a great experience for me."[17]

With the arrival of tens of thousands of Jews from the former Soviet Union in the 1990s, the Hochschule suddenly took on a new function. Because the vast majority of these new arrivals were Jews in name only, with dim memories, if any, of Jewish life or tradition, the communities felt themselves responsible for providing the elements of a Jewish education to their new members and their families. In 2000 they established twenty stipends at the Hochschule for prospective teachers for the new Russians, to be drawn from the immigrants themselves.[18]

The Hochschule is, however, only one of the new educational phenomena in Germany as the Jewish communities add new services designed to intensify Jewish life: day schools for young children, high schools, youth centers, institutes, and courses in Jewish studies at the community centers. In Potsdam, the historian Julius Schoeps heads the Moses Mendelssohn Center, which has an ambitious program of seminars and publications on contemporary Jewish life. In 1998 it took under its wing the newly founded Abraham Geiger College, which opened in 2001 as the first rabbinical seminary to function in Germany since the end of the war. Founded under the auspices of the London-based World Union for Progressive Judaism, it continues the tradition of the Seminary for the Science of Judaism, which had flourished in Berlin under Leo Baeck until 1942. The new rabbinical institute accepts both men and women students as part of its Liberal program, a revolutionary change in the conservative religious scene in Germany.[19]

In contrast with the older generation, which was immersed in the organization of the community, broadening its services to its members, and building its relation to the government, the children of the postwar immigrants moved along a different path. As they reached the universities in the 1960s, they were drawn into the radical orbit of the student revolution that dominated the atmosphere and disrupted the classrooms. Activism attracted many Jewish followers because the various movements not only professed noble aims but also attacked the everyday injustices that agitated the students' lives: authoritarianism in the universities, discrimination against women, and the "materialism" of the West Germans—a theme very popular among students, whether poor or middle class. Their devotion lasted until the 1970s, when many of the Jewish followers suddenly realized that they themselves had become targets of the Left.

Hostility erupted in 1967 after the Six-Day War in Israel when the student Left declared itself on the side of the "Palestinian Revolution in its anti-imperialistic struggle for freedom." A Maoist group even advocated violence against the Jews in West Germany and did not hesitate to spread anti-Semitic propaganda.[20]

A brilliant and controversial spokesman for disappointed Jewish leftists was the journalist Henryk Broder, who was born in Poland in 1946 and brought to Germany by his parents in 1958.[21] At the university he was just in time to join the radical movements that dominated student life. But by the end of the 1970s, having experienced the Left's response to the Six-Day War, he was disillusioned with his former comrades. He published his conclusions in March 1981 in a devastating article in *Die Zeit:* "You Remain the Children of Your Parents." There came a moment when he realized that the "alternative" way of life devised by the students was no less compulsive in its disorder and ideology than the compulsive orderliness of the bourgeois households out of which these students had come. In these households, said Broder accusingly, the students had absorbed the prejudices of their parents without even realizing it. Even more significant was their total submission to Marxist-Leninism, which had blinded them to the murderousness of the Stalin regime. The final betrayal, for Broder and many other Jews, was the unquestioning acceptance by the Left of the Soviet condemnation of Israel and of Zionism, and with it, all too lightly veiled, a strong dose of anti-Semitism.

In his article Broder painstakingly demonstrates how the Left descended to this vile condition. He shows two caricatures, one from the Nazi magazine *Der Stürmer* for 1943 and the other from a Soviet newspaper, *Gudok,* in August 1973. Each shows the identical figure, a fat Jew recognizable by his hooked nose and with a six-pointed star on his vest. In the *Stürmer* drawing he is shown sitting on a throne and the caption reads "The Ruler of the World." In the Soviet caricature, his vest, stretched over a big belly, carries the legend "International Zionism," with two pendants on his watch chain, one for Israel and the other for South Africa.

"I only want to concern myself here," Broder writes to his former comrades, "with one point in your racial reservoir, one that affects me in particular: your anti-Semitism. That a Leftist . . . cannot be an anti-Semite, because that is the domain of the Right, is a much cherished lying excuse to which you cling . . . a further excuse for the poverty of your historical knowledge. I would bet that the names of Slansky and Rajk mean nothing to you, nor the Doctors' Trials of 1953." Broder's long and detailed list of particulars in his condemnation of the Left ends with a declaration that he intends to leave Germany and emigrate to Israel. In his summary statement, "Why I Am Going"—*Warum Ich Gehe*—he describes how the Left's lack of understanding for the position of the Jews had finally made his life in Germany intolerable. "The leftists here in this country," he concludes, "have reflected very fundamentally on many topics: about the position of the Left in a constitutional state; about women in a society dominated by men; about workers in the capitalist system; about art and commercialization. Only how the Jews feel amid the hostile uproar of the Left, living in a post-Auschwitz landscape—this is a question that has never occurred to them."[22]

Not many Jews chose to follow the extreme example of Broder and Lea Fleischmann in abandoning Germany. But Broder's manifesto in *Die Zeit,* followed by additional books and articles, helped to awaken some Jews from their naive infatuation with Marxism. The fall of the regimes in East Germany and then the Soviet Union and its satellite states brought an end for most to that romance.

The new Jewish organizations that sprang up in the 1970s and 1980s reflected a distinction that Julius Carlebach, director of the Heidelberg Hochschule for Jewish studies, once made. "The main problem of Jews in Germany," he observed, "is that they want to be Jews, but not Jewish."[23] Feeling that the officially organized communities did not really represent them, in either interests or age, many of the young Jews sought more informal ways of meeting and learning about their heritage. These "Jewish Groups" preferred the private to the official in the celebration of holidays, joining with other families and inventing new personal forms. The historian Marion Kaplan has called these practices a move in the direction of cultural Judaism, where connectedness and personal participation is prized above the strict observance of formal religious ritual. By the mid-1990s branches of these Jewish groups had been established in Frankfurt, Berlin, Cologne, Hamburg, Munich, and Düsseldorf.[24] Their great appeal for their members is their spontaneity and the way they reflect both the members' origins and the problematic history of the country in which they lived.

In East Germany the first tentative steps toward self-examination and learning came with the formation of the group *Wir für Uns*— We for Ourselves—which was originally loosely attached to the Gemeinde but whose purpose was study and discussion rather than prayer. The biophysicist Käte Leiterer, who was born in 1943, joined when the group was formed in 1984. As she described it: "At the 'Wir für Uns' group, I had the feeling that talk proceeded in a discerning and intelligent way about issues. Interesting people with interesting ideas meet here and one can enjoy oneself considering these ideas together. And that's why I went." But as time went on, the Gemeinde began to pressure the free-floating members of the new group to join. Leiterer found this demand "repellent, especially because I had felt myself on such intimate ground and so much at home."[25]

Vincent von Wroblewsky, another member of the group, had a political interpretation of its tense relation with the Gemeinde. To begin with, he reported, the Gemeinde welcomed the new group, hoping ultimately to bring these nonreligious Jews into the community. "On the other hand," he noted, "it was naturally a problem for them, even a threat, because these were mostly younger people and more dynamic than those in the Gemeinde. The group compromised them also as regards the outside world, because the Gemeinde shared the official GDR definition that Jews were adherents of the Jewish religion. . . . And that naturally left us out. We could not accept [that definition] because we had a Jewish self-consciousness without being religious. This was exactly our problem: What is it to be Jewish when it is not only a matter of religion?"[26]

Leiterer and Wroblewsky were not alone. Other nonreligious Jews were also looking for a Jewish affiliation based on ethnic or cultural affinity rather than the strict religious commitment that the Gemeinde in East Germany required. One of the unexpected pendants to the opening of the Berlin wall on November 9, 1989, was a reorganization of Wir für Uns, which now felt free from the Gemeinde. In December a group of five members who had objected to the Gemeinde's demands for membership met to organize a Jewish cultural group that would be broad-based and nonreligious. The Jewish Cultural Union, as it was called, would be open, as one of its organizers put it, "to people who biographically have some relationship to Judaism."[27] This was aimed at the Gemeinde's strict classification, following Orthodox Jewish law, that only the child of a Jewish mother was a Jew. Broadening the definition opened the door for many others to come in.

Irene Runge, who subsequently became the leading force in the Jewish Cultural Union, joined it immediately after its founding. She had been born in New York City to German-Jewish parents in 1949. When she was ten, her parents, who were distressed by and perhaps fearful of the consequences of McCarthyism, decided to return to East Germany. Once in Berlin, her father was given a job in the Ministry of Information as an editor and writer for radio. In the secular atmosphere of her parents' home, Runge got to know many of East Germany's leading intellectuals, as well as visitors who were survivors of the concentration camps. Her growing interest in Judaism and also her support for Soviet Jews is reflected vividly in the Jewish Cultural Union. The group has made strong efforts to attract the Russian immigrants who have been coming to Berlin in ever greater numbers since the 1970s. Although the Cultural Union started without any religious affiliation, by 1996, with three hundred members, it arranged for regular visits from two Orthodox rabbis. The union began to sponsor services at the holidays and offer classes in the Bible and other sacred texts. Among its advisers are rabbis from the Chabad, the missionary arm of the Hasidic sect known as the Lubavitchers. These services are so far removed from what the secular Russian Jews have experienced that they almost have the quality of Jews watching other Jews perform, especially as otherwise independent women find themselves relegated to the back of the room.[28]

Vadim Isaakow, a Russian Jew who joined the union in 1996, was rather bemused in reporting his participation in the religious services. "In Moscow," he wrote, "I went to the synagogue only very rarely. Here I go almost every Sabbath. Not so often to the Jewish community— the Gemeinde—where they are very cold and unfriendly toward newcomers. I really feel comfortable [at the Union], very much accepted. They have no real synagogue, but frequently they have a rabbi over from New York from the Lubavitch community. These Hasids are very orthodox and I am not, obviously, I couldn't [be]."

Isaakow becomes then, in his religious life, as in its secular aspect, a witness to the lives of others who are rooted in their religion or in their country. This poignant sense of loss has afflicted refugees of every generation and every nation. When a Berlin Jew who had fled Germany in the 1930s returned for a visit after the war, he was deeply affected by a walk on Tauentzienstrasse, which had been the main shopping and promenade boulevard in his youth. On weekends, he recalled, people had strolled on the boulevard and greeted one another, flirted a little and, as he put it in three short words: *"Man war wer"*—One was somebody. What overwhelmed him on his return was that he could no longer find anyone who knew him. Vadim Isaakov copes with the same sense of anonymity, using almost the same words. "I came here and refound my Jewish identity," he says, "but doing so I lost my position in society. In Moscow I was someone, here I am no one."[29]

After years of suffering a dearth of rabbis, the Jews in Germany are now being besieged by representatives of Jewish denominations from abroad, ranging from the most liberal approach—Reform Judaism, as it is known in the United States—to the most conservative, the Lubavitcher Hasidim. With a new and powerful missionary movement, the once-closeted scholars of the Lubavitch movement now seem to be blanketing Germany with emissaries and services designed to teach their form of Orthodox Judaism.

In dramatic contrast to strict Orthodoxy, with its myriad minutely defined observances, the women's movement has added a bold dimension to the search for how to be Jewish in Germany. Running counter to the Orthodox practice, in which women have no role in the public services and do not even count in making up a quorum of worshipers, the women's movement has fostered "egalitarian services," promoted the religious education of girls, and encouraged women to aspire to the rabbinate.

Showing the special vitality of a grassroots organization is the Bet Debora movement, whose founders define it as "a place of encounter and of learning, a spiritual centre." Its first conference, held in Berlin in May 1999 was designed to bring together "European rabbinically educated and interested women," and gave young women rabbis, cantors, lay preachers, and other community workers an opportunity to meet and exchange experiences. In Germany there is only one woman rabbi, Bea Wyler, who is based in Oldenburg but also serves the communities of Braunschweig and Delmenhorst. Born in Switzerland and ordained at the Conservative Jewish Theological Seminary in the United States, Rabbi Wyler has emphasized that much of her work involves teaching her congregation the fundamentals of Judaism. This very newness of Jewish observance, repeated all across Germany, almost guarantees a freshness of approach and a reinvention of Jewish practices.

As the organizers of Bet Debora state very openly, "We are three women living in Germany, in the country which nobody imagined would give rise to an authentic Jewish life again. . . . We were tired of being told time and again about what was lacking in this place, what was assumed to be impossible in this place, because we had lost knowledge of the tradition. . . . We wanted to do something. Each of us had learned, had acquired Jewish knowledge, each had tackled her own fragmentary Jewish family history, a painful task, leading however to one result: Here we are and here we will stay for good." In confining the guests to European women and some men, the organizers indicated in no uncertain terms what they did not want. "We did not want to model ourselves yet again," they wrote, "on situations abroad, and we did not want to be lectured by Jews from the USA or Israel about what our Judaism was to look like."[30]

Amid all the uncertainty about ritual, liturgy, and simple education, some descendants of a class of Germans defined by the Nazis as "Christian 'non-Aryans'" are also attempting to find their way back to the elusive Jewish element in their heritage. As we saw in Chapter 3, the Nazis, with their minutely divided racial categories, were able to place more than 300,000 people in this class. Their children and grandchildren are still wrestling with the consequences of these classifications. The sociologist Franklin A. Oberlaender, who has done the definitive study of this group, has called them "orphans in history" and has discovered that while they are not, on the whole, storming the Jewish communities for admission, their special history has left them with strong anti-German feelings. Many of these descendants of the "Christian 'non-Aryans,'" he discovered, were marrying outsiders as a "diffuse protest against everything German." They tended to choose neither German Christian nor Jewish partners, but rather Turks, Arabs, Africans, or African Americans.[31] They remain permanently attracted to Jewish life, however, and attend public events at the Gemeinde centers in significant numbers. In 1996, when Oberlaender spoke at the Gemeinde in Berlin, the room was filled with perhaps eighty people who were exactly the ones he was writing about. Many of those who stood up to speak echoed the phrase used by their parents or grandparents *"Wir aber sind nicht Fisch und nicht Fleisch"*—We are neither fish nor fowl—and described with great emotion their sense of disorientation in a society that still drew sharp lines between its subgroups.[32]

On the official level, the institutionalization of the memory of Jewish life in Germany and the remembrance of the Holocaust have become overwhelming parts of the landscape and of public discussion. In Berlin, where there has been extended controversy on an appropriate Holocaust memorial, it has been suggested that perhaps the best memorial might be an endless debate. Countless small towns whose Jews have vanished have restored the still-standing synagogues for use as museums or other ceremonial purposes. Others have published extensively researched studies of the Jewish communities that once existed in their midst, the writers sometimes searching across the globe to track down every single surviving member for a biographical entry. In Frankfurt, Fürth, Munich, and elsewhere, handsome museums commemorate the history of the Jews who once lived there, with extensive explanations of Jewish ritual and religious customs for the mostly non-Jewish visitors. And in a particularly dramatic gesture, the city of Osnabrück commissioned a museum dedicated to the painter Felix Nussbaum, who was killed in Auschwitz in 1944.

Berlin's Jewish Museum, which opened in 1933 in a building on Oranienburger Strasse adjoining the New Synagogue, was closed by the Nazis in 1938. Since the war, the contents of the museum have been lost, and its picture collection, which did survive, has been scattered across the world.[33] In the postwar years artifacts that had been rescued or rediscovered were exhibited in a few rooms of the Berlin Museum and in the Martin Gropius Bau, the former Decorative Arts Museum, both in West Berlin.

By 1988, with the Berlin Museum running out of room, a competition was advertised to design an extension which would provide 44,500 square feet of new exhibition space, of which about a third was designated for the Jewish section of the museum. The winner, in a field of 189 entries, was the American architect Daniel Libeskind, who, following the design requirements, allocated only the ground floor of his building to the Jewish section.[34] The foundation stone was laid in 1992, and the building was formally opened for viewing—empty—in January 1999. But by this time the director of the Jewish Museum, Michael Blumenthal, began to have doubts about the plan. Appointed as the second director of the museum in November 1997, Blumenthal is a native Berliner who had fled with his parents to Shanghai to escape Hitler. In 1947 the family emigrated to the United States, where Blumenthal had an illustrious career. Among other posts, he held a professorship of economics at Princeton University and an appointment as secretary of the treasury in President Jimmy Carter's cabinet. By the time the museum was finished, Blumenthal had resolved that it not be divided. With its powerful sculptural qualities, it needed to be organized as a whole.

In 1998 Blumenthal was able to persuade the Berlin Senate that the new building in its entirety should be devoted to a Jewish Museum. And by the year 2000 the Senate also agreed to add the original baroque building of the Berlin Museum to the new Jewish Museum.[35] Even before its official opening, Libeskind's building had become a landmark in Berlin, with its striking zigzag design, its bright metal cladding, and its insistent reminder to the visitor of the Holocaust with its seven "voids"—one ninety feet high—and its intermittent black walls. To Libeskind these "voids represent Germany's post-Holocaust cultural vacuum."[36] Before the staff could place a single artifact in the exhibition areas, the museum began to draw thousands of visitors who wanted to tour the empty building. In its first twenty months after completion, 330,000 people came to see it. With its somber design, it has even been suggested as a Holocaust memorial just as it stands, without exhibits or artifacts. This sentiment is perhaps an attempt to ward off the official Berlin Holocaust memorial, which has had a controversial history.

The many voices that have spoken for the memorial, about it, or against it are a measure of the still-unresolved place of the Holocaust

The Jewish Museum in Berlin, designed by Daniel Libeskind. The columns in the foreground compose the "Garden of Exile." Photographer Klaus Lehnartz. Landesarchiv Berlin.

in German life. The proposal for a monument began significantly enough in 1988 with Lea Rosh, a television personality who, despite her Jewish-sounding name, is not Jewish. Her Initiative Berlin, backed by a Sponsors' Club for the Construction of a Memorial to the Murdered Jews, proposed that Berlin build a memorial on the site of the former Gestapo headquarters. The proposal, once made, was like a genie that could not be crammed back into its bottle and left Berlin struggling with the question of what to do about it.

What had seemed at first an eccentric personal whim suddenly became a political issue. Where was the politician who would risk opposing it, who would want to offend the Jews in Germany, in the world, by opposing a memorial to the dead? As many journalists have pointed out, Germany is in the unique position of raising memorials to its own victims.

In 1994 the regional government of Berlin finally opened a competition for a memorial and was flooded with 528 designs. The winning entry called for a concrete "Gravestone" the size of a football field, on which would be engraved the names of the six million Jews who had been murdered by the Nazis. It would have cost 15 million marks. Although the design in its scale and aesthetics confirmed the worst fears of the doubters, who hoped for something more human and less monumental, it won the backing of Rosh and her Sponsors' Club. But now with something tangible before them, the opponents mounted a fervent campaign in newspapers and magazines outlining the reasons for their opposition and offering alternatives. In addition to objecting to the design, critics asked why other persecuted groups were not also being remembered: the Sinti and Roma (Gypsies), the Russian war prisoners, the homosexuals, the mentally and physically disabled who were among the first victims of the Nazis. Others were concerned about the cost, pointing out that the former concentration camps Sachsenhausen and Buchenwald, which now provided important educational programs for schoolchildren, were vastly under-financed.

In the face of so much opposition, in 1997 the donors of the design prize, which now included the national Bundestag and the city of Berlin, as well as Rosh's Sponsors' Club, decided to run a second competition. This time, the field was limited in advance, and only twenty-five entries were offered to the judges. In a long, drawn-out process of decision making, the winner was a joint entry by the American architect Peter Eisenman and the sculptor Richard Serra, which they titled "Field of Memory."

But their design aroused no popular enthusiasm, instead becoming the source of constant discussion and controversy. In essence their plan called for undulating rows of concrete stele, four thousand in all, each eight feet high, filling a square block near the Brandenburg Gate. The Sponsors' Club offered to provide a third of the necessary money.[37] Then Chancellor Helmut Kohl, who favored the design, asked for two changes: that the height of the stones be reduced to about four feet and their number to about twenty-five hundred. Eisenman accepted these modifications, but Serra resigned from the project in protest.

As a national election neared, the final decision about the memorial was postponed, and it received a further setback from one of its three sponsors. In June 1998 the mayor of Berlin, Eberhard Diepgen, declared that he opposed building the memorial and turning Berlin, the new capital of Germany, into the "capital of repentance." At the same time, he maintained that the proliferation of memorials would only lead to "a deadening of the senses of the observer."[38]

It was not until January 1999, with the new Social Democratic government in place, that final modifications were made on the Eisenman plan. Led by Minister for Culture Michael Naumann, the government's changes included a further reduction in the number of stele to between eighteen hundred and twenty-one hundred. The area thus freed would be used to build a "house of remembrance," an archive, and an information center, as well as providing further exhibition space.[39] In March 1999 the Bundestag declared that the final decision on the monument lay within its authority, and in June the Cultural Committee of the Bundestag presented two new proposals for a vote: the Eisenman design and another by the theologian Richard Schroeder for a simple memorial stone with the inscription: "Thou shalt not kill." In the final vote on June 25, 1999, the Eisenman plan won in a sharply divided legislature, although with a reduced house of

Model for the Holocaust Memorial in Berlin, by Peter Eisenman.
Photographer Klaus Lehnartz. Landesarchiv Berlin.

remembrance. The count showed 314 representatives for the Eisenman proposal and 209 against.[40] Mayor Diepgen remained true to his principles and refused to attend the groundbreaking ceremony in January 2000.

Although the controversy about the Holocaust memorial has occupied more than ten years, it is not as if Berlin has tried to hide its past. Dotting the city are a variety of memorials, which often take the visitor by surprise. In the pleasant area of the Bayerische Platz, with its colorful gardens and radiating shopping streets, for example, are eighty signs affixed to the lampposts, each one detailing, with words on one side and a symbol on the reverse, the regulations that increasingly constricted the life of the Jews under the Hitler regime. Installed in 1993, the memorial was intended to commemorate the six thousand Jews who had lived in that neighborhood and had been deported by the Nazis. The earliest notice, dated March 18, 1933, begins by depriving a whole class of Jews of their livelihood. It states that "Jewish lawyers and notaries may no longer appear in court cases in the city of Berlin." The last, issued on February 2, 1945, as the Russians were approaching Berlin, is in a totally different vein. It warns all citizens: "Files containing information of anti-Jewish acts are to be destroyed."[41] And in between is a sampling of the regulations large and small that gradually transformed the remaining Jews from citizens to marked targets for abuse.

On the site of the demolished Levetzow Strasse synagogue, from which thirty-five thousand Berlin Jews were deported to their deaths, the passerby sees a playground, and at its edge a tall, pierced-metal screen, on which are listed every transport, its destination, and the number of Jews it took away. Leaving nothing to the imagination, on the street itself is a full-sized concrete replica of a boxcar. A much simpler reminder at Wittenberg Platz, the heart of Berlin's shopping center, is a stark black and gold sign listing the death camps, with the legend "Sites of terror that we must never forget." And then, totally unexpected, are the bronze plaques in Kreuzberg, in northeast Berlin, set in cobblestones in front of the homes of former Jewish residents, each bearing the name of those who had been deported to their deaths.

Equally surprising is the remembrance at the subway station of the Hausvogteiplatz—the prewar center of the garment-manufacturing district in Berlin. As the passenger comes to the exit, he sees a bronze plaque affixed to each riser of the twenty-eight steps leading to the street, each with the name and address of a Jewish firm that had once operated in the district. On the street level, he is confronted with three long mirrors, alluding again to the vanished fashion industry, and bronze plaques in the sidewalk tell its story. "Under increasing pressure, the Jewish owners were driven out of their firms or forced to sell them to Aryans," the legend states. "And thus, the tradition and the economic significance of this, the second-largest industry in Berlin, was permanently destroyed. The Jewish owners and workers in the Berlin clothing industry were driven to emigrate or were deported to camps where they were murdered."

In the residential suburb of Steglitz, a reflecting wall of polished steel was erected in 1995, but not before some of the ugly undercurrents of contemporary German life had displayed themselves. The wall, which is some thirty-three feet in length and ten feet high, lists the names, addresses, and birthdates of each of the two thousand Jewish residents of Steglitz and the neighboring suburbs of Lankwitz and Lichterfelde who were deported. The architects describe their work as having an interactive quality: "Only a few of those named have survived," they wrote in their presentation essay.

> Engraved into this "flood of names" on every third panel are texts and pictures relating to Jewish life past and present. One of these panels contains a chronicle of the Steglitz Synagogue. . . . In the wall are mirrored the heavens, trees, birds . . . and human occupations, the market, traffic. . . . The observer of the wall is himself mirrored in the steel plates. He is confronted with the past and the present. The reaction of the observer can range from offering a bouquet of flowers to smearing the wall with Nazi slogans. In this way the past becomes the mirror image of the present. Every flower, every insulting slogan becomes a part of the memorial.[42]

This project did not have a smooth passage through the local council. It faced, in fact, an unholy alliance of the conservative Christian Democratic Party (CDU) and the Free Democratic Party (FDP) with the far-right Republicans, who made a counterproposal to reduce the monument to a panel twenty-one feet long. When the artists resisted this suggestion, the CDU offered a "compromise" to abandon the idea of the wall entirely and simply affix a plaque to the wall of the surviving synagogue.

By now the controversy had drawn international attention, and the chairman of the Building and Housing Committee of the Berlin City Council, Wolfgang Nagel, intervened to save the project. With the help of the city of Berlin, the Reflecting Wall was finally built as designed and unveiled in June 1995. But as Hermann Simon, the director of the Centrum Judaicum, has written: "There remains the unpleasant aftertaste of an 'imposed' memorial."[43]

Jewish life in Berlin proceeds on many levels. The memorials we have discussed were not, after all, the work of the Jewish community but of local, city, or national governments, a part of the unending reflection in Germany on the twelve years of Nazi rule. Within the Jewish community the major concern in the last decade of the twentieth century was not the past, but how to cope with the powerful new wave of immigration of Jews from Russia that in numbers, at least, overwhelmed the 35,000 Jews settled in Germany. Between 1990 and 1998 some 100,000 Jews from the former Soviet Union emigrated to Germany, encouraged by the special conditions of the Refugee Quota Law. In 1991 the heads of the federated German states had agreed to accept Jewish immigrants from the Soviet Union on the basis of the Geneva Refugee Treaty. The "quota" referred to the proportional allocation of the new arrivals to the various states in Germany. This agreement gives the immigrants the right to live in Germany without any time limitation. It also gives them the right to work and help in furthering their education.[44] Although some of the immigrants remained in Germany only temporarily, some of the smaller Jewish communities have discovered the radical effect the influx of Russian Jews can have on the makeup of community membership. The leaders of the Düsseldorf Jewish community bravely welcomed the arrival of young immigrants "even if it means that the language of the Gemeinde becomes Russian."[45]

When these immigrants talk about why they left, it is clear that seventy years of Communism did not dim the long-held anti-Semitism in the Soviet lands. At times, as during the Stalin era, it received official and murderous support. In less bloody times, the prejudice was exercised to restrict the lives of Jews. It kept them from places in the university, it excluded them from jobs, and it held them back from professional advancement. Jewish identity was hard to hide in Russia, as we know, because the internal passport carried information on nationality on the notorious "fifth line." Here we come to the first of a series of paradoxes. Many Jews, well aware of the discrimination that faced them if they identified themselves accurately, entered "Russian" on the fifth line. Children of mixed marriages, for example, could choose at the age of sixteen which nationality they wanted to adopt. Others took more drastic measures, destroying family papers that could reveal their Jewish origin. In the postwar years survivors of the death camps who no longer had any papers would frequently adopt a new "Russian" identity when they acquired their replacement passports. But then when they wished to emigrate as Jews in the 1990s, they had only their false identity in their official papers and no way to prove their actual family history.

The second paradox is probably the greatest reversal of the twentieth century. In the 1930s and 1940s a Jewish passport in Central and Eastern Europe was nothing less than a passport to death. In the 1990s in Russia it became a passport to freedom and prosperity. A black market in forged Jewish passports grew up quickly in the former

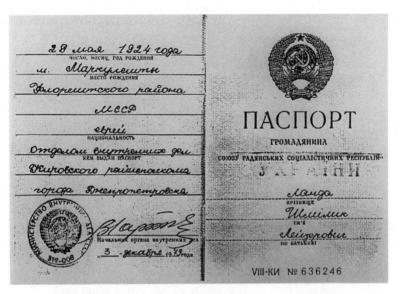

Russian internal passport showing the "fifth line," with "Evreil"—
Hebrew—written in. Photographer Margit Billeb. Stiftung
"Neue Synagogue Berlin. Centrum Judaicum," Berlin.

Soviet Union, entitling the non-Jewish owners and their families to
leave. On arriving in Germany, it gave them protected immigrant status as well as the support of the Jewish community. In Israel the proportion of new Russian arrivals on dubious passports has been estimated at one third, in Germany perhaps a bit lower.

The third great paradox is that Russia, which until the Revolution was the cradle of Jewish life and culture, is now sending forth
Jews who have never seen a Yiddish book or set foot in a synagogue
and who lack even an elementary acquaintance with Jewish history,
life, and customs. On the whole, Russian Jews are urban, well-
educated, and secular. Seventy percent of the immigrants in Berlin
have at least a college education. But doctors, engineers, and academ-

ics arriving in the West often find that their degrees are not recognized and have to struggle to find new careers.[46]

One of the first conflicts between the Russian immigrants and the Jewish communities in Germany arose because the community expected that the immigrants would want a closer connection with Jewish religion and Jewish practices. The host communities have been disappointed to discover that the newcomers have not arrived as apprentices. They need the social services of the Gemeinde, but they are not ready to accept new beliefs or to reorganize their way of life according to a religious model proposed by the community. Without any acquaintance with Jewish learning, a number of the Russian immigrants are so convinced of the superiority of Slavic culture that they are not interested in exploring a world they do not know.

The inevitable differences that emerge from this collision of cultures may be resolved ultimately in a reversal of the usual immigrant experience. In the confines of the official Jewish communities, the Russians are changing the style of communal life, rather than bowing to the prevailing mores. In Berlin the monthly *Gemeinde* bulletin appears in a bilingual format. All the notices in the Gemeinde building are in both languages—or sometimes only in Russian. The staff is also changing from German-speaking to Russian personnel. By the year 2000 only one member of the staff in the Gemeinde library was a native German speaker.

Emblematic of the change is a small confrontation that took place in the offices of the Gemeinde in Berlin as the number of Russians gradually overwhelmed the others. One longtime member, a rather grand lady whose family had lived for generations in Berlin, knew that an era had come to an end when she waited at a desk while the clerk conducted a long telephone conversation in Russian. When the phone call was over, she informed the speaker in an icy tone that she did not understand Russian. The clerk, instead of apologizing, as the visitor

Wedding of Russian Jews in the Pestalozzistrasse Synagogue in Berlin in 1992.
Photographer Margrit Schmidt, Berlin.

had expected, answered rather sharply, "Well, then, it's high time you did. Now it's our turn!"

The old generation of German Jews finds that the Gemeinde festivals—the Purim Ball, the Hanukkah festivities—are now being conducted by the newcomers, who set the tone in dress and food and who hire bands that play Russian music. The Gemeinde library in Berlin has set aside a section for Russian books and periodicals, while the kosher restaurant in the building advertises that it subscribes to both German and Russian newspapers.

Language, however, has been the great barrier, particularly for the older immigrants, separating them from the new world to which they have come. Although the Gemeinde offers classes to teach German at all levels and retains the services of a social worker to help the immigrants solve the problems of everyday life, integration is slow. One survey found that after five years of residence in Germany more than half of those interviewed conceded that they did not speak German adequately. This difficulty only heightens the tendency of the immigrants to withdraw into a self-constructed world. As with immigrant groups everywhere, the first arrivals find true comfort and understanding with those who come from the same background, speak the same language, share the same ideas. What appears to the native-born, then, as an unwillingness to mingle—as when the Russians sit together at Gemeinde festivities—may instead be attributed to the newcomers' inability to talk comfortably in German.

The Gemeinde in Berlin has been undergoing other radical changes. Nineteen ninety-seven was a watershed year, when for the first time the postwar generation took over the leadership from the generation of the survivors. Heinz Galinski's successor in 1992 was Jerzy Canal, who served as interim chairman and retired in 1997. The subsequent election of Andreas Nechama, born in 1951 as the son of the highly esteemed Greek-born cantor Estrongo Nechama, signaled a sweeping change in the Gemeinde. In the same election, Hermann Simon, head of the Centrum Judaicum, was elected chairman of the representatives' council. Simon is a descendant of one of Berlin's oldest Jewish families, and brings to the new joint Gemeinde the perspective of someone who lived in East Germany in the postwar years.

But more than a generational change was in play at this election. For the first time Gemeinde members were confronted with an organized attempt by the Russian Jews to achieve a substantial place in the council. For many of the new immigrants it was their first encounter with the way democracy works. Although it had long been the practice in Gemeinde elections for different parties to present candidates as a "list," in 1997 the election committee insisted that "this election is being conducted as a personal election" and deplored the fact that some of the candidates had chosen to see this election as a competition between parties or lists. The Russians, however, insisted that they were indeed running as a list, as did Hermann Simon, who called his group a "team," which included a number of Russians. The official election bulletin issued by the Gemeinde carried a photograph of each candidate, and a statement by each—in Russian and German— in which the rivalry was made plain.

One of the Russian candidates, Jakov Sterenberg, denounced what he called the lulling tactics of the longtime majority and pointed out that his was in fact an opposition list, which called itself Voice. Appealing directly to the Russian members he wrote: "The Gemeinde members have an opportunity to become a force with which one must reckon. Do not miss out on your chance. Until now, you did not have your own Voice in the Gemeinde, and that is why you were dealt with as second-class persons. Only when you have your own Voice in the Parliament of the Gemeinde will you become equal members of the Gemeinde. Take this list with the names of the nine candidates with you to the election. Only when you vote for each of these will you be voting for yourself and for your Voice in the Gemeinde."[47] Despite the numerical majority of the Russians in the Gemeinde, the Voice list lost. The newcomers had not yet learned to come out and vote. Of the 8,787 members entitled to vote, only 3,634 took part in the election.

The election in 2001, which was also fiercely contended, brought a bridge candidate into office as the head of the Gemeinde. Alexander Brenner was born in Poland in 1932 into a Yiddish-speaking family. Following the German invasion of Poland in 1941, the family fled east to Siberia, where Brenner was educated. After the war he came to Berlin, where he took a degree in chemistry and began working for the government. But because of his technical skills and his perfect command of Russian, he was invited to join the German diplomatic mission in Moscow as its scientific adviser. Upon his retirement, he returned to Berlin and became active in the Gemeinde. With his combination of extensive experience of Russian life and a German background, he was a candidate who could appeal to many different elements in the community. During the election campaign Brenner reproached the previous regime with not doing enough for the integration of the Russian immigrants and thereby cast his lot with the newcomers.[48]

By 2001 Berlin had the largest Jewish community in Germany, with 12,000 members. Many of the Soviet Jews who had been allocated to small towns under the official quota system managed to leave after a while for the opportunities and the social comfort of life in Berlin or other large cities. In 1998 the official roster of members registered in the Jewish communities all across Germany counted 74,289 members, of whom 53,559 were from the former Soviet Union.[49] Most observers put the number of Jews in Germany even higher, at 100,000, because not all who are residents are members of the community, and the rather large number of Israelis who come for varying periods of time do not register but form a kind of shadow community of their own.

Like voting, job hunting is yet another aspect of life for the former Soviet Jews in the West that requires more than simple compliance with official directives, which for many marked the good citizen at home. And Western approaches to job hunting and to finding an apartment take time to learn. Growing up in the tightly controlled life of the Soviet Union, where not only behavior but ways of thinking were drummed into the population from their earliest childhood, the immigrants have discovered unimaginable contrasts on encountering the West. Svetlana Kalinina, a young woman who emigrated to Berlin from St. Petersburg, described her sense of betrayal when she took her first trip abroad—not to a Western European country, but to Hungary—just before she and her husband emigrated to Germany. In an interview after she had settled in Berlin, she recalled, "During the whole trip, I cried and cried. I was so shaken and I kept thinking, I had thought that we live so well and then I saw how badly we live. . . . I particularly observed the women and children. How happy they are, how easy, how jolly. And in Russia it's totally different, the women are exhausted. And I was so surprised when I saw how the children were dressed, and the women, and the way they behaved with one another. For me it was all surprising. When I came home, I couldn't speak, I could only cry. 'How rotten things are with us. How badly we live and how we have been betrayed, always!'"[50]

When they first arrived in Berlin, many of the Russian Jews were confronted for the first time in their lives with the option of living their lives openly as Jews, of "becoming Jews." In the case of Svetlana and her husband, this desire to "live as Jews" was a decision they reached while they were still in Russia. "For me," she said, "this was an absolutely new feeling, because I had always been ashamed that I was a Jew."[51] Svetlana and her husband found the Orthodox Adass Israel community in Berlin as the place that would support them in their desire to change their lives. Adass Israel energetically sought out the new arrivals, hoping to attract them to their Gemeinde with special programs. Like the larger Gemeinde in Fasenenstrasse, Adass too organized language classes and opened a tea room that rapidly became a social center with its Russian and German books and newspapers. Understanding the disorientation of the immigrants, Adass also engaged two professional psychiatric social workers to help them sort out their problems.[52] But companionship and compassion were not enough in the struggle to find work and become self-supporting.

For some of the immigrants, that problem was to become insoluble. They had come from what one immigrant from Uzbekistan called a "caste society. In it" he said of the Soviet Union, "every nation knows quite precisely which place is reserved for it and which places they would never be able to enter. . . . The smallest Jewish child has already completely internalized the realization that an administrative post will never be for him. I myself was never under any illusion that I would ever receive a high position in science . . . although for Jews in Uzbekistan, science is the only area that they are permitted to enter, because trade, a traditional Jewish vocation, is here closed to them."[53]

Although Germany is not a caste society, it is highly organized, and as those seeking work discovered, it is bounded by regulations at every level. Workers do not have their occupations prescribed from above, but each branch has its own rules for admission, training, and the conditions of work. Immigrant craftsmen and factory workers have to deal with the trade unions; those who wanted to enter commerce faced the requirements of the trade associations, and in the professions, the first stumbling block was the acceptance of their diplomas. One woman who had taught mathematics in the Soviet Union for fifteen years, for example, could not get a job because in Germany teachers are required to have a second area of specialization. She had to spend several years working as a cleaning woman while she earned a degree in Slavic linguistics in order to qualify for a teaching position. Nor could every engineer from Russia expect to be accepted at the level at which he had worked. Doctors had a particularly hard time, because they could not practice unless they were citizens, and in the early 1990s it took sixteen years before they could even apply. The Social Democratic government, elected in 1998, succeeded in reducing the waiting period for citizenship for ordinary immigrants to twelve years. But even this reduced interval, which was still more than a decade, was an insuperable barrier for Russian doctors and too long to wait to start a new life.

In contrast, the ethnic German "returnees" were granted citizenship immediately on their taking up residence in the Federal Republic. The returnees, who came from a variety of countries, were privileged because they could lay claim to native German ancestors. Some are indeed Germans who had lost their citizenship as a result of the change of borders at the end of the war. Others, like the Volga Germans, whose forefathers had migrated to Russia three hundred years earlier, had a more ephemeral connection. Still others came from Czechoslovakia or the Baltic countries.

Although some Russian Jews have visibly found their way to prosperity in the new society, the picture for the others is rather darker. In 1997, after five years in Germany, a quarter of the Russian immigrants had not been able to find any kind of regular employment and were dependent on their families or on social help. At least two-thirds of those who were employed reported that they were working in positions below their actual level of achievement. As in many immigrant situations, women turned out to be more adaptable than men in finding places to work or in their willingness to change careers. In part, they showed their flexibility in their willingness to take part-time jobs; although these positions were inferior to the workers' level of qualifications, they at least provided some income.[54]

Youth, however, is the key to success, as is demonstrated in the histories of those who have arrived in Germany between the ages of sixteen and thirty. The younger members of this group can resume their interrupted education in Germany and with a German university or technical degree can move smoothly into the workforce. Others in the under-thirty group have been able to integrate by taking language and technical courses, which also qualify them to meet German requirements. But the difference in cultures has remained one of the main sources of difficulty for the immigrants. In their old society they did not go job hunting but were allotted work. But their new world demands a radical change in attitude, requiring them to seek out work, to be flexible in assessing what they can do, and in general to adopt a far more independent life strategy. For the younger immigrants, of course, this is easier.[55]

Children have other strategies for fitting into the new world. Many of them have ugly experiences of anti-Semitism in their homelands, and all share the experience of being uprooted and subsequently moving between two worlds. Natascha Ronkine, who came to Germany from the Ukraine in 1992, when she was fifteen, wrote eloquently about how language and Jewish identity were the key criteria for her in Germany: "The best is to be among people who speak Russian. And mostly these are also Jews. Since my emigration, my circle of friends has hardly changed; they have the same interests and the same education as I do. . . . If I do communicate with someone in German, then I find it easier to be with Jews than with non-Jews. For me, Jewish people are simply closer than the others, even though the German Jews are no easier to know than the others."

Like many other Jews, she finds her reversed identity ironic. Although in their homeland the immigrants suffered for being Jewish, "In Germany, I am not the Jew," as one of them put it, "but the Russian."[56] For Natascha, part of her odyssey in coming to Germany was to have the right to live as a Jew. More than that she wanted to learn about the "culture, tradition, religion, and history of my people. One is not born with this information," she says firmly, "one must acquire it." When she was sixteen she began to study, and she reports: "I felt myself as newborn. I was not only a Jew, but also Jewish."

The dark side of being in Germany, however—remembering its history—is never far from her thoughts. "Sometimes," she writes, "I feel a kind of aversion to myself, because we have betrayed the memory of the victims by coming to this country. At the same time I believe that the newly blooming Jewish communities in Germany are a sign of our vitality, our ability to carry on with life."[57]

Natascha's clinging to the Russian language is unusual in her generation, where entering the mainstream of German youth culture tends to dominate young immigrants' lives. With their opportunities to meet German contemporaries at school, in sports, and at clubs, they are inevitably drawn into their generation's orbit. But it will be some time before they become the leaders. The dominant group within the Jewish community continues to be the children of the survivors and the descendants of the original German-Jewish community. Many decades after the war, however, they persist in seeing themselves as "Jews in Germany," unlike the prewar generation. Yet their position is a reflection not only of their own history but also of changing political perceptions.

In the new millennium, the idea of the nation-state, which dominated the imagination of state makers and patriots in previous centuries, has fallen into dubious repute. The reality of the modern world has shown us that, with the possible exception of Iceland, every nation is a conglomerate of peoples. This is a recognition that has been liberating for Jews in every part of the world. To be a citizen in their country of birth no longer requires them to mask their history, to suppress their idiosyncracies of belief or practice, to give up their languages. This sense of personal freedom pervades the writing and the films of the new generation in Germany. It is so new that there is still an atmosphere of daring about it, which shows itself particularly in the their magazines. The very titles are at once an affront and an affirmation of self.

The first of the "second-generation" magazines was *Babylon,* which was founded in 1986 with ambitions beyond the literary scene in Germany. The cover of its first issue was a photograph deliciously chosen to put the reader off balance. Babylon, of course, evokes the first great place of exile of the Jews, and in Germany we might expect

BABYLON
Beiträge zur jüdischen Gegenwart

TRACK 18

12:40 P M OFF PEAK

BABYLON

JAMAICA

Dan Diner Negative Symbiose • **Norman Birnbaum** Zur gegenwärtigen Situation der amerikanischen jüdischen Intellektuellen **Claus E. Bärsch** Das Urteil von Nürnberg • **Jürgen Habermas** Die Schrecken der Autonomie. Zu Carl Schmitt • **Harold Bloom** Scholem: Unhistorischer oder jüdischer Gnostizismus • "Red keinen Quatsch, mein Kind . . ." Gespräch mit **Marek Edelman**

neue kritik   Heft 1/1986

Cover of the first issue of *Babylon*, October 1986.
Verlag Neue Kritik.

some weighty reflections on the theme. The photograph, however, shows a signboard of the Long Island Rail Road in New York City, listing the departure times of the train for the suburban town of Babylon. In the first issue the magazine offered translations of articles by the American literary critic Harold Bloom on Scholem and Norman Birnbaum about American Jewish intellectuals. It also featured an interview with Marek Edelman, one of the survivors of the Warsaw ghetto. Under its editors, Dan Diner and Micha Brumlik, *Babylon* has continued a high standard of literary and political criticism.

Of a quite different order are the so-called youth magazines, with their exuberantly brash Yiddish names: *Chuzpe* (Impudence), *Tachlis* (Basics), and *Nudnik* (Nag). They are both irreverent and caustic, standing outside the official Jewish community and ready to satirize the high officials who are always treated with solemn deference in the publications of the Gemeinde.

The summer 1990 issue of *Tachlis,* which appeared at the moment when the two Germanies were uniting their currencies, and Jews in Berlin were hoping for the first meeting in Germany of the World Jewish Congress, presented an imaginary telephone conversation between Heinz Galinski and Edgar Bronfman, head of the World Jewish Congress. Galinski tries to persuade Bronfman that if he will indeed arrange for the congress to meet in Berlin, Galinski will arrange for Bronfman to trade in his East German Great Star of Peoples' Friendship for a Federal Republic Cross of Honor. This is all made possible, Galinski assures Bronfman, by the fact that the going rate of exchange for East to West currency is 1:1, and Bronfman would simply be exchanging an East medal for one from the West. "I'll take care if it with my friend Helmut," promises Galinski.[58] (His readers know, of course, that he is referring to Helmut Kohl, the Chancellor of Germany.)

As much as they enjoy roasting the Gemeinde officials, the editors of *Tachlis* can be equally severe toward their own literary contemporaries. The reviewer of a new book of short stories by Maxim Biller, *When I Am Finally Rich and Dead,* is caustic about Biller's attacks on Ignatz Bubis. Bubis, who was a well-known and controversial real estate developer in Frankfurt, was an obvious and easy target for an irreverent intellectual. But Bubis also had a sense of civic responsibility which was most dramatically demonstrated in 1985, when he and others prevented the performance of a scurrilous anti-Semitic Fassbinder play in Frankfurt by occupying the stage on opening night. Uncharacteristically, the reviewer objects to Biller's stream of invective: "Bordello-owner and stage occupier, speculator, Holocaust survivor, nouveau riche—well, if you please! And their children, naturally likewise, the problems of the second generation—charming." Despite the attractions of Biller's satire, the editors are critical. "He presents the 'truth,'" they note, "but at the cost of the Jews."

Nudnik, first issued in Munich in 1988, lasted only a year despite its promising name.[59] *Chuzpe,* founded in 1994 in Frankfurt by two students, Filipp Goldscheider and Oliver Viest, appeared quarterly and lived up to its name by treating serious topics in bold language. It dared to discuss homosexuality, mixed marriages, whether kosher slaughtering was humane, and, of course, the history of anti-Semitism. The magazine had only thirty-five hundred subscribers, and its editors were aware than many of its readers were not Jewish.[60] Its most widely reproduced article appeared on the two hundredth anniversary of the death of Freiherr von Knigge, the classic eighteenth-century arbiter of correct behavior. The homage published by *Chuzpe* at the end of 1996 was titled "The Kosher Knigge: On Deportment with 'Jewish Fellow Citizens'" and was intended as a guide to non-Jews on how to behave toward Jews.

One of the most awkward aspects of relations between Jews and non-Jews in postwar Germany is a sense of self-consciousness that somehow invades any social situation. *Chuzpe* addressed this problem directly with a list of nine hints to non-Jews. A few of the "tips" give a sense of their tone:

1. It is quite permissible to say "Jew." The word is not insulting. If, nonetheless, it is hard for you to say it, then it means that somewhere in your head are ideas from the past. In any case, that's your problem, not ours. . . .

4. We are not all Israelis. Most Israelis are Jews. But to deduce from that that most Jews are Israelis is not logical. Therefore, when you have some criticism of Israel's security policies, your nearby optician Levy is not the most appropriate and expert discussant. And also he can probably not teach your Women's Group how to dance the hora.

5. We are also not all rich. Statistically, riches among Jews are exactly as unevenly distributed as they are among the rest of the population. Therefore when there is a discussion about the current hard times, you shouldn't pound the nearest Jew on the shoulder and say, "But of course none of this affects you!"

6. And we are also not all geniuses. Most Jews are just as dumb as the majority of the rest of mankind. The chance, therefore, that your conversational partner, because he is a Jew, is an expert on the Frankfurt School (since after all they were all Jews, etc.) is relatively small. It is much more plausible that he thinks "Adorno" is the name of a Tuscan wine.

The final "hint" makes the most serious point:

9. You must deal with the past yourself. If you suffer from continual feelings of guilt because your great uncle was in the SS, the Jew who happens to be around is not necessar-

ily interested in hearing the details. In such cases, it is preferable to seek out a good therapist (preferably not Jewish).[61]

The tone of these "tips" is remarkable when we remember that the writers are of a generation largely made up of the children of the Polish Jews who arrived in rags in Germany in 1945. These new Jews have grown up in a remade Germany: one of the strongest, most stable, and most democratic countries in Europe, with an exemplary policy on human rights. Perhaps that has helped to make them so confident and tough-minded. The two generations of Germans who have grown up since the end of the war have thought long and hard about the Nazi past. And it is just this thoughtfulness that has created the atmosphere of self-consciousness in social situations that both Jews and non-Jews find so trying.

While these encounters keep Jewish self-consciousness more in the forefront than they would like, the prevailing liberal democracy is one in which Jews can flourish and Jewish life goes on steadily within a thriving community. But the worm in the apple, as we shall see, is that Germany has become, unwillingly and to its own surprise, a multicultural nation. The Jews are no longer the only minority in an otherwise homogeneous population; the presence of many new minorities has made the "foreigner problem" a touchy political issue.

Some of this tension has extended to the Jewish community. For the last three decades of the twentieth century, the Jews in Germany accepted as a given that their institutions were fortresses. Since 1972, when eleven Israeli athletes were murdered by Arab terrorists at the Olympic Games in Munich, Jews have lived in a state of siege. Synagogues and Jewish museums, libraries, schools, and community buildings are under constant guard. One cannot attend a synagogue service or visit a Jewish museum without submitting one's bag and coat pockets to a search. Although this may seem a comforting, protective procedure to many, one young mother had a different reaction on the morning that she brought her toddler for the first time to his kindergarten class in a Jewish school. When she saw the armed guards at the entrance, the police vans parked at the curb, the barbed wire around the perimeter of the schoolyard, she broke down in tears. This was not normal life.

What further darkened Germany for the Jews was the persistent growth of antiforeigner politics and of violence by neo-Nazis, along with a disturbing sense of their threatening physical presence, particularly in the small towns of the former East Germany. Visitors to these towns report that carefully costumed young men, outfitted in leather, adorned in heavy metal, with shorn heads and wearing lethal boots, congregate visibly and provocatively in central public places. Although for a long time, the attacks on foreigners were attributed to the high unemployment in the East and the disorientation resulting from the change of political systems, more than a decade after reunification these explanations can no longer account for the sheer volume of activity.

Paul Spiegel, who succeeded Ignatz Bubis as the head of the Central Council of Jews in Germany, had a simpler explanation. "No child," he said in an interview, "is born as a right extremist, an anti-Semite, or neo-Nazi. Something wrong happened in the way they were brought up." And here he lays the responsibility for their ideas squarely on their families and the schools.[62]

Despite candlelit protest demonstrations by concerned Germans and countermarches against the neo-Nazis parades, the amount of violence has continued to grow year by year, causing concern not only to Jews but also to Germans who cherish their democracy. In the year 2000, right-wing crimes rose by 40 percent; in the first eleven months, the police recorded 13,735 extremist antiforeigner and anti-Semitic acts.[63] The preferred targets of the neo-Nazis have been the racially visible foreigners: Africans, Asians, Indians. Although many incidents remain invisible, recorded only in the police blotter, some are brutal enough to reach the newspapers. In 1999 in Guben, a town on the Polish border, an Algerian immigrant died when he plunged through a glass door attempting to escape his pursuers, who were shouting, "Immigrants out." Some months later an African was killed in Dessau, and a year later a group of skinheads knifed an Asian-looking man in Cottbus, a town also in the east of Germany.[64] These pointed acts of violence were troubling not only in themselves but because they took place against a widely perceived background of threats and intimidation. In August 1998, for example, as a group of soccer fans with shaved heads filled a train leaving from the center of Berlin, they began to sing, "We're building a subway to Auschwitz." Although the police had been forewarned and had sent along security forces, they did not confront the skinheads directly, but instead gathered up all the regular passengers and segregated them into the first-class compartment.[65] What was disturbing to the passengers was the helplessness of the police against the potentially violent, drunken mob and that their only way of protecting members of the public was to put them out of the mob's reach.

In Rostock, one of the first centers of antiforeigner violence, some five thousand supporters of the National Party of Germany (NPD) paraded through the streets in September 1998 in old Nazi style on the occasion of an election. Beating drums, carrying flags, some in paramilitary uniforms, they shouted rehearsed slogans in unison: "Here the national resistance is marching." "Whether East or West, down with the Red Pest." "Citizens, don't just stare. Come and join us."[66] Such events were all too reminiscent of the 1930s and the Nazi paramilitary corps, the Brown Shirts, who, chanting and singing as they marched in military formation, had also intimidated the civilian population.

These scenes caused open concern in Germany, even leading the

Bundestag to consider banning the NPD "because of its actively aggressive attitude against the existing civil order."[67] But the Bundestag has been reluctant to take such strong action, and apart from occasional peaceful citizen protests, no clear consensus has emerged regarding how best to combat this new phenomenon.

A turning point for the Jews in Germany came in the first week of October 2000, at the time of the Jewish New Year. Throwing Molotov cocktails, vandals attacked the synagogue in Düsseldorf, where Paul Spiegel is a member. The damage was controlled and no one was hurt, but the attackers escaped leaving no trace. The government immediately offered a reward of 25,000 marks (about $15,000) for information leading to their arrest. On the same day the Holocaust Memorial building at the former Buchenwald concentration camp was smeared with swastikas and several windows were broken. Finally, on the same night, eleven gravestones in the Jewish cemetery in Schwäbisch Hall were sprayed with swastikas.

The Düsseldorf bombing was solved six months later with the arrest of two terrorists who had acted to protest Israeli policy toward the Palestinians. One of the arsonists, Belal Thiab, was a Palestinian, and his companion, Khalid Zaouaghia, was a Moroccan-born German citizen who had also been implicated in a riot at another synagogue five days after the Düsseldorf attack.[68] Although the arrests cleared the neo-Nazis as suspects, it did not ultimately diminish the basic unease of Jewish life in Germany. As we have seen, since 1972 the Jewish community has been wary of the constant possibility of Arab attacks, and these two sources of anxiety remain a permanent feature of the Jewish landscape.

There had been other acts of vandalism aimed at the Jews over the years—cemeteries desecrated, Nazi slogans painted on the windows of Jewish stores or the walls of Jewish community buildings. All had been viewed with concern, but not yet with alarm. The situation grew uglier in 1993, when the grave of Heinz Galinski was spray-painted, leading Ignatz Bubis to stipulate in his will that he be buried in Israel. Toward the end of his life, in fact, Bubis had become quite pessimistic about the situation of Jews in Germany. Since the elections in 1997, when the right-wing German People's Union (DVU) gained 32 percent of the votes in Saxony-Anhalt, Bubis had observed that the taboo against outspoken anti-Semitism was extinct, that "people were no longer embarrassed to admit that they were anti-Semites."[69]

This growing uneasiness among Jews took place against the background of escalating antiforeigner feeling, including large public demonstrations purportedly demanding jobs for Germans instead of foreigners, as well as outspoken slogans by the right-wing parties against foreigners. The real wish or fantasy of these demonstrators was clear—even if not based in reality. They simply wished them away.

By 1998 Germany had 7.3 million foreigners in a population of 82 million, many of whom had been invited as "guest workers" in the 1960s, when Germany had a labor shortage. Nearly half of the foreigners—3.5 million—had been in the country for more than ten years, and another 2 million for between four and ten years. To the radical right it does not matter that a German economic institute has demonstrated that the taxes and social insurance paid by immigrant entrepreneurs and workers far exceeded the costs to the government for welfare and other social benefits to the needy. In 1995, for example, the German government came out ahead in payments from foreigners by 2.4 billion marks.[70] But in the rhetoric of the radical right there are only contradictory and inflammatory images: either the foreign worker is living on welfare, costing the German worker money, or if he is working, he is taking a job from a German. While Jews have not been the primary targets of the attacks from the radical right, they are made uneasy by its growth, knowing that xenophobia is not compatible with freedom and civil rights.

The events on the first Jewish New Year of the twenty-first century in Düsseldorf, with its 3,500 Jews, were unnerving not only locally but to the Jews in all of Germany who had tolerated decades of sporadic, if minor, violence. Following the attack, Paul Spiegel issued a statement in which he raised the fundamental question of whether it had been right after all for the Jews to have once again built up communities in Germany after the war.[71] Although mildly and thoughtfully phrased, the statement spoke for a shaken community that was beginning to doubt whether Jews should be living within German borders.

The writer Richard Chaim Schneider greeted Spiegel's statement almost with relief. Although Schneider, with his vehement style, may not be entirely representative of his generation, his passionate statements contain a kernel of truth that every member of that generation would acknowledge. "At last," he wrote in the *Berliner Zeitung*,

> a member of the older generation has said openly what we, the children of the survivors, have long reproached them with: Was it right, after the war, once again to build a Jewish life in the land of the murderers? . . . Our problem is: a hybrid identity, a divided relationship to this country that is also the country of our birth—our "homeland." This homeland, however, only a few years earlier destroyed our entire people and our families, and yet we were inoculated with its "culture" in our schools. A culture that led to Auschwitz. . . . No, we, the children of the survivors, know all too well where we are living and even before the fall of the Berlin wall had no illusions. We, the children of the survivors, know that we live in the society of the children of the murderers and that we had better not rely on this society.

And then, perhaps without realizing that he was returning to one of the oldest, longest-held Jewish ideas—the idea of *goles*—Schneider restated it for Jews in contemporary Germany: "We were not asked whether we wanted to grow up in this country, with this language, with this culture, with this dreadful ambivalence, with this inner homelessness. Now, we are homeless, right here in the middle of Germany. And not just since Düsseldorf, but always. . . . We are here, but in actuality we are free." Finally Schneider turned to address the Germans directly:

> What security does any form of "homeland" give us? It doesn't give us any, and thus we live always in the eye of the hurricane, in the center of an existential demand on our lives with all its imponderability. That is our opportunity and our advantage over you who are still gnawing on the ideas of "homeland and nation." . . . We are here, but in reality we are free. Free in a way that you will never be. And that is why you envy us in secret and that is why you hate us. But that is your problem. And when you have reduced all the synagogues and cemeteries in Germany to rubble and ashes: then it is your earth that will burn and smoke. We, however, will long be gone and leave you to yourselves.[72]

Rachel Salamander, who was born to Polish Jewish parents in the displaced persons camp of Deggendorf, is another member of that second generation who takes a similarly wary, if less vehement, view of Jewish life in Germany. What is most important for her, and for her ability to live in Germany, is that she lives in a state governed by law. This is the fundamental requirement shared by the members of her generation. On being awarded the Prize for Culture by the city of Munich in 1999, she described graphically the conditions under which her generation can live in Germany. "What does it mean," she asked, "to put down one's roots here? For me, there is one thing above all else: The guarantees of the Constitution are more important than the goodwill offered by Germans. . . . If the guarantees of the Constitution depended only on goodwill, then I would have to begin looking around for another country."

She, like Schneider, also relates the sense of discomfort that she had as a schoolchild being inducted into German culture. While she sat in her German classroom, she could only feel the great emptiness left by the loss of Eastern European Jewish culture. This loss, she said, "has left a vacuum" in its place, and in order to fill this vacuum, she resolved in 1982 to open a bookstore in Munich specializing in Jewish literature. Fulfilling her broad program, her store also became a Jewish cultural center for the presentation of new books and for forums of interest to her readers. Since then she has opened two branches, in Berlin and Fürth, each of which continues the tradition of the original *Literaturhandlung* (literature exchange) with readings, receptions, and discussions.[73]

It has not been easy to be a German with a sense of the past. Buffeted by a tragic history at home and a cool reception abroad, Germans traveling in Europe have realized that their collective history has been made part of their personal biographies. Having experienced cold and even hostile receptions, they know that the memories of German army occupation even so many decades ago has left behind deep-seated animosity. Growing up, as Schneider pointed out, they were part of that generation he has called the "children of murderers." Whether literally or not, they had to contemplate this possibility. On their own home ground, too, German awkwardness in dealing with the Jewish community is an intractable problem, and all the formal obeisances to Christian-Jewish brotherhood do little to close the gap.

But many Germans have moved on from the rather sober attempts at reconciliation to a more lighthearted way of simply enjoying the special culture and picturesque aspects of Jewish life—its music, its food, its customs. Nowhere in the world is klezmer music—the Jewish wedding music of Eastern Europe—more popular than in Berlin, which has been the hospitable host to bands from abroad, as well as fostering its own. Similarly, nowhere else in the world is the interest in converting to Judaism greater than in Germany. But oddly enough, this adoption of Jewish culture has not made Jews feel easier or more accepted. Indeed, it has elicited instead a certain discomfort. Julius Schoeps, the head of the Moses Mendelssohn Center in Potsdam, in fact, believes that the entire movement "has nothing to do with the Jews . . . but is the result of the fact that the non-Jewish society has not come to terms with history." Hartmut Bomhoff, who had formerly been active in the movement for Jewish-Christian Dialogue, is more specific. "It is easier," he writes, "to go to dinner at Tabuna [a Jewish restaurant in Berlin] than to talk to one's grandparents about what happened in the 1940s. The more Jewish culture is popularized, the greater the gap for me [between Jews and Christians]." The journalist Henryk Broder puts it in an even more reprehensible light. He sees the attempt to make the Jews picturesque as part of a wave of nostalgia that has a sinister political purpose. He compares it to the movement to restore the Berlin Palace, the Hohenzollern Stadtschloss, that was torn down by the East German government in the 1950s. "If one were to rebuild the Stadtschloss," he said in an interview, "and also had a few visible Jews with their sidelocks walking about, then one could rock oneself into the illusion that between '33 and '98 there was only a little gap. And also that nothing had happened."[74]

At the beginning of the twenty-first century, the Jews from the former Soviet Union have easily overwhelmed in sheer numbers the tiny minority of surviving German Jews, as well as the Eastern European Jews who settled in Germany after the war. For the former Soviet Jews, nostalgia for the old Eastern European secular traditions—

its klezmer music, its ballads, theatre, poetry, and literature—has no resonance. And with religion banned in the Soviet Union, the fundamentals of Jewish observance had long vanished from their view. Nor can the subtle pattern of the old German-Jewish style, with its balance of separateness and intertwining with the German world, be a model for the new immigrants. At the same time, there is no lack of Jewish missionaries seeking to bring the Soviet Jews into various religious folds. By all reports, however, these emissaries have been greeted with a certain skepticism. So far the interest in Jewish culture and the attendance at Jewish events is greater among the German public than it is among the new immigrants.

Many of the Soviet Jews came to Germany to escape the overt anti-Semitism that was part of the Soviet system and continued to prevail in the post-Soviet world. Others, as we have seen, thought of the West as a place in which they could explore and reclaim their Jewish heritage. What they did not expect is the subtle style of Western social anti-Semitism which lies in wait almost invisibly, but ready to spring at unexpected moments. They also learned that they are not alone as a minority and that attacks on foreigners, on blacks, and on Asians are warning signals to the Jewish community of a changing mood in the country, of a diminished tolerance for difference.

More fundamentally, in arriving in Germany they are being asked to look into themselves, to ask themselves what kind of Jews they are, what kind of commitment they are ready to make to their own past and to their new community—or whether they feel permanently alienated from their Jewish history. But whether they wish it or not, by the sheer force of numbers the new immigrants will be the creators of the next phase of Jewish culture in Germany. The postwar world that was crafted by the immigrants from Eastern Europe was designed to fulfill their special needs for community; their synagogue services were remembrances of the ones they knew, their way of life was a continuation of what they had grown up with before the war. These patterns can hardly suit the new immigrants who bring no remembrances of these forms of Jewish life with them. It is also a question whether the imported styles brought in by the Lubavitchers, the Orthodox, the Conservative, or the Reform movements will be adopted by the Soviet Jews. Or will they find it necessary to develop their own way of living a Jewish life in the Western world?

The majority of the synagogues in Germany, for example, follow the traditional Orthodox ritual. Whether they are using the old German-Jewish prayer books or the style of Eastern Europe, the men and women are separated during the services, with the women sitting along the sides of the sanctuary or in the balcony. Women are in a subordinate position not only in their place in the synagogue, but also in their exclusion from active participation in the services. They are essentially onlookers. For secular Russian Jews, then, the very form of synagogue worship begins with an alienating effect.

It is possible that sheer ignorance, sheer lack of acquaintance with tradition and with the languages that have defined Jewish life for millennia, will lead to the invention of something quite original. Whether they wish it or not, the immigrant generation will bear the burden for defining the future. It is a task they did not expect when they emigrated to Germany, yet inescapably they will be shaping the nature of Jewish life and culture there for the foreseeable future. Bound neither by memories of the Eastern European past nor by those of the German Jews, the new immigrants have the opportunity to create a fresh way of living as Jews in modern times—an original way of being a Jew in Germany.

Notes

ONE

Where They Came From

1. Martin Gilbert, *The Macmillan Atlas of the Holocaust* (New York: Macmillan, 1982), map 5, p. 16.
2. Celia S. Heller, *On the Edge of Destruction: Jews of Poland Between the Two World Wars* (New York: Columbia University Press, 1977), p. 59.
3. Cited in David Rosental, "The Polish Offence That Doesn't Go Away," *Forverts*, January 30, 1998, p. 19.
4. Chone Shmeruk, "A Trilingual Jewish Culture," in *The Jews of Poland Between Two World Wars*, ed. Yisrael Gutman et al. (Hanover, N.H.: University Press of New England, 1989), p. 311.
5. Nicholas Dawidoff, "Shura and Shaya: An Afternoon with Sir Isaiah Berlin," *American Scholar*, vol. 67, no. 2 (Spring 1998), p. 103.
6. Lucjan Dobroszycki, ed., *The Chronicle of the Lodz Ghetto, 1941–1944* (New Haven: Yale University Press, 1984), pp. xi, xxiii, xxxiv.
7. Avraham Barkai, "German Speaking Jews in Eastern European Ghettos," *Leo Baeck Institute Yearbook XXXIV* (1989), p. 254.
8. Jacqueline Dewell Giere, "Wir sind Unterwegs, aber nicht in der Wüste: Erziehung und Kultur in den jüdischen Displaced Persons- Lagern der Amerikanischen Zone in Nachkriegsdeutschland 1945–1949," Ph.D. diss., Johann Wolfang Goethe–Universität zu Frankfurt am Main, Aberdeen, S.D., 1993, p. 70.

9. Emmanuel Ringelblum, *Notes from the Warsaw Ghetto: The Journal of Emanuel Ringelblum,* ed. and trans. Jacob Sloan (New York: McGraw-Hill, 1958), p. xxi.

10. Marcel Reich-Ranicki, *Mein Leben* (Stuttgart: Deutsche Verlags-Anstalt, 1999), p. 216.

11. Nochum Polinowski, "Die 'Brenner' aus Bialystok: Bericht der Arbeiter Simon Amiele und Salman Edelman aus der Stadt Bialystok," in *Das Schwarzbuch: Der Genozid an den sowjetischen Juden,* ed. Wassili Grossman, Ilya Ehrenburg; Arno Lustiger, ed. of German edition (Reinbeck: Rowohlt Verlag, 1994), p. 398.

12. Richard Glazar, *Die Falle mit dem grünen Zaun: Überleben in Treblinka* (Frankfurt: Fischer Taschenbuch Verlag, 1992), p. 175.

13. Ibid., pp. 27, p. 116.

14. Harry Maor, "Über den Wiederaufbau der jüdischen Gemeinden in Deutschland seit 1945," Ph.D. diss., Mainz, 1961, p. 33.

15. Ibid., pp. 35, 36.

16. Cited in Heller, *Edge of Destruction,* p. 225.

17. Ben-Cion Pinchuk, *Soviet Jews Under Soviet Rule: Eastern Poland on the Eve of the Holocaust* (Padstow, Cornwall: Basil Blackwell, 1990), p. 16.

18. Yehiel Yeshaiah Trunk, *Poyln: Zkhroynes un Bilder. Varshe tsvishen beyde welt mlhomes* (New York: Varlag Undzer Tsayt, 1953), vol. 7, pp. 42, 43.

19. *Forverts,* February 9, 1996. p. 5.

20. Ibid., p. 22.

21. Ezra Mendelsohn, *The Jews of East Central Europe Between the World Wars* (Bloomington: Indiana University Press, 1983), p. 57.

22. Paul R. Mendes-Flohr and Jehuda Reinharz, eds., *The Jew in the Modern World: A Documentary History* (New York: Oxford University Press, 1980), p. 529.

23. Mendelsohn, *Jews of East Central Europe,* p. 61.

24. Jacob Lestschinsky, *Di ekonomishe lage fun Yidn in Poyln* (Berlin: Buchdruckerei Viktoria, 1931), p. 11.

25. Isaac Lewin, *The Jewish Community in Poland: Historical Essays* (New York: Philosophical Library, 1985), p. 217.

26. Mendelsohn, *Jews of East Central Europe,* p. 74.

27. Ibid., p. 42.

28. Heller, *Edge of Destruction,* p. 44.

29. Mendelsohn, *Jews of East Central Europe,* p. 74.

30. Seymon Rudnicki, "From Numerus Clausus to Numerus Nullus," *POLIN*, vol. 2 (1987), p. 262.

31. Moshe Prywes (as told to Haim Chertok), *Prisoner of Hope* (Hanover, N.H.: Brandeis University Press, 1996), p. 71.

32. Heller, *Edge of Destruction*, p. 9.

33. Quoted in Mendelsohn, *Jews in East Central Europe*, p. 76.

34. Solomon M. Schwarz, *The Jews in the Soviet Union* (Syracuse: Syracuse University Press, 1951), p. 13.

35. Adam Yarmolinsky, 1928: p. 48. Quoted in Victor Zaslavksy and Robert J. Brym, *Soviet Jewish Emigration and Soviet Nationality Policy* (New York: St. Martin's, 1983), p. 11.

36. Zaslavsky and Brym, *Soviet Jewish Emigration*, p. 11.

37. Ilya Trotzky, "Jewish Pogroms in the Ukraine and in Byelorussia (1918–1920)," in *Russian Jewry 1917–1967*, ed. Gregor Aronson et al. (New York: Thomas Yoseloff, 1969), vol. 2, p. 87.

38. Zaslavsky and Brym, *Soviet Jewish Emigration*, p. 7.

39. Gregor Aronson, "Jewish Communal Life in 1917–1918," in Aronson, *Russian Jewry*, p. 31.

40. Isaac Babel, *Collected Stories*, trans. or rev. by Walter Morison (London: Methuen, 1957; reissued in Penguin Modern Classics, 1974, rpt. 1983), pp. 167, 168.

41. Schwarz, *Jews in the Soviet Union*, pp. 35, 40.

42. Judel Mark, "Jewish Schools in Soviet Russia," in Aronson, *Russian Jewry*, vol. 2, p. 255.

43. Solomon M. Schwarz, "Birobidzhan . . .," in Aronson, *Russian Jewry*, vol. 2, p. 342.

44. Robert Weinberg, Zvi Gitlman, and Bradley Herman, *Stalin's Forgotten Zion: Birobidzan and the Making of a Soviet Jewish Homeland* (Berkeley: University of California Press), p. 31.

T W O

Return to the World

1. Michael Marrus, *The Unwanted: European Refugees in the Twentieth Century* (New York: Oxford University Press, 1985) p. 298. See also Malcolm Proudfoot, *European Refugees, 1939–1952,* (London: Faber and Faber, 1957), p. 158.

2. Stephan Stolze, *Innenansicht: Eine bürgerliche Kindheit, 1938–1945* (Berlin: Suhrkamp, 1981), p. 152.

3. Gita Glazer, interviewed by author, New York, January 8, 1998.

4. Koppel S. Pinson, "Jewish Life in Liberated Germany," in *Jewish Social Studies,* vol. 9, no. 2 (April 1947), p. 103.

5. Martin Gilbert, *The Macmillan Atlas of the Holocaust* (New York: Macmillan, 1982), p. 195.

6. The phrase, as so many of their allusions, is from the Bible—1 Chronicles 4:43.

7. Martha Brixius quoted in Alexandra Richie, *Faust's Metropolis: A History of Berlin* (London: HarperCollins, 1998), p. 633–4.

8. Marrus, *Unwanted,* p. 298.

9. Klemens Nussbaum, "Jews in the First Polish Army," in *Jews in Eastern Poland and the USSR, 1939–1946,* ed. Norman Davies and Antony Polonsky (London: Macmillan Academic and Professional, 1991) p. 194; Yosef Litvak, "Polish-Jewish Repatriates from the USSR," ibid., p. 230. Nussbaum reports that there were 12,000 Jews in the army, while Litvak estimates between 16,000 and 20,000.

10. Jack Pomerantz and Lyric Wallwork Winik, *Run East: Flight from the Holocaust* (Urbana: University of Illinois Press, 1997), p. 140.

11. Ibid., p. 141.

12. Ibid., p. 159.

13. Yosef Litvak, "Jewish Refugees from Poland in the USSR," in *Bitter Legacy: Confronting the Holocaust in the USSR,* ed. Zvi Gitelman (Bloomington: Indiana University Press, 1997), p. 127.

14. Jan Tomasz Gross, "The Sovietization of Western Ukraine and Western Byelorussia," in Davies and Polonsky, *Jews in Eastern Poland,* p. 73; and Keith Sword, "The Welfare of Polish Jewish Refugees in the USSR, 1941–1943: Relief Supplies and their Distribution," ibid., p. 145. The editors of the cited volume estimate that 400,000 Jews were deported to the Soviet interior (p. 34), while Sword sets the number at 500,000.

15. Raul Hilberg, *The Destruction of the European Jews* (New York: Harper Torchbooks, 1961), p. 192.

16. Litvak, "Jewish Refugees," p. 135.

17. Moshe Prywes (as told to Haim Chertok), *Prisoner of Hope* (Hanover, N.H.: Brandeis University Press, 1996), p. 113.

18. Litvak, "Polish-Jewish Repatriates," pp. 230–35.

19. Prywes, *Prisoner of Hope*, p. 176.

20. *Encyclopedia Judaica* (Jerusalem, 1972), vol. 10, p. 989.

21. Gerson Chanachovski, "Fifty-two Years After the Pogrom Against the Jews in Kielce," in *Forverts*, July 3, 1998, p. 8.

22. Michael Steinlauf, *Bondage to the Dead: Poland and the Memory of the Holocaust* (Syracuse: Syracuse University Press, 1997), pp. 52, 55.

23. Leo Schwarz Papers, YIVO Microfilm 488, reel 45.

24. International Refugee Organization, Yearbook 1947. Geneva, p. 806.

25. Samuel Gringauz, "A grus di jidn fun Pojln," in *Jidisze Cajtung*, November 5, 1946, p. 6, 23.

26. *Hemshekh (Continuation)* (Literary journal printed by the Farlag Bafreiung, Munich), Report for the Year 1947, p. 69. In microfilm: Jewish Displaced Persons Periodicals from the Collection of the YIVO Institute, University publications of America, Bethesda, Md., reel 1.

27. *Hemshekh* Report, p. 151.

28. Jacqueline Dewell Giere, "Wir Sind Unterwegs, aber nicht in der Wüste: Erziehung und Kultur in den Jüdischen Displaced Persons Lagern der Americanischen Zone im Nachkriegsdeutschland, 1945–1949," Ph.D. diss., Johann Wolfgang Goethe-Universität zu Frankfurt am Main, Aberdeen, S.D., 1993, pp. 211–17.

29. Herman Yablokoff, *Der Payatz: Around the World with the Yiddish Theatre* (Silver Spring, Md.: Bartleby, 1995), p. 31.

30. Nahma Sandrow, *A World History of Yiddish Theatre* (New York: Seth, 1986) p. 354.

31. Joseph Gar, "Bafrayte Yidn," *Fun noentn ovar* (New York: Congress for Jewish Culture, 1959), vol. 3, p. 157.

32. Leo W. Schwarz, *The Redeemers: A Saga of the Years 1945–1952* (New York: Farrar Straus and Young, 1953), p. 311.

33. Gar, *Fun noentn over*, pp. 167–68.

34. "Tetikajts-Baricht fun der centraler historicer komisje," in *Jidisze Cajtung*, May 20, 1947, p. 5.

35. Gar, *Fun noentn over*, p. 127.

36. S. Katcherginsky, "Among His People," in *Undzer Weg*, January 16, 1948, p. 5.

37. "Staff study relating to winter care and planning for Jewish displaced person in Germany by the UNRRA Jewish Council," August 1946, pp. 1, 2, United

Nations Archives, PAG 4/422.2 (UNRRA) Office of the Historian-Monographs, box 80.

38. Abraham S. Hyman, "Displaced Persons," in *American Jewish Year Book*, vol. 51, 1950, p. 317.

39. Angelika Königseder and Juliane Wetzel, *Lebensmut im Wartesaal: Die jüdischen DPs (Displaced Persons) im Nachkriegsdeutschland* (Frankfurt: Fischer Taschenbuch Verlag, 1994), pp. 247–68.

40. Koppel Pinson, "Jewish Life in Liberated Germany: A study of the Jewish DPs," in *Jewish Social Studies*, vol. 9, no. 2 (April 1947), pp. 105–6.

41. Irving Heymont, *Among the Survivors of the Holocaust, 1945: The Landsberg DP Camp Letters of Major Irving Heymont, United States Army* (Cincinnati: American Jewish Archives, 1982), p. 109.

42. Ibid., pp. 56, 75.

43. Joseph Gar, *Fun noentn ovar*, p. 157.

44. Zalman Grinberg, speech at St. Ottilien, May 27, 1945, in the YIVO Library 3/48033.

45. Michael Brenner, *Nach dem Holocaust: Juden in Deutschland, 1945–1950* (Munich: Verlag C. H. Beck, 1995), p. 35.

46. *Jidisze Cajtung*, December 24, 1946, p. 7.

47. Comrade Cholawski, in a report on the "General Debate at the 2nd Congress of the Szejris-Haplejto," *Jidisze Cajtung*, March 7, 1947, p. 3.

48. Jacob Olejski, speech at Landsberg, August 24, 1945. In the private collection of Abraham J. Peck. Cited by Jacqueline Giere in the *Jahrbuch 1997 zur Geschichte und Wirkung des Holocaust* (Frankfurt: Campus Verlag, 1997), pp. 15–16.

49. Yehuda Bauer, *Flight and Rescue: Brichah* (New York: Random House, 1970), p. 26ff.

50. Walter Laqueur, *A History of Zionism* (New York: Holt, Rinehart, and Winston, 1972), p. 567.

51. Leonard Dinnerstein, "Britishe und amerikanische DP-Politik," in *Überlebt und Unterwegs: Jüdische Displaced Persons in Nachkriegsdeutschland*, ed. Fritz Bauer Institut (Frankfurt: Campus Verlag, 1997), p. 111.

52. Leonard Dinnerstein, "The United States and the Displaced Persons," *Sh'erit Hapletah, 1944–1948: Rehabilitation and Political Struggle*, from the proceedings of the Sixth Yad Vashem International Historical Conference, Yisrael Gutman and Avital Saf, eds. (Jerusalem: Yad Vashem, 1990), p. 357.

53. Harry Truman, "Message of the President to the Congress," July 7, 1947, *De-*

partment of State Bulletin, *July 20* (Washington: U.S. Government Printing Office, 1947), p. 2.

54. Dinnerstein, "The United States and the Displaced Persons," pp. 361, 364.

55. Judith Tydor Baumel, "Kibbutz Buchenwald," in *She'erit Hapletah,* Gutman and Sat, eds., p. 442.

56. Leo W. Schwarz, *Redeemers,* (New York: Farrar, Straus, and Young, 1953), p. 298.

57. Wolfgang Koeppen, *Tauben im Gras* in *Drei Romane* (Frankfurt: Suhrkamp Verlag, 1972), pp. 19, 20.

58. In the Victor Cooper Papers, Leo Baeck Institute, New York, Ar 10113 A37/3.

59. Königseder and Wetzel, *Lebensmut,* p. 136.

60. Ibid., p. 138.

61. Samuel Gringauz, "Di greste lager-einhajt in Dajczland: Landsberg, Feldafing, Föhrenwald, Neu-Freiman, Gauting," in *Jidisze Cajtung,* November 22, 1946, p. 3.

62. Jim G. Tobias, "Die Juden hatten ein Recht, sich zu rächen," *Aufbau,* no. 20, October 1, 1999, p. 20. See also a book by one of the conspirators: Joseph Harmatz, *From the Wings: A Long Journey, 1940–1960* (New York: Book Guild, 1998).

63. Discussion in *She'erit Hapletah,* pp. 532, 534.

64. Pomerantz and Winik, *Run East,* p. 158.

65. Ruth Klüger, *Weiter Leben: Eine Jugend* (Göttingen: Wallstein Verlag, 1992), p. 195.

66. Bunim Heller, "On jidn," in *Jidisze Cajtung,* November 29, 1946, p. 5.

67. Mirian Shmulevitz-Hoffman, "Hindenberg Kazerne," in *Forverts,* April 8, 1996, p. 15.

68. Klüger, *Weiter Leben,* pp. 211–12.

69. Abraham S. Hyman, *The Undefeated* (Jerusalem: Gefen, 1970), p. 276.

THREE

The Last German Jews

1. Samuel Gringauz, "'Bejlis-Proces' un frejlicher Purim in Deggendorf," *Jidisze Cajtung,* March 14, 1947, p. 2.

2. Konrad Kwiet, "Suicide in the Jewish Community," *LBI Yearbook XXIX,* 1984, pp. 154, 155.

3. Victor Klemperer, *Ich will Zeugnis ablegen bis zum letzten: Tagebücher, 1942–1945* (Berlin: Aufbau Verlag, 1998 [c. 1995]), vol. 2, p. 675. When Klemperer's diary was published, it became an instant best-seller for its almost unbearable day-by-day description of how the Nazis squeezed him and his wife out of their world and brought them almost to the brink of death.

4. Victor Klemperer, *Und so ist alles Schwankend: Tagebücher Juni bis Dezember 1945* (Berlin: Aufbau Verlag, 1997 [c. 1995]), pp. 74, 96.

5. Ibid., pp. 221–22.

6. Ibid., p. 30.

7. Walter Besser, interviewed by Dieter Heger and Edgar Pankow Berlin, June 16, 1995, Fortunoff Video Archive in Berlin, Yale University Manuscripts and Archives, T3135.

8. Marcel Reich-Ranicki, *Mein Leben* (Stuttgart: Deutsche Verlags-Anstalt, 1999), p. 292.

9. Ilselotte Themal geb. Urbach, "Meine Erlebnisse während der Zeit der Judenverfolgungen in Deutschland 1933–1945," ms. in possession of the author; private conversations with Themal.

10. Michael A. Meyer, ed., *German-Jewish History in Modern Times* (New York: Columbia University Press, 1996), vol. 4, Avraham Barkai and Paul Mendes-Flohr, *Renewal and Destruction, 1918–1945,* p. 387.

11. Bruno Blau, in Monika Richarz, *Jüdisches Leben in Deutschland: Selbstzeugnisse zu Sozialgeschichte, 1918–1945,* vol. 3, p. 470.

12. Inge Deutschkron, *Ich trug den gelben Stern* (Cologne: Verlag Wissenschaft und Politik, 1980 [c. 1978]), p. 199.

13. Karl Marx, *Fünfzehn Jahre danach: Beweise der Nächstenliebe gegen Unmenschlichkeit* (Düsseldorf: Allgemeine Wochenzeitung, 1960).

14. Lili Marx, "Die Anfänge der Allgemeinen Jüdische Wochenzeitung," in Michael Brenner, *Nach dem Holocaust: Juden in Deutschland, 1945–1950* (Munich: Verlag C. H. Beck, 1995), pp. 179, 184.

15. Constantin Goeschler, "Jews in Bavaria After the War," in *Leo Baeck Yearbook XXXVI* (1991), p. 448.

16. Quoted in Rolf Vogel, *Ein Stück von uns. Deutsche Juden in deutsche Armeen, 1813–1976. Eine Dokumentation* (Mainz: v. Hase und Köhler Verlag, 1977), p. 67.

17. Philipp Auerbach, "Zum Geleit," in *Jüdisches Gemeindeblatt für die Nord-Rheinprovinz und Westfalen,* vol. 1, no. 1. April 15, 1946, p. 1.

18. Richard Lichtheim, *Rückkehr: Lebenserinnerungen aus der Frühzeit des deutschen Zionismus* (Stuttgart: DTV, 1970), pp. 51, 55.

19. *Jüdisches Gemeindeblatt*, no. 1/21, February 5, 1947, p. 4.

20. *Neue Welt, Mitteilungsblatt der jüdischen Gemeinden in Bayern*, vol. 1, no. 1, mid-September 1947, issued by Landesverband der israel. Kultusgemeinden in Bayern, ed. Kurt Neumark, pub. Hans Frey.

21. *Aufbau*, no. 26, December 18, 1998, p. 3.

22. Ernst Landau, "Um die jüdische Zukunft in Deutschland," March 16, 1947, p. 5, YIVO, Leo Schwarz Papers, MK488, reel 46.

23. Ibid., pp. 2, 3.

24. *UNRRA CENTRE ZEHLENDORF*, no. 1, March 1946, p. 1.

25. "Political Poland," in *Repatriation News*, District 3 H.Q., vol. 1, no. 11, December 14, 1946, p. 1.

26. Ernst Landau, "Wir Juden und die Umwelt: Ein Beitrag zum Problem der Kollektivschuld," in *Jüdische Rundschau* 1, no. 6, July 1946, pp. 23–25.

27. Landau, "Um die jüdische Zukunft," p. 5.

28. Landau, "Wir Juden und die Umwelt," p. 25.

29. R.R., "Katzetnikes zoln sikh farshtendikn mit . . . Daitshland!" *Undzer Weg*, vol. 1, no. 51, November 15, 1946.

30. Landau, "Wir Juden und die Umwelt," pp. 23–25.

31. *Jüdisches Gemeindeblatt für die Nord-Rhein Provinz und Westfalen*, vol. 1, no. 21, February 5, 1947, p. 1.

32. Ibid., vol. 2, no. 20, May 10, 1947, p. 12.

33. Harry Maor, "Über den Wiederaufbau der jüdischen Gemeinden in Deutschland seit 1945," Ph.D diss., University of Mainz, 1966, p. 40.

34. Hans Frey, "Auswandern oder Hierbleiben?" in *Jüdisches Gemeindeblatt*, vol. 1, no. 15, November 9, 1946, p. 1.

35. Ernst Landau, "Im DP Lager," in Brenner, *Nach dem Holocaust*, p. 128.

36. Deutschkron, *Ich trug*, pp. 213, 214.

37. Brenner, *Nach dem Holocaust*, p. 242 n.28.

38. Letter by the "Aktionskomitee zur Vorbereitung democratischer Wählen in der Israelitischen Kultusgemeinde Augsburg," to the Landesverband der Israelitischen Kultusgemeinden in Bayern, Augsburg, January 15, 1954, p. 1, Leo Baeck Archive (New York), AR 5890/3.

39. Brenner, *Nach dem Holocaust*, p. 133.

40. Franklin A. Oberlaender, *"Wir aber sind nicht Fisch und nicht Fleisch"*:

Christliche "Nichtarier" und ihre Kinder in Deutschland (Opladen: Leske and Budrich, 1996), p. 61.

41. Ibid., p. 109.

42. Philip Friedman, *Roads to Extinction: Essays on the Holocaust* (New York: Jewish Publication Society of America, 1980), p. 42.

43. Oberlaender, *Wir aber,* p. 100.

44. Quoted from Harry Maor in Erica Burgauer, *Zwischen Erinnerung und Verdrängung: Juden in Deutschland nach 1945* (Hamburg: Rowohlts Enzyklopaedie, 1993) p. 53; Maor, "Über den Wiederaufbau," quoting a report of the American Jewish Committee, p. 96.

45. Quoted in Julius Posner, *In Deutschland 1945–1946* (Jerusalem, 1947), p. 115.

46. *Jüdisches Gemeindeblatt,* vol. 3, no. 7, July 1948, pp. 2, 3.

47. Quoted in Brenner, *Nach dem Holocaust,* pp. 113–16.

48. Interview in *Jahrbuch für Antisemtismusforschung,* 1993.

FOUR

Jews Again in Berlin

1. Inge Deutschkron, *Unbequem . . . Mein Leben nach dem Überleben* (Bielefeld: Verlag Wissenschaft und Politik, 1992), p. 18.

2. Reinhard Rürup, ed., Berlin 1945, *Eine Dokumentation,* (Berlin: Verlag Willmuth Arenhövel, 1995), p. 59.

3. Erica Fischer, *Aimée und Jaguar: Eine Liebesgeschichte Berlin 1943* (Cologne: Kiepenheuer and Witsch, 1997), p. 281.

4. Angelika Königseder, *Flucht nach Berlin: Jüdische Displaced Persons, 1945–1948* (Berlin: Metropol Verlag, 1998), p. 31.

5. H. G. Sellenthin, *Geschichte der Juden in Berlin und des Gebäudes Fasanenstrasse 79/80: Festschrift anlässlich der Einweihung des jüdischen Gemeindehauses,* Published by the Jewish Community of Berlin, 1959, pp. 84, 85.

6. Phillip Skorneck, "Report on the Institutions of the Gemeinde to the American Joint Distribution Committee" February 21, 1946, p. 3. In the Leo Schwarz Papers in YIVO, MK 488, reel 45. See similar figures for June 1946 given in the JDC report by Eli Rock, director of JDC office in Berlin, pp. 5, 6.

7. Gad Beck, *Und Gad ging zu David: Die Erinnerungen des Gad Beck, 1923–1945* (Berlin: Zebra Literaturverlag, 1995), p. 97.

8. Richard Breitman, *Official Secrets: What the Nazis Planned, What the British and Americans Knew* (New York: Hill and Wang, 1998), p. 162.

9. Nathan Stoltzfus, *Resistance of the Heart: Intermarriage and the Rosenstrasse Protest in Nazi Germany* (New York: Norton, 1996), p. xx.

10. Ibid., p. 243.

11. Ibid., p. 244.

12. Bruno Blau, "Vierzehn Jahre Not und Schrecken," in Monika Richarz, Hrg., *Jüdisches Leben in Deutschland: Selbstzeugnisse zur Sozialgeschichte 1918–1945* (Stuttgart: Deutsche Verlags-Anstalt, 1982), vol. 3, p. 474.

13. Ernst Günter Fontheim, "Postwar recollections of a Berlin Jew" (unpublished manuscript in possession of the author), p. 4.

14. A. Schwersenz, Letter of August 3, 1945 to Pfarrer Buchholz, Beirat für kirchliche Angelegenheiten des Magistrats der Stadt Berlin (Berlin: Siegmund Weltlinger Papers at Landesarchiv Berlin), B Rep.001 Acc 2685, no. 4617.

15. Ulrike Offenberg, *"Seid vorsichtig gegen die Machthaber": Die jüdischen Gemeinden in der SBZ und der DDR 1945 bis 1990* (Berlin: Aufbau Verlag, 1998), p. 20.

16. Program in Siegmund Weltlinger Papers, Landesarchiv Berlin.

17. Andreas Nachama, "Nach der Befreiung: Jüdisches Leben in Berlin, 1945–1953," in *Jüdische Geschichte in Berlin: Essays und Studien,* ed. Reinhard Rürup (Berlin: Edition Hentrich, 1995), p. 271.

18. It is worth noting that although Lustig was outspoken in his letter, he nonetheless complied with the accepted official language. Both the Soviets and later the East Germans used the word *Fascist* instead of *National Socialist* in referring to the Hitler regime, presumably so as not to confuse their socialism with that of the Nazis. However, its usage soon became a signal of adherence to or sympathy with the Soviet position.

19. Walter Lustig, Letter to the Magistrat, June 6, 1945, Siegmund Weltlinger Papers at Landesarchiv Berlin.

20. Andreas Nachama, "Nach der Befreiung," in Rürup, *Jüdische Geschichte,* p. 271.

21. Offenberg, *"Seid vorsichtig,"* p. 292, n. 35; Rivka Elkin, "The Jewish Hospital in Berlin," in *Leo Baeck Institute Yearbook XXXVIII* (1993) pp. 190–91.

22. Günter Kunert, "Rohstoff, unsichtbar," in *Aufbau nach dem Untergang: Deutsch-jüdische Geschichte nach 1945,* ed. Andreas Nachama und Julius H. Schoeps (Berlin: Argon Verlag, 1992), p. 248.

23. Personal communication, Ingeborg Glier, New Haven, February 22, 1999.

24. Although Blum was chosen by General Bersarin to begin organizing the Jewish community, his name does not appear again among the community officers. It is possible that he emigrated and thus dropped from sight. My reference to him comes in a letter from the general secretariat of the Jewish community to the Soviet central command on December 12, 1945. This is essentially a year-end report detailing the history of the formation of the Jüdische Gemeinde. In the archives of the Centrum Judaicum, Berlin. 5A1, 1.

25. Nachama, "Nach der Befreiung," pp. 267–68.

26. Heinz Knobloch, *Der beherzte Reviervorsteher: Ungewöhnlich Zivilcourage am Häckeschen Markt* (Berlin: Morgenbuch Verlag, 1993), 2d ed., p. 7.

27. Ibid., p. 90.

28. Nicola Galliner, ed., *Wegweiser durch das jüdische Berlin: Geschichte und Gegenwart* (Berlin: Nicolai, 1987), p. 155.

29. Offenberg, *"Seid vorsichtig,"* pp. 18, 21.

30. "Auszug aus dem Protokoll der Sitzung des Vorstandes und der Repräsentanten vom 24.July 1945"; and Letter to Schwersenz from the Gemeinde, dated August 10, 1945, signed by Erich Mendelsohn, Centrum Judaicum, Bestand 511, Signatur no. 2.

31. Papers relating to the activities of Siegmund Weltlinger, Landesarchiv Berlin, B Rep 002 Acc 2685, no. 4617; Letter to Magistrat der Stadt Berlin, October 4, 1945.

32. Ernst G. Lowenthal, *Juden in Preussen: Ein biographisches Verzeichnis* (Berlin: Bildarchiv Preussischer Kulturbesitz, 1981), p. 144.

33. Sellenthin, *Geschichte der Juden,* p. 97.

34. Offenberg, *"Seid vorsichtig,"* p. 24.

35. Fontheim, "Postwar recollections," p. 4.

36. Eli Rock, "Quarterly Report: Berlin Office AJDC. March 1, 1946–June 1, 1946," p. 10.

37. Beck, *Und Gad,* pp. 180–81.

38. In Leo Schwarz Papers, YIVO, MK488, reel 45.

39. Philip Skorneck, "Report on Berlin," Paris, February 21, 1946, Leo Schwarz Papers, YIVO, MK 488, reel 45.

40. Nathan Peter Levinson, "Von den Aufgaben eines Rabbiners im Nachkriegsdeutschland," in Michael Brenner, *Nach dem Holocaust: Juden in Deutschland 1945–1950* (Munich: Verlag C. H. Beck, 1995), p. 159.

41. *Der Weg,* vol. 1, no. 1, March 1, 1946, p. 2.

42. Ibid., vol. 1, no. 6, April 5, 1946, p. 3.

43. Hans-Erich Fabian, *Der Weg,* vol. 1, no. 24, August 9, 1946, pp. 1, 2.

44. *Die Welt,* August 22, 1997, reproduced in *Das Ende des Exils in Shanghai* (Berlin: Verein Aktives Museum, 1997).

45. Christine Hoss, "Kein sorgenfreies Leben: Erfahrungen mit dem neuen Deutschland," in *Leben im Wartesaal: Exile in Shanghai, 1938–1947,* Amnon Barzel, ed. (Berlin: Jüdisches Museum, 1997), p. 101.

46. *Der Weg,* vol. 1, no. 5, March 24, 1946, p. 1.

47. Norman Bentwich, "Nazi Spoliation and German Restitution: The Work of the United Restitution Office," in *Leo Baeck Institute Yearbook X* (1965), p. 204.

48. Joachim Nawrocki and Johannes Volkers, *30 Jahre Wiedergutmachung. Und eine Chronik der Berlin-Besuche emigrierter Mitbürger* (Berlin: Berliner Forum, 1981), p. 13.

49. Ibid., p. 33.

50. Rolf Vogel, ed., *It Began in Luxembourg: 25 Years of German Israeli Relations, A Documentation* (Bonn: Deutschland Berichte, 1977), pp. 12–14.

51. Ibid., p. 11.

52. Ibid., p. 5.

53. Henry Ashby Turner, Jr., *The Two Germanies Since 1945* (New Haven: Yale University Press, 1987), p. 13.

54. Offenberg, *"Seid vorsichtig,"* p. 37.

55. Letter of the Jüdische Gemeinde to the Magistrat der Stadt Berlin, February 11, 1946, Betriff: Bildung der Jüdische Gemeinde zu Berlin (Centrum Judaicum Archives, Berlin), 5A 1, no. 1.

56. Jehuda Reinharz, *Fatherland or Promised Land: The Dilemma of the German Jew* (Ann Arbor: University of Michigan Press, 1975), p. 10.

57. Centrum Judaicum Archives, Berlin, 5A 1, no. 73.

58. Offenberg, *"Seid vorsichtig,"* p. 26.

59. Andreas Nechama, "Der Mann in der Fasanenstrasse," in *Aufbau nach dem Untergang: Deutsche-jüdische Geschichte nach 1945. In memoriam Heinz Galinski* (Berlin: Argon Verlag, 1992), p. 29.

60. Ibid., p. 32.

61. Charles Rappaport. "Report on UNRRA D.P. Operation in Berlin, Germany: July 1945–June 1947," UNRRA Team 1027 Berlin, Germany, p. 3 (United Nations Archives), UNRRA Germany Mission, PAG-4/3.0 11.3.2, box 48.

62. H. J. Fishbein, Director UNRRA Team 597, Berlin, "Report for Anglo-American Committee of Inquiry" (n.d.—before April 1946), p. 2.

63. Yehuda Bauer, *Flight and Rescue: Brichah* (New York: Random House, 1970), p. 133.

64. Ibid., p. 135.

65. "JDC Report from Berlin." May 31, 1946, p. 9 (Leo Schwartz Papers at YIVO), MK 488, reel 45.

66. Rappaport. "Report on UNRRA D.P. Operation," pp. 5, 6.

67. Königseder, *Flucht nach Berlin*, p. 61.

68. *Undzer Lebn*, nos. 3–4, August 25, 1946, pp. 15, 16.

69. David Kohn, "Menachem-Mendl in Berlin," in *Undzer Lebn*, nos. 15–16, April 1, 1947, pp. 42–48.

70. *Undzer Lebn*, nos. 11–12, January 15, 1947, p. 34.

71. Susan Pettiss, Zone Child Welfare Officer for Jewish Children, in "History of Child Welfare. Report—DP #US 22," February 1, 1948, p. 81 (United Nations Archives), PAG 4/3.0.11.1.1.:15.

72. Simon Schochet, *Feldafing,* (Vancouver: November House, 1983), p. 24.

73. Samuel Pisar, *Of Blood and Hope,* (Boston: Little, Brown, 1979), pp. 99–129 passim.

74. M. Chait, "Undzer gaystiger renesans," *Undzer Lebn*, no. 2, August 10, 1946, p. 1.

75. *Undzer Lebn*, no. 2, December 27, 1946, p. 5.

76. Yehudi Menuhin, *Unfinished Journey,* (New York: Knopf, 1977), p. 224.

77. Quoted ibid., p. 220.

78. Ibid., p. 225.

79. Quoted in Abraham S. Hyman, *The Undefeated* (Jerusalem: Gefen, 1953), p. 341.

80. Ibid., p. 342.

81. *Der Weg*, Berlin, vol. 2, no. 41, October 10, 1947, p. 5.

82. Alexandra Richie, *Faust's Metropolis: A History of Berlin* (London: Harper-Collins, 1998), pp. 663–73.

FIVE

Jews in East Berlin

1. Quoted in Helmut Eschwege, *Fremd unter meinesgleichen: Erinnerungen eines Dresdner Juden* (Berlin: Christoph Links Verlag, 1991), p. 121.

2. Harry Maor, "Über den Wiederaufbau der jüdischen Gemeinden in Deutschland seit 1945," inaugural diss., University of Mainz, 1961, p. 176.

3. Eschwege, *Fremd unter*, p. 59.

4. Mario Kessler, *Zwischen Repression und Toleranz: Die SED und die Juden* (Berlin: 1993), p. 66.

5. Henry Ashby Turner, Jr., *Germany from Partition to Reunification* (New Haven: Yale University Press, 1992), pp. 30–51 passim.

6. American Jewish Committee, *American Jewish Year Book*, vol. 52 (1951), pp. 366, 367.

7. Ibid., p. 68.

8. Ulrike Offenberg. *"Seid vorsichtig gegen die Machthaber": Die jüdischen Gemeinden in der SBZ und der DDR, 1945–1990* (Berlin: Aufbau Verlag, 1998), p. 63.

9. Nathan Peter Levinson, *Ein Ort is mit wem du bist: Lebensstationen eines Rabbiners* (Berlin: Edition Hentrich, 1996), p. 111.

10. Ibid., p. 127.

11. *American Jewish Year Book*, vol. 54 (1953), p. 347; vol. 55 (1954), pp. 292, 293.

12. Jeffrey Herf, "East German Communists and the Jewish Question: The Case of Paul Merker," Fourth Alois Mertes Memorial Lecture, 1994, (Washington: German Historical Institute, 1994), p. 8. For a full treatment of the case and the situation in East Germany, see also Jeffrey Herf, *Divided Germany: The Nazi Past in the Two Germanies* (Cambridge: Harvard University Press, 1997).

13. Offenberg, *"Seid vorsichtig,"* pp. 84–87.

14. Eschwege, *Fremd unter*, p. 72.

15. Nathan Peter Levinson, "Von den Aufgaben eines Rabbiners in Nachkriegsdeutschland," in Michael Brenner, *Nach dem Holocaust: Juden in Deutschland, 1945–1950* (Munich: Verlag C. H. Beck, 1995), p. 160.

16. Ibid., p. 136.

17. Offenberg, *"Seid vorsichtig,"* pp. 84, 88.

18. Levinson, "Von den Aufgaben eines Rabbiners," p. 127.

19. Offenberg, *"Seid vorsichtig,"* p. 93.

20. Ibid., p. 90.

21. Jürgen Landeck, "Jude, Deutscher—deutscher Jude," in *Fremd im Eigenen Land: Juden in der Bundesrepublik*, ed. Henry M. Broder and Michel R. Lang (Frankfurt: Fischer Taschenbuch Verlag, 1979), p. 25.

22. Offenberg, *"Seid vorsichtig,"* p. 100.

23. Brenner, *Nach dem Holocaust,* p. 201.

24. Berlin Museum, *Synagogen in Berlin, Zur Geschichte einer zerstörten Architektur* (Berlin: Verlag Wilmuth Arenhövel, 1983), vol. 1, pp. 126–28.

25. Lothar Mertens, *Davidstern unter Hammer und Zirkel: Die jüdischen Gemeinden in der SBZ/DDR und ihre Behandlung durch Partei und Staat, 1945–1990* (Hildesheim: Georg Olms Verlag, 1997), p. 160.

26. Martin Riesenburger, *Das Licht verlöschte nicht: Dokumentation aus der Nacht des Nazismus* (Berlin: Berlin Union Verlag, 1960), p. 26.

27. Ibid., p. 27.

28. Salomea Genin, "Wie ich in der DDR aus einer Kommunistin zu einer Jüdin wurde," in *Das Exil der kleinen Leute: Alltagserfahrung deutscher Juden in der Emigration,* ed. Wolfgang Benz (Munich: Verlag C. H. Beck, 1991), pp. 315, 316.

29. Mertens, *Davidstern,* p. 203.

30. Offenberg, *"Seid vorsichtig,"* p. 326.

31. Arnim Stiller, "Judisches Gemeindeleben in der DDR," in *Allgemeine Jüdisches Wochenzeitung,* vol. 29, no. 24, June 14, 1974, p. 3.

32. Quoted in Erica Burgauer, *Zwischen Erinnerung und Verdrängung: Juden in Deutschland nach 1945* (Hamburg: Rowohlt Taschenbuch, 1993), p. 177–78.

33. Eschwege, *Fremd unter,* pp. 66, 76.

34. Quoted in Robert Weinberg, *Stalin's Forgotten Zion: The Making of a Soviet Jewish Homeland* (Berkeley: University of California Press, 1998), p. 14.

35. Quoted in Burgauer, *Zwischen Erinnerung,* pp. 187, 188.

36. Quoted in Kessler, *Zwischen Repression,* pp. 116, 117.

37. Peter Lust, *Two Germanies: Mirror of an Age* (Montreal: 1966), pp. 209, 212, 214.

38. Quoted in Offenberg, *"Seid vorsichtig,"* p. 114.

39. Peter Kirchner, "Die jüdische Gemeinde in Berlin (Ost)," in *Juden in Berlin, 1671–1945: Ein Lesebuch* (Berlin [West], 1988), pp. 328–33.

40. Offenberg, *"Seid vorsichtig,"* p. 126.

41. Ibid., p. 111.

42. Mertens, *Davidstern,* pp. 83–85.

43. Hermann Simon, "Die Neue Synagogue Einst und Jetzt," in *"Tuet auf die Pforten": Die Neue Synagogue, 1866–1995* (Berlin: Stiftung Neue Synagoge—Centrum Judaicum, 1995), p. 36.

44. Peter Kirchner, interviewed in Robin Ostow, *Jüdisches Leben in der DDR* (Frankfurt: Athenaum Verlag, 1988), p. 37.

45. Offenberg, "*Seid vorsichtig*," p. 120.

46. Kirchner, "Die jüdische Gemeinde," pp. 330, 332.

47. Kirchner interview, p. 35.

48. Offenberg, "*Seid vorsichtig*," pp. 128, 129.

49. Thomas Eckert, interviewed in Ostow, *Jüdisches Leben*, p. 157.

50. Heinz Rothholz, interviewed in Robin Ostow, *Juden aus der DDR und in die deutsche Wiedervereinigung: Elf Gespräche* (Berlin: Wichern Verlag, 1996), p. 36.

51. Eschwege, *Fremd unter*, pp. 169–75 passim.

52. Jalda Rebling, interviewed in Ostow, *Jüdisches Leben*, pp. 90, 94.

53. Ibid., p. 92.

54. Weinberg, *Stalin's Forgotten Zion*, pp. 31, 43, 82, 84, 85.

55. Mertens, *Davidstern*, p. 328.

56. Burgauer, *Zwischen*, p. 223.

57. Ibid.

58. Ibid., pp. 230, 231.

59. Max Sinasohn, ed., *Adass Jisroel Berlin: Entstehung, Entfaltung, Entwurzelung* (Jerusalem, 1966), p. 24.

60. Robert Liberles, *Religious Conflict in Social Context: The Resurgence of Orthodox Judaism in Frankfurt am Main, 1838–1877* (Westport, Conn.: Greenwood, 1985), p. 167.

61. Rahel Heuberger, "Orthodoxy versus Reform" in *Leo Baeck Institute Yearbook XXXVII* (London: Secker and Warburg, 1992), p. 46.

62. For the parliamentary debate on this law, see James F. Harris, "Eduard Lasker: The Jew as National German Politician," in *Leo Baeck Institute Yearbook XX* (1973), pp. 159–65.

63. Sinasohn, *Adass Jisroel Berlin*, p. 26.

64. Ibid., pp. 37, 131.

65. Quoted ibid., p. 134.

66. Ibid., p. 41.

67. Henryk M. Broder, *Ebarmen mit dem Deutschen* (Hamburg: Hoffmann und Campe, 1993), p. 86.

68. Daniel Dagan, "Erich Honecker und die Juden," trans. from the Hebrew newspaper *Ha'aretz*, Tel Aviv, March 3, 1986, in *Adass Jisroel: Die jüdische*

Gemeinde in Berlin (1869–1942), Vernichtet und Vergessen, ed. Mario Offenberg (Berlin: Museumpädagogischer Dienst Berlin, 1986), pp. 292–95.

69. Offenberg, *"Seid vorsichtig,"* p. 249.
70. Ibid., p. 263.
71. Mertens, *Davidstern,* p. 373.
72. Ibid., p. 375.
73. Offenberg, *"Seid vorsichtig,"* p. 264.
74. *Nachrichten von Adass Israel, Bulletin der jüdischen Gemeinde Adass Israel,* Berlin, no. 15, October 1997, pp. 11–13.
75. Simon, *"Tuet auf die Pforten,"* p. 36.
76. Barbara Welker, "Das Gesamtarchiv der deutschen Juden," in Simon, *"Tuet auf die Pforten,"* pp. 227–32.
77. Mertens, *Davidstern,* p. 199.
78. Quoted in Simon, *"Tuet auf die Pforten,"* p. 40.

S I X

New Generations in Germany

1. Max Hermann Friedländer, *Tiferet Jisrael: Schilderungen aus dem innern Leben der Juden in Mähren in vormärzlichen Zeiten* (Brunn, 1878). Quoted in W. G. Sebald, *Unheimliche Heimat: Essays zur Österreichischen Literatur* (Frankfurt: Fischer Taschenbuch Verlag, 1995), p. 46.
2. Erica Burgauer, *Zwischen Erinnerung und Verdrängung: Juden in Deutschland nach 1945* (Hamburg: Rowohlt Taschenbuch Verlag, 1993), p. 34.
3. Michael Brenner, *Nach dem Holocaust: Juden in Deutschland, 1945–1950* (Munich: Verlag C. H. Beck, 1995), p. 198.
4. Burgauer, *Zwischen,* p. 42.
5. Brenner, *Nach dem Holocaust,* p. 109.
6. Lea Fleischmann, *Dies ist nicht mein Land: Eine Jüdin verlässt die Bundesrepublik* (Hamburg: Hoffmann und Campe Verlag, 1980), p. 111.
7. Burgauer, *Zwischen,* p. 100.
8. Michael Wolffsohn, *Meine Juden-Eure Juden* (Munich: Piper Verlag, 1997), p. 10.
9. Franz Xaver Schönhuber is the head of the Republican Party, which is outspokenly anti-immigrant and is widely regarded as keeping alive many elements of Nazi ideology.

10. Rafael Seligmann, *Mit Beschränkter Hoffnung: Juden, Deutsche, Israelis* (Hamburg: Hoffmann und Campe, 1991), p. 165.

11. Ignatz Bubis, *Ich bin ein deutscher Staatsbürger jüdischen Glaubens: Ein autobiographischen Gespräch mit Edith Kohn* (Cologne: Kiepenheuer und Witsch, 1993), p. 110.

12. Richard Chaim Schneider, *Fetish Holocaust: Die Judenvernichtung verdrängt und vermarktet* (Munich: Kindler Verlag, 1997), p. 161.

13. Geoffrey Hartman, Berlin Address to the UJA Premission, October 21, 1993. Unpublished ms.

14. Ignatz Bubis, with Peter Sichrovsky, *"Damit bin ich noch längst nicht fertig": Die Autobiographie* (Berlin: Ullstein, 1998), p. 247.

15. Brenner, *Nach dem Holocaust*, pp. 105, 107.

16. Marion Kaplan, "What Is 'Religion' Among Jews in Contemporary Germany," in Sander L. Gilman and Karen Remmler, eds., *Reemerging Jewish Culture in Germany: Life and Literature Since 1989* (New York: New York University Press, 1994) pp. 89, 107.

17. Quoted in Robin Ostow, *Juden aus der DDR und die deutsche Wiedervereinigung: Elf Gespräche* (Berlin: Wichern Verlag, 1996), p. 85.

18. Gabriele Döhring, "Jüdische Alphabetisierung: Rabbinerausbildung in Deutschland: Verschiedene Standpunkte prallen aufeinander," *Der Tagesspiegel*, June 18, 2000.

19. Ibid.

20. Mario Kessler, *Antisemitismus, Zionismus, und Sozialismus* (Mainz: Decaton Verlag, 1994), p. 85.

21. Henryk Broder, "Warum ich gehe," *Die Zeit*, no. 10, March 6, 1981, pp. 8, 9.

22. Ibid. See also Nikolaus Simon. "Deutsche Geschichte und Solidarität: Die Israel-Palästinadiskussion in der deutschen Linken und der neuen Friedensbewegung," in *Äthetik und Kommunkation: Deutsche, Linke, Juden*, vol. 51, no. 14. June 1983, pp. 101–10.

23. Quoted in Kaplan, "What Is 'Religion,'" p. 89.

24. Ibid., pp. 85, 87.

25. Quoted in Ostow, *Juden aus der DDR*, p. 131.

26. Vincent von Wroblewsky, "Wir hatten ja ein jüdisches Selbstbewusstsein," in *Zwischen Thora und Trabant: Juden in der DDR*, ed. Vincent von Wroblewsky (Berlin: Aufbau Verlag, 1993), pp. 201, 202.

27. Ostow, *Juden aus der DDR*, p. 48.

28. I owe these observations to Marion Kaplan.

29. Quoted in Jeroen Doomernik, *Going West: Soviet Jewish Immigrants in Berlin Since 1990* (Aldershot, England: Avebury, 1997), p. 101.

30. Lara Dämmig, Rachel Monika Herweg, Elisa Klapheck, Editorial, *Journal Bet Debora,* Berlin, January 2000, pp. 4, 5.

31. Franklin A. Oberlaender, *"Wir aber sind nicht Fisch und nicht Fleisch": Christliche "Nichtarier" und ihre Kinder in Deutschland* (Opladen: Leske und Budrich, 1996), pp. 348, 349.

32. Personal observation of the author.

33. Hermann Simon, "Das Jüdische Museum," in *"Tuet auf die Pforten": Die Neue Synagoge, 1866–1995* (Berlin: Centrum Judaicum, 1995), p. 224.

34. *Die Zeit,* June 18, 1998, pp. 37–38.

35. Thomas Lackmann, "Die Kiwis kommen," *Der Tagesspiegel,* May 25, 2000.

36. *Forward,* September 19, 1997, pp. 13, 14.

37. Rainer Hoeynck, "Denkpause für das Denkmal," *Aufbau,* August 28, 1998, pp. 1, 2.

38. Stefanie Endlich and Rainer Hoeynck, "Resignative Grundhaltung von Schadensbegrenzung," *Aufbau,* July 3, 1998, p. 1.

39. Roger Cohen, "Schröder Backs Design for a Vast Berlin Holocaust Memorial," *New York Times,* January 18, 1999.

40. "Holocaust-Mahnmal: Der deutsche Bundestag beschliesst den Bau," *Kulturchronik,* no. 5, 1999, p. 5.

41. Kunstamt Schöneberg et al., *Orte des Erinnern: Das Denkmal im Bayerischen Viertel, Beiträge zur Debatte um Denkmäle und Erinnerung* (Berlin: Edition Hentrich, 1994), vol. 1, p. 8, and back cover.

42. Wolfgang Göschel, Joachim v. Rosenberg, Hans-Norbert Burkert, "Erläuterung der Kunstler" in Horst Seferens, *Ein deutscher Denkmalstreit: Die Kontroverse um die Spiegelwand in Berlin Steglitz* (Berlin: Edition Hentrich, 1995), p. 16.

43. Ibid., pp. 7, 96.

44. Franz Bertsch, *Migration in Deutschland und Europa* (Bonn: Internationes, 2000), p. 6.

45. "'Jüdische Zuwanderer aus der GUS—zur Problematik von sozio-kultureller und generationsspezifischer Integration.' Eine empirische Studie des Moses Mendelssohn Zentrums, 1997–1999," in *Ein neues Judentum in Deutschland? Fremd- und Eigenbilder der russisch-jüdischen Einwanderer,* ed. Julius

H. Schoeps, Willi Jasper, and Bernhard Vogt (Potsdam: Verlag fur Berlin-Brandenburg, 1999), p. 28. Also Lothar Mertens, *Alija: Die Emigration der sowjetischen Juden* (Bochum: Universitätsverlag Dr. N. Brockmeyer, 1991), p. 202.

46. Judith Kessler, "Identitätssuche und Subkultur: Erfahrungen der Sozialarbeit in der Jüdischen Gemeinde zu Berlin," in Schoeps, Jasper, and Vogt, *Ein neues*, p. 142.

47. Jakov Sterenberg, *Wahl 1997* (Berlin: Wahlausschuss, Jüdische Gemeinde zu Berlin, 1997), p. 53.

48. "Neuer Vorsitzender der Jüdischen Gemeinde zu Berlin," *Aufbau*, May 10, 2001, p. 1.

49. Schoeps, Jasper, and Vogt, *Ein neues*, p. 9.

50. Franziska Becker, "Ankommen in Deutschland: Eine Ethnographie über Migrationsprozesse 'jüdische Kontingentflüchtlinge' aus der Sowjetunion," Ph.D. diss., Humboldt University, Berlin, 1999, p. 161.

51. Ibid., p. 174.

52. Ulrike Offenberg, *"Seid vorsichtig gegen die Machthaber": Die jüdischen Gemeinden in der SBZ und der DDR 1945 bis 1990* (Berlin: Aufbau Verlag, 1998), p. 268.

53. Schoeps, Jasper, and Vogt, *Ein neues*, p. 45.

54. Ibid., p. 71.

55. Ibid., p. 64ff.

56. Becker, "Ankommen," p. 81.

57. Natascha Ronkine, "Mit russischer Kultur und jüdischem Akzent," in *Zuhause, keine Heimat? Junge Juden und ihre Zukunft in Deutschland*, ed. Micha Brumlik (Gerlingen: Bleicher Verlag, 1998), pp. 131, 133, 134.

58. "Eins zu Eins," *Tachlis*, no. 4, 1990, p. 17.

59. Martin Löw-Beer, "From Nowhere to Israel and Back: The Changing Self-Definition of Periodicals of German-Jewish Youth Since 1960," in Y. Michal Bodemann, ed., *Jews, Germans, Memory: Reconstructions of Jewish Life in Germany* (Ann Arbor: University of Michigan Press, 1996), p. 120.

60. Paul Behrens, "Auch der Knigge ist koscher. 'Chuzpe—Das junge jüdische Magazin' aus Frankfurt am Main," *Die Zeit*, January 10, 1997, p. 19.

61. "Der koschere Knigge. Über den Umgang mit 'jüdischen Mitbürgern,'" rpt. in *Allgemeine Jüdische Zeitung*, no. 10, 1996, p. 16.

62. "Wie viele Verrückte verträgt eine Demokratie?" *Aufbau*, August 24, 2000, p. 1.

63. "Germany: Rightists on Rise," *New York Times,* February 8, 2001.

64. Roger Cohen, "Young Asian Knifed by German Neo-Nazis," *New York Times,* December 27, 2000.

65. Jürgen Heppner, "Rassistische Pöbeleien und die Polizei schaut zu," letter in *Der Tagesspiegel,* August 24, 1998, p. 12.

66. Frank Jansen, "Braunes Spektakel: Rostocker äussern sich abfällig über Ausländer—aber vor Neonazis haben sie angst," *Der Tagesspiegel,* September 20, 1998, p. 3.

67. *Berliner Zeitung,* October 7–8, 2000, p. 1.

68. "Palestinian sentenced for synagogue arson," cnn.com/world, March 7, 2001.

69. *Der Tagesspiegel,* September 8, 1998, p. 4.

70. *Der Spiegel,* no. 36, 1998, pp. 79, 83.

71. Quoted in *Berliner Morgenpost,* October 5, 2000, p. 1.

72. Richard Chaim Schneider, "Wir sind frei: Juden nach Düsseldorf. Sie sind, was sie immer waren—heimatlos mitten in Deutschland," *Berliner Zeitung,* October 6, 2000, pp. 13, 14.

73. Rachel Salamander, "Man kann nicht Wurzeln im Nichts schlagen," *Frankfurter Allgemeine Zeitung,* January 27, 1999, p. 42.

74. Meike Wohlert, "Der Hype um den Davidstern," *Zitty,* no. 16, 1998, pp. 16–18 passim.

Acknowledgments

This book began more than fifty years ago when I first met Gita and Chaim Baigelman and Rosa and Leo Glazer. They arrived in New York in the hot summer of 1949 under the special Truman-inspired legislation to admit displaced persons outside the restrictive American quotas. In 1939 the war had caught them in Lodz, where with other Jews they were soon imprisoned in the ghetto. Then with youth, energy, and large doses of luck on their side, they survived a succession of Nazi concentration and work camps. After the war, finding Lodz no longer possible for Jews, they had fled to the safety of the American occupation zone in Bavaria. They were starting over again in Munich when new displaced persons legislation permitted them to come to the United States to join their remaining family. Over the next years, I heard more and more of their story.

This book is essentially that story writ large. What happened to the Jews in the cauldron of postwar Europe has not been subjected to the close scrutiny that has been accorded the war years in all their horror. Dramatically, the period seems like the denouement of a great saga. Details without a plot, and yet for those who lived to experience it, it was the beginning, which they took up sometimes joyfully, sometimes dazedly, of the rest of their lives. For Jews after the war the fundamental truth was not only that most had lost family, friends, and community. They had also lost their country. Friendless and unwelcome in what had once been home, they began their postwar lives not as citizens but as displaced persons.

I particularly want to thank Gita and Chaim Baigelman for their willingness to talk about their past and reflect on it. Rosa and Leo Glazer died all too early. But in the years that I was fortunate enough to know them, they were wry and witty commentators on their unimaginable experiences.

Others who had passed through the horrors of the war and the camps also agreed to talk to me about their experiences, among them Samuel Bak, Roma Ben-Atar, Inge Deutschkron, Ernest Günter Fontheim, and Ruth Galinski. Samuel Bak kindly permitted me to use a cartoon that he made as a fourteen-year-old, commenting on Yehudi Menuhin's appearance in Berlin in 1947.

For the situation of Jews in Germany today, well-informed friends, historians, and other observers of the current scene were generous with their information. I want particularly to thank Dr. Chana Schütz and Dr. Hermann Simon at the Centrum Judaicum for opening their restored archive to me, and for their knowledgeable observations on the history of Jewish life in Berlin. Dr. Simon, with his intimate understanding of the new immigration of Russian Jews, served as a valuable and instructive guide to that community. Dr. Schütz was a patient friend, answering faxes and letters out of her inexhaustible store of information and saving me from many errors. She was also immensely helpful in finding rare pictures for use in this book.

Arkady Fried, Nicola Galliner, and Elisa Klapheck at the Jüdische Gemeinde were good company during my visits to Berlin and were invaluable sources of information. Dr. Jürgen Wetzel at the Berlin Landesarchiv was, as ever, liberal with his time, and both he and Dr. Klaus Dettmer were thoughtful guides to the resources of the archive. The staff at the Bildarchiv was inventive and efficient in finding the pictures I was looking for. Mark Gelber showed me around the newly rebuilt Adass Israel complex and described the hopes and plans of the new community.

Franziska Becker, Ilan Diner, Myriam Halberstam, Robin Ostow, Sibylle Quack, Irmtrud Wojak, and Thea Wolffsohn were all wonderful informants in their individual fields. My visits to Berlin over nearly twenty years have been enriched by my friendship with Gabriele Katwan. Her delightful company, combined with her astute observations on the passing scene, have made for memorable times together.

In New York, Frank Mecklenburg and Diane Spielman at the Leo Baeck Institute, Zachary Baker and Krysia Fisher at YIVO, and the librarians at the superb Judaica Room of the New York Public Library provided me scholarly resources and the help that I needed for my research. Aurora Tangkeko at the United Nations Archives guided me to valuable material in the massive historical files of that organization. Abraham Peck, as one of the pioneer researchers on the She'erith Hapletah, offered useful advice and information. Marion Kaplan was a wonderful source of the latest bulletins from Germany that arrived in a steady stream of photocopies, offprints, and clippings. Talking with her was always enlightening. Joanne Rudof at the Fortunoff Video Archive for the Holocaust at Yale University was an unfailing source of information. I benefited greatly from her intimate knowledge of the period. Linda Abrahams with her penetrating observations sharpened my sense of what I needed to say in this book. Professor Saul Touster kindly allowed me to use the illustration of the letter Beth from the *Survivors' Haggadah*. The photographer Henry Ries permitted me to use a moving photograph that he had made in Berlin in 1947 of Jews returning from Shanghai.

I especially want to thank my editor at Yale University Press,

Gladys Topkis, for a close and careful reading of my manuscript with her famous no. 2 black pencil. She was adventurous in accepting the proposal for this book, and without that encouragement I could not have written it. I also want to thank Dan Heaton for a meticulous reading that helped to clarify many points in the manuscript.

On a personal level, I have benefited in more ways than I know how to describe from conversation with my sister Shirley Gorenstein, part of our lifelong dialogue. I was also sustained by long talks and the interest of Doron and Jo Ben-Atar, Linda Collins, and Peggy and Dick Kuhns. My daughters, Sarah, Sophie, and Lizzie, read portions of the manuscript in early stages and gave me thoughtful and informed advice. I am especially grateful to my grandson Eli Shaoul Khedouri, who came to my rescue on several occasions when my computer failed, and with sovereign competence was able to restore the vanished text with a few telephoned instructions. He was also able to retrieve obscure information from the depths of the Internet, material that I had despaired of finding. Few writers are as fortunate as I am to have both a live-in editor and cook-extraordinary right on the premises. My loving thanks, as ever, go to my husband, Peter Gay.

Index

335

234–35, 262, 267–72, 305–6; in GDR, 225; and Russian Jews, 306–8

Jewish education, 26, 30, 66, 241, 243, 262, 264

Jewish feminist learning, 271

Jewish Hospital and Nazi deportation, 154–55

Jewish immigration: to Germany, 281–82; from GDR, 222–23. *See also* immigration

Jewish Marxism, 264–66. *See also* Communism

Jewish Museum (Berlin), 273–74

Jewish nationalism, 37

Jewish newspapers: *Undzer Weg,* 60–63; in D.P. camps, 71–74, 169; *Jüdisches Gemeindeblatt,* 113–15, 120, 130, 132, 135; *Neue Welt,* 119; *Jüdische Rundschau,* 126; Ernst Landau, 133–34; *Der Weg,* 166–70, 173, 198; *Undzer Lebn,* 186–89, 193–94; in GDR, 228–29; and Eastern Europeans, 257

Jewish orthodoxy, 240

Jewish passport, 39, 282–83

Jewish postwar adjustments: education, 66, 241, 243, 262, 264; homelessness, 92–94; vocational training, 120; assimilation, 127; historical awareness, 192–93; identity in Germany, 124, 125, 166–67, 257–60, 306–8; homecoming, 131–32; orphans and trauma, 189–93; identity in

GDR, 223–24; identity in Russia, 282–83; identity and Russian Jews, 289–90; and children, 292–93; etiquette, 296–98

Jewish reconciliation, 260–61

Jewish Reform Movement, 239–40

Jewish Restitution Successor Organization (JRSO), 174

Jewish schools: prohibition of, 7, 38; in Poland, 14, 31; in D.P. camps, 185; and Zionism, 193–94; and secularism, 194

Jewish separateness, 13, 127

Jewish student activism, 264–66

Jewish testimony, 73

Jewish theater in Germany, 61–62

Jewish youth magazines, 294–96

Jews: Polish postwar metamorphosis, x; numbers killed, deported, xii; return to Germany, xii–xiii; disapproval of, xii–xiii, 12, 133–34, 140–42; and modernity, 15–16; separateness of, 16–17; religious conversion of, 20; and revenge, 89–90; in Germany, future of, 142; cultural identity of, 124–25, 166–67, 189–90, 223–24, 257–60, 282–83, 289–90; status of, 154–55, 163–64, 174; definition of, 179–80; and Communist Party, 203; and concentration camps, 226–27; Soviet, 237, 282–83. *See also* Anti-Semitism; Concentration camps; Jewish postwar adjustments; Victims of Fascism